SANDWORM

ALSO BY ANDY GREENBERG

This Machine Kills Secrets

SANDWORM

A New Era of Cyberwar and

the Hunt for the Kremlin's

Most Dangerous Hackers

ANDY GREENBERG

DOUBLEDAY  NEW YORK

Portions of this work originally appeared, in different form, in
Wired magazine as "The Untold Story of NotPetya, the Most
Devastating Cyberattack in History" on August 22, 2018.

Book design by Michael Collica
Jacket design by Emily Mahon
Front-of-jacket image © filo/DigitalVision Vectors / Getty Images

Library of Congress Cataloging-in-Publication Data
Names: Greenberg, Andy, author.
Title: Sandworm : a new era of cyberwar and the hunt for the
Kremlin's most dangerous hackers / Andy Greenberg.
Description: First edition. | New York : Doubleday,
[2019] | Includes bibliographical references.
Identifiers: LCCN 2019006755 (print) | LCCN 2019015885 (ebook) |
ISBN 9780385544412 (Ebook) | ISBN 9780385544405 (hardcover)
Subjects: LCSH: Computer crimes—Russia
(Federation) | Hackers—Russia (Federation)
Classification: LCC HV6773.R8 (ebook) |
LCC HV6773.R8 G74 2019 (print) | DDC 364.16/80947—dc23
LC record available at https://lccn.loc.gov/2019006755

MANUFACTURED IN THE UNITED STATES OF AMERICA

1 3 5 7 9 10 8 6 4 2

First Edition

In memory of my father,
Gary Greenberg

CONTENTS

INTRODUCTION

On June 27, 2017, something strange and terrible began to ripple out across the infrastructure of the world.

A group of hospitals in Pennsylvania began delaying surgeries and turning away patients. A Cadbury factory in Tasmania stopped churning out chocolates. The pharmaceutical giant Merck ceased manufacturing vaccines for human papillomavirus.

Soon, seventeen terminals at ports across the globe, all owned by the world's largest shipping firm, Maersk, found themselves paralyzed. Tens of thousands of eighteen-wheeler trucks carrying shipping containers began to line up outside those ports' gates. Massive ships arrived from journeys across oceans, each carrying hundreds of thousands of tons of cargo, only to find that no one could unload them. Like victims of a global outbreak of some brain-eating bacteria, major components in the intertwined, automated systems of the world seemed to have spontaneously forgotten how to function.

At the attack's epicenter, in Ukraine, the effects of the technological doomsday were more concentrated. ATMs and credit card payment systems inexplicably dropped off-line. Mass transit in the country's capital of Kiev was crippled. Government agencies, airports, hospitals, the postal service, even scientists monitoring radioactivity levels at the ruins of the Chernobyl nuclear power plant, all watched helplessly as practically every computer in their networks was infected and wiped by a mysterious piece of malicious code.

This is what cyberwar looks like: an invisible force capable of striking out from an unknown origin to sabotage, on a massive scale, the technologies that underpin civilization.

For decades, the Cassandras of internet security warned us this was coming. They cautioned that hackers would soon make the leap beyond mere crime or even state-sponsored espionage and begin to exploit vulnerabilities in the digitized, critical infrastructure of the modern world. In 2007, when Russian hackers bombarded Estonia with cyberattacks that tore practically every website in the country off-line, that blitz hinted at the potential scale of geopolitically motivated hacking. Two years later, when the NSA's malicious software called Stuxnet silently accelerated Iran's nuclear enrichment centrifuges until they destroyed themselves, the operation demonstrated another preview of what was in store: It showed that tools of cyberwar could reach out beyond the merely digital, into even the most closely guarded and sensitive components of the physical world.

But for anyone watching Russia's war in Ukraine since it began in early 2014, there were clearer, more direct harbingers. Starting in 2015, waves of vicious cyberattacks had begun to strike Ukraine's government, media, and transportation. They culminated in the first known blackouts ever caused by hackers, attacks that turned off power for hundreds of thousands of civilians.

A small group of researchers would begin to sound the alarm—largely in vain—that Russia was turning Ukraine into a test lab for cyberwar innovations. They cautioned that those advancements might soon be deployed against the United States, NATO, and a larger world that remained blithely unprepared for this new dimension of war. And they pointed to a single force of Kremlin-backed hackers that seemed to be launching these unprecedented weapons of mass disruption: a group known as Sandworm.

Over the next two years, Sandworm would ramp up its aggression, distinguishing itself as the most dangerous collection of hackers in the world and redefining cyberwar. Finally, on that fateful day in late June 2017, the group would unleash the world-shaking worm known as NotPetya, now considered the most devastating and costly malware in history. In the process, Sandworm would demonstrate as never before that highly sophisticated, state-sponsored hackers with the motivations of a military sabotage unit can attack across any distance to undermine the foundations of human life, hitting interlocked, interdependent systems with unpredictable, disastrous consequences.

Today, the full scale of the threat Sandworm and its ilk present looms over the future. If cyberwar escalation continues unchecked, the victims of state-sponsored hacking could be on a trajectory for even more virulent and destructive worms. The digital attacks first demonstrated in Ukraine hint at a dystopia on the horizon, one where hackers induce blackouts that last days, weeks, or even longer—intentionally inflicted deprivations of electricity that could mirror the American tragedy of Puerto Rico after Hurricane Maria, causing vast economic harm and even loss of life. Or one where hackers destroy physical equipment at industrial sites to cause lethal mayhem. Or, as in the case of NotPetya, where they simply wipe hundreds of thousands of computers at a strategic moment to render brain-dead the digital systems of an enemy's economy or critical infrastructure.

This book tells the story of Sandworm, the clearest example yet of the rogue actors advancing that cyberwar dystopia. It follows the years-long work of the detectives tracking those hackers—as Sandworm's fingerprints appeared on one digital disaster scene after another—to identify and locate them, and to call attention to the danger the group represented in the desperate hope that it could be stopped.

But *Sandworm* is not just the story of a single hacker group, or even of the wider threat of Russia's reckless willingness to wage this new form of cyberwar around the world. It's the story of a larger, global arms race that continues today. That race is one that the United States and the West have not only failed to stop but directly accelerated with our own headlong embrace of digital attack tools. And in doing so, we've invited a new, unchecked force of chaos into the world.

SANDWORM

PROLOGUE

The clocks read zero when the lights went out.

It was a Saturday night in December 2016, and Oleksii Yasinsky was sitting on the couch with his wife and teenage son in the living room of their Kiev apartment. The forty-year-old Ukrainian cyber-security researcher and his family were an hour into Oliver Stone's film *Snowden* when their building abruptly lost power.

"The hackers don't want us to finish the movie," Yasinsky's wife joked. She was referring to an event that had occurred a year ear-lier, a cyberattack that had cut electricity to nearly a quarter-million Ukrainians two days before Christmas in 2015.

Yasinsky, a chief forensic analyst at a Kiev cybersecurity firm, didn't laugh. He looked over at a portable clock on his desk: The time was 00:00. Precisely midnight.

Yasinsky's television was plugged into a surge protector with a bat-tery backup, so only the flicker of images on-screen lit the room now. The power strip started beeping plaintively. Yasinsky got up and switched it off to save its charge, leaving the room suddenly silent.

He went to the kitchen, pulled out a handful of candles, and lit them. Then he stepped to the kitchen window. The thin, sandy-blond engineer looked out on a view of the city as he'd never seen it before: The entire skyline around his apartment building was dark. Only the gray glow of distant lights reflected off the clouded sky, outlining blackened hulks of modern condos and Soviet high-rises.

Noting the precise time and the date, almost exactly a year since the December 2015 grid attack, Yasinsky felt sure that this was no normal blackout. He thought of the cold outside—close to zero degrees Fahrenheit—the slowly sinking temperatures in thousands of homes, and the countdown until dead water pumps led to frozen pipes.

That's when another paranoid thought began to work its way through Yasinsky's mind: For the past fourteen months, he had found himself at the center of an enveloping crisis. A growing list of Ukrainian companies and government agencies had come to him to analyze a plague of cyberattacks that were hitting them in rapid, remorseless succession. A single group of hackers seemed to be behind all of it. Now he couldn't suppress the sense that those same phantoms, whose fingerprints he had traced for more than a year, had reached back, out through the internet's ether, into his home.

PART I

EMERGENCE

Use the first moments in study. You may miss many an opportunity for quick victory this way, but the moments of study are insurance of success. Take your time and be sure.

1

THE ZERO DAY

Beyond the Beltway, where the D.C. intelligence-industrial complex flattens out to an endless sea of parking lots and gray office buildings marked with logos and corporate names designed to be forgotten, there's a building in Chantilly, Virginia, whose fourth floor houses a windowless internal room. The room's walls are painted matte black, as if to carve out a negative space where no outside light penetrates.

In 2014, just over a year before the outbreak of Ukraine's cyberwar, this was what the small, private intelligence firm iSight Partners called the black room. Inside worked the company's two-man team tasked with software vulnerability research, a job that required focus intense enough that its practitioners had insisted on the closest possible office layout to a sensory-deprivation chamber.

It was this pair of highly skilled cave dwellers that John Hultquist first turned to one Wednesday morning that September with a rare request. When Hultquist had arrived at his desk earlier that day in a far-better-lit office, one with actual windows on the opposite side of the iSight building, he'd opened an email from one of his iSight colleagues in the company's Ukraine satellite operation. Inside, he found a gift: The Kiev-based staff believed they might have gotten their hands on a zero-day vulnerability.

A zero day, in hacker jargon, is a secret security flaw in software, one that the company who created and maintains the software's code doesn't know about. The name comes from the fact that the company has had "zero days" to respond and push out a patch to protect users.

A powerful zero day, particularly one that allows a hacker to break out of the confines of the software application where the bug is found and begin to execute their own code on a target computer, can serve as a kind of global skeleton key—a free pass to gain entrance to any machine that runs that vulnerable software, anywhere in the world where the victim is connected to the internet.

The file Hultquist had been passed from iSight's Ukraine office was a PowerPoint attachment. It seemed to silently pull off exactly that sort of code execution, and in Microsoft Office, one of the world's most ubiquitous pieces of software.

As he read the email, Klaxons sounded in Hultquist's mind. If the discovery was what the Ukrainians believed it might be, it meant some unknown hackers possessed—and had used—a dangerous capability that would allow them to hijack any of millions of computers. Microsoft needed to be warned of its flaw immediately. But in a more self-interested sense, discovering a zero day represented a milestone for a small firm like iSight hoping to win glory and woo customers in the budding security subindustry of "threat intelligence." The company turned up only two or three of those secret flaws a year. Each one was a kind of abstract, highly dangerous curiosity and a significant research coup. "For a small company, finding a nugget like this was very, very gratifying," Hultquist says. "It was a huge deal for us."

Hultquist, a loud and bearish army veteran from eastern Tennessee with a thick black beard and a perpetual smile, made a point of periodically shouting from his desk into a room next door known as the bull pen. One side of that space was lined with malware experts, and the other with threat analysts focused on understanding the geopolitical motives behind digital attacks. As soon as Hultquist read the email from iSight's Ukrainian staff, he burst out of his office and into the bull pen, briefing the room and assigning tasks to triage what would become, unbeknownst then to any of them, one of the biggest finds in the small company's history.

But it was down the hall, in the black room, that the hacker monks within would start to grapple with the significance of iSight's discovery: a small, hidden marvel of malicious engineering.

■

Working on computers whose glowing monitors were the room's only light source, the reverse engineers began by running the Ukrainians' malware-infected PowerPoint attachment again and again inside a series of virtual machines—ephemeral simulations of a computer housed within a real, physical one, each one of them as sealed off from the rest of the computer as the black room was from the rest of the iSight offices.

In those sealed containers, the code could be studied like a scorpion under an aquarium's glass. They'd allow it to infect its virtual victims repeatedly, as the reverse engineers spun up simulations of different digital machines, running varied versions of Windows and Microsoft Office, to study the dimensions and flexibility of the attack. When they'd determined that the code could extract itself from the PowerPoint file and gain full control of even the latest, fully patched versions of the software, they had their confirmation: It was indeed a zero day, as rare and powerful as the Ukrainians and Hultquist had suspected. By late in the evening—a passage of time that went almost entirely unmarked within their work space—they'd produced a detailed report to share with Microsoft and their customers and coded their own version of it, a proof-of-concept rewrite that demonstrated its attack, like a pathogen in a test tube.

PowerPoint possesses "amazing powers," as one of the black room's two reverse engineers, Jon Erickson, explained to me. Over years of evolution, it's become a Rube Goldberg machine packed with largely unnecessary features, so intricate that it practically serves as its own programming language. And whoever had exploited this zero day had deeply studied one feature that allowed anyone to place an information "object" inside a presentation, like a chart or video pulled from elsewhere in the PowerPoint file's own bundle of data, or even from a remote computer over the internet.

In this case, the hackers had used the feature to carefully plant two chunks of data within the presentation. The first it loaded into a temporary folder on the target computer. The second took advantage of PowerPoint's animation feature: PowerPoint's animations don't merely allow speakers to bore audiences with moving text and cartoons but actually execute commands on the computer on which the presentation is running. In this case, when the presentation loaded that animation file, it would run an automated script that right-clicked on the first file the presentation had planted on the machine and click "install" on the resulting drop-down menu, giving that code a foothold on the computer without tipping off its user. The result was something like a harmless-looking package left on your doorstep that, after you bring it inside, sprouts an arm, cuts itself open, and releases tiny robots into your foyer. All of this would happen immediately and invisibly, the instant the victim double-clicked the attachment to open it.

Erickson, the reverse engineer who first handled the zero day in iSight's black room, remembers his work disassembling and defusing the attack as a somewhat rare, fascinating, but utterly impersonal event. In his career, he'd dealt with only a handful of real zero days found in the wild. But he'd analyzed thousands upon thousands of other malware samples and had learned to think of them as specimens for study without considering the author behind them—the human who had rigged together their devious machinery. "It was just some unknown guy and some unknown thing I hadn't seen before," he said.

But zero days do have authors. And when Erickson had first begun to pull apart this one in his blacked-out workshop that morning, he hadn't simply been studying some naturally occurring, inanimate puzzle. He was admiring the first hints of a remote, malevolent intelligence.

2

BLACKENERGY

Once iSight's initial frenzy surrounding its zero-day discovery had subsided, the questions remained: Who had written the attack code? Whom were they targeting with it, and why?

Those questions fell to Drew Robinson, a malware analyst at iSight whom John Hultquist described as a "daywalker": Robinson possessed most of the same reverse-engineering skills as the black room's vampire crew but sat in the sunlit bull pen next to Hultquist's office, responsible for a far wider angle analysis of hacking campaigns, from the personnel who carried them out to their political motives. It would be Robinson's job to follow the technical clues within that PowerPoint to solve the larger mysteries of the hidden operation it represented.

Minutes after Hultquist had walked into the bull pen to announce the all-hands-on-deck discovery of the PowerPoint zero day that Wednesday morning, Robinson was poring over the contents of the booby-trapped attachment. The actual presentation itself seemed to be a list of names written in Cyrillic characters over a blue-and-yellow Ukrainian flag, with a watermark of the Ukrainian coat of arms, a pale blue trident over a yellow shield. Those names, Robinson found after using Google Translate, were a list of supposed "terrorists"—those who sided with Russia in the Ukrainian conflict that had begun earlier that year when Russian troops invaded the east of the country and its Crimean peninsula, igniting separatist movements there and sparking an ongoing war.

That the hackers had chosen an anti-Russian message to carry their zero-day infection was Robinson's first clue that the email was likely a Russian operation with Ukrainian targets, playing on the country's patriotism and fears of internal Kremlin sympathizers. But as he searched for clues about the hackers behind that ploy, he quickly found another loose thread to pull. When the PowerPoint zero day executed, the file it dropped on a victim's system turned out to be a variant of a piece of notorious malware, soon to become far more notorious still. It was called BlackEnergy.

BlackEnergy's short history up to that point already contained, in some sense, its own primer on the taxonomy of common hacking operations, from the lowliest "script kiddies"—hackers so unskilled that they could generally only use tools written by someone more knowledgeable—to professional cybercriminals. The tool had originally been created by a Russian hacker named Dmytro Oleksiuk, also known by his handle, Cr4sh. Around 2007, Oleksiuk had sold BlackEnergy on Russian-language hacker forums, priced at around $40, with his handle emblazoned like a graffiti tag in a corner of its control panel.

The tool was designed for one express purpose: so-called distributed denial-of-service, or DDoS, attacks designed to flood websites with fraudulent requests for information from hundreds or thousands of computers simultaneously, knocking them off-line. Infect a victim machine with BlackEnergy, and it became a member of a so-called botnet, a collection of hijacked computers, or bots. A botnet operator could configure Oleksiuk's user-friendly software to control which web target its enslaved machines would pummel with spoofed requests as well as the type and rate of that digital bombardment.

By late 2007, the security firm Arbor Networks counted more than thirty botnets built with BlackEnergy, mostly aiming their attacks at Russian websites. But on the spectrum of cyberattack sophistication, distributed denial-of-service attacks were largely crude and blunt. After all, they could cause costly downtime but not the serious data breaches inflicted by more penetrating hacking techniques.

In the years that followed, however, BlackEnergy had evolved. Security firms began to detect a new version of the software, now equipped with an arsenal of interchangeable features. This revamped version of the tool could still hit websites with junk traffic, but it could also be programmed to send spam email, destroy files on the computers it had infested, and steal banking usernames and passwords.*

Now, before Robinson's eyes, BlackEnergy had resurfaced in yet another form. The version he was looking at from his seat in iSight's bull pen seemed different from any he'd read about before—certainly not a simple website attack tool, and likely not a tool of financial fraud, either. After all, why would a fraud-focused cybercrime scheme be using a list of pro-Russian terrorists as its bait? The ruse seemed politically targeted. From his first look at the Ukrainian BlackEnergy sample, he began to suspect he was looking at a variant of the code with a new goal: not mere crime, but espionage.†

Soon after, Robinson made a lucky find that revealed something further about the malware's purpose. When he ran this new Black-Energy sample on a virtual machine, it tried to connect out over the internet to an IP address somewhere in Europe. That connection, he could immediately see, was the so-called command-and-control server that functioned as the program's remote puppet master. And when Robinson reached out himself via his web browser to that faraway machine, he was pleasantly shocked. The command-and-

---

* As that more sophisticated cybercriminal use of BlackEnergy spread, its original creator, Oleksiuk, had been careful to distance himself from it—particularly after BlackEnergy was connected to financial fraud against Russian banks, a dangerous move in a country otherwise known to look the other way when cybercriminals focused on Western victims. "The fact that its source code was available to many people in all sorts of (semi) private parties, can mean that someone took it for their own needs," Oleksiuk tried to explain in a post—titled "Fuck me I'm famous"—on the blogging site LiveJournal in 2009. "To suspect that the author of this bot software, whose autograph was written on publicly accessible versions of it 3 years ago, is involved in criminal machinations, you'd have to be a complete idiot."

† In fact, security analysts at the Russian security firm Kaspersky had quietly suspected someone had been using BlackEnergy for sophisticated spying since early 2013. Versions of the tool had begun appearing that were no longer offered for sale on hacker forums, and some were designed to infect machines that run Linux—an operating system rare enough that the hackers must have been using it for precision spy operations, not indiscriminate theft. "The crimeware use was gone," the Kaspersky analyst Maria Garnaeva told me. "That was when the hackers using this became a unique targeted attack group."

control computer had been left entirely unsecured, allowing anyone to browse its files at will.

The files included, amazingly, a kind of help document for this unique version of BlackEnergy that conveniently listed its commands. It confirmed Robinson's suspicion: The zero-day-delivered version of BlackEnergy had a far broader array of data-collection abilities than the usual sample of the malware found in cybercrime investigations. The program could take screenshots, extract files and encryption keys from victim machines, and record keystrokes, all hallmarks of targeted, thorough cyberspying rather than some profit-focused bank-fraud racket.

But even more important than the contents of that how-to file was the language it was written in: Russian.

3

ARRAKIS02

The cybersecurity industry constantly warns of the "attribution problem"—that the faraway hackers behind any operation, especially a sophisticated one, are very often impossible to pinpoint. The internet offers too many opportunities for proxies, misdirection, and sheer overwhelming geographic uncertainty. But by identifying the unsecured command-and-control server, Robinson had broken through iSight's BlackEnergy mystery with a rare identifying detail. Despite all the care they'd displayed in their PowerPoint hacking, the hackers seemed to have let slip a strong clue of their nationality.

After that windfall, however, Robinson still faced the task of actually delving into the innards of the malware's code in an effort to find more clues and create a "signature" that security firms and iSight's customers could use to detect if other networks had been infected with the same program. Deciphering the functionality of the malware's code wasn't going to be nearly as easy as tracing its command-and-control server. As Robinson would painstakingly learn over the next days of solid, brain-numbing work, it had been thoroughly scrambled with three alternating layers of compression and encryption.

In other words, getting to the malware's secrets was something like a scavenger hunt. Although Robinson knew that the malware was self-contained and therefore had to include all the encryption keys necessary to unscramble itself and run its code, the key to each layer of that scrambling could only be found after decoding the layer on top of it. And even after guessing the compression algorithm the hackers had used by scanning the random-looking noise for recognizable patterns, Robinson spent days longer working to identify the encryption scheme they'd used, a unique modification of an existing system. As he fell deeper and deeper into that puzzle, he'd look up from his desk and find that hours had seemingly jumped forward. Even at home, he'd find himself standing fixated in the shower, turning the cipher over and over in his mind.

When Robinson finally cracked those layers of obfuscation after a week of trial and error, he was rewarded with a view of the Black-Energy sample's millions of ones and zeros—a collection of data that was, at a glance, still entirely meaningless. This was, after all, the program in its compiled form, translated into machine-readable binary rather than any human-readable programming language. To understand the binary, Robinson would have to watch it execute step-by-step on his computer, unraveling it in real time with a common reverse-engineering tool called IDA Pro that translated the function of its commands into code as they ran. "It's almost like you're trying to determine what someone might look like solely by looking at their DNA," Robinson said. "And the god that created that person was trying to make the process as hard as possible."

By the second week, however, that microscopic step-by-step analysis of the binary finally began to pay off. When he managed to decipher the malware's configuration settings, they contained a so-called campaign code—essentially a tag associated with that version of the malware that the hackers could use to sort and track any victims it infected. And for the BlackEnergy sample dropped by their Ukrainian PowerPoint, that campaign code was one that he immediately recognized, not from his career as a malware analyst, but from his private life as a science fiction nerd: "arrakis02."

In fact, for Robinson, or virtually any other sci-fi-literate geek, the word "Arrakis" is more than recognizable: It's as familiar as Tatooine or Middle-earth, the setting of a central pillar of the cultural canon. Arrakis is the desert planet where the novel *Dune,* the 1965 epic by Frank Herbert, takes place.

The story of *Dune* is set in a world where Earth has long ago been ravaged by a global nuclear war against artificially intelligent machines. It follows the fate of the noble Atreides family after they've been installed as the rulers of Arrakis—also known as Dune—and then politically sabotaged and purged from power by their evil rivals, the Harkonnens.

After the Atreides are overthrown, the book's adolescent hero Paul Atreides takes refuge in the planet's vast desert, where thousand-foot-long sandworms roam underground, occasionally rising to the surface to consume everything in their path. As he grows up, Atreides learns the ways of Arrakis's natives, known as the Fremen, including the ability to harness and ride the sandworms. Eventually, he leads a spartan guerrilla uprising, and riding on the backs of sandworms into a devastating battle, he and the native Fremen take the capital city back from the Harkonnens, their insurgency ultimately seizing control of the entire global empire that had backed the Harkonnens' coup.

"Whoever these hackers were," Robinson remembers thinking, "it seems like they're Frank Herbert fans."

■

When he found that arrakis02 campaign code, Robinson could sense he'd stumbled onto something more than a singular clue about the hackers who had chosen that name. He felt for the first time that he was seeing into their minds and imaginations. In fact, he began to wonder if it might serve as a kind of fingerprint. Perhaps he could match it to other crime scenes.

Over the next days, Robinson set the Ukrainian PowerPoint version of BlackEnergy aside and went digging, both in iSight's archives of older malware samples and in a database called VirusTotal. Owned by Google's parent company, Alphabet, VirusTotal allows any security researcher who's testing a piece of malware to upload it and check it against dozens of commercial antivirus products—a quick and rough method to see if other security firms have detected the code elsewhere and what they might know about it. As a result, VirusTotal has assembled a massive collection of in-the-wild code samples amassed over more than a decade that researchers can pay to access. Robinson began to run a series of scans of those malware records, searching for similar snippets of code in what he'd unpacked from his BlackEnergy sample to match earlier code samples in iSight's or VirusTotal's catalog.

Soon he had a hit. Another BlackEnergy sample from four months earlier, in May 2014, was a rough duplicate of the one dropped by the Ukrainian PowerPoint. When Robinson dug up its campaign code, he found what he was looking for: houseatreides94, another unmistakable *Dune* reference. This time the BlackEnergy sample had been hidden in a Word document, a discussion of oil and gas prices apparently designed as a lure for a Polish energy company.

For the next few weeks, Robinson continued to scour his archive of malicious programs. He eventually wrote his own tools that could scan for the malware matches, automate the process of unlocking the files' layers of obfuscating encryption, and then pull out the campaign code. His collection of samples slowly began to grow: BasharoftheSardaukars, SalusaSecundus2, epsiloneridani0, as if the hackers were trying to impress him with their increasingly obscure knowledge of *Dune*'s minutiae.

Each of those *Dune* references was tied, like the first two he'd found, to a lure document that revealed something about the malware's intended victims. One was a diplomatic document discussing Europe's "tug-of-war" with Russia over Ukraine as the country struggled between a popular movement pulling it toward the West and Russia's lingering influence. Another seemed to be designed as bait for visitors attending a Ukraine-focused summit in Wales and a NATO-related event in Slovakia that focused in part on Russian espionage. One even seemed to specifically target an American academic researcher focused on Russian foreign policy, whose identity iSight decided not to reveal publicly. Thanks to the hackers' helpful *Dune* references, all of those disparate attacks could be definitively tied together.

But some of the victims didn't look quite like the usual subjects of Russian geopolitical espionage. Why exactly, for instance, were the hackers focused on a Polish energy company? Another lure, iSight would later find, targeted Ukraine's railway agency, Ukrzaliznytsia.

But as Robinson dug deeper and deeper into the trash heap of the security industry, hunting for those *Dune* references, he was most struck by another realization: While the PowerPoint zero day they'd discovered was relatively new, the hackers' broader attack campaign stretched back not just months but years. The earliest appearance of the *Dune*-linked hackers' lures had come in 2009. Until Robinson had managed to piece together the bread crumbs of their operations, they'd been penetrating organizations in secret for half a decade.

■

After six weeks of analysis, iSight was ready to go public with its findings: It had discovered what appeared to be a vast, highly sophisticated espionage campaign with every indication of being a Russian government operation targeting NATO and Ukraine.

As Robinson had painstakingly unraveled that operation, his boss, John Hultquist, had become almost as fixated on the work of the Russian hackers as the malware analysts scrutinizing its code were. Robinson sat on the side of the bull pen closest to Hultquist's office, and Hultquist would shout questions to him, his Tennessee-accented bellow easily penetrating the wall. But by the middle of October, Hultquist now invaded the bull pen on an almost daily basis to ask for updates from Robinson as the mystery spun out from that first PowerPoint zero day.

For all the hackers' clever tricks, Hultquist knew that getting any attention for their discovery would still require media savvy. At the time, Chinese cyberspies, not Russian ones, were public enemy number one for the American media and security industry. Companies from Northrop Grumman to Dow Chemical to Google had all been breached by Chinese hackers in a series of shocking campaigns of data theft—mostly focused on intellectual property and trade secrets—that the then NSA director, Keith Alexander, called the "greatest transfer of wealth in history." A Russian espionage operation with unsurprising eastern European targets like this one, despite all its insidious skill and longevity, nonetheless risked getting lost in the noise.

Their hackers would need a catchy, attention-grabbing name. Choosing it, as was the custom in the cybersecurity industry, was iSight's prerogative as the firm that had uncovered the group.* And clearly that name should reference the cyberspies' apparent obsession with *Dune*.

Robinson, a *Dune* fan since he was a teenager, suggested they label the hacking operation "Bene Gesserit," a reference to a mystical order of women in the book who possess near-magical powers of psychological manipulation. Hultquist, who had never actually read Frank Herbert's book, vetoed the idea as too abstruse and difficult to pronounce.

Instead, Hultquist chose a more straightforward name, one he hoped would evoke a hidden monster, moving just beneath the surface, occasionally emerging to wield terrible power—a name more fitting than Hultquist himself could have known at the time. He called the group Sandworm.

---

* In fact, iSight wasn't necessarily the first to piece together this hacker group's fingerprints. The Slovakian firm ESET was, around the same time, making the same discoveries, including even the *Dune*-themed campaign codes in the group's malware. ESET even presented its findings at the Virus Bulletin conference in Seattle in September 2014. But because ESET didn't publish its findings online, iSight's analysts told me they weren't aware of its parallel research, and iSight has been widely credited—perhaps mistakenly—with discovering Sandworm first.

4

FORCE MULTIPLIER

Six weeks after they'd first discovered Sandworm, iSight's staff held a round of celebratory drinks in the office, gathering at a bar the company kept fully stocked down the hall from the analysts' bull pen. Sandworm's debut onto the world stage had been everything Hultquist had hoped for. When the company went public with its discovery of a five-years-running, zero-day-equipped, *Dune*-themed Russian espionage campaign, the news had rippled across the industry and the media, with stories appearing in *The Washington Post*, *Wired*, and countless tech and security industry trade publications. Robinson remembers toasting Hultquist with a glass of vodka, in honor of the new species of Russian hacker they'd unearthed.

But that same evening, 2,500 miles to the west, another security researcher was still digging. Kyle Wilhoit, a malware analyst for the Japanese security firm Trend Micro, had spotted iSight's Sandworm report online that afternoon, in the midst of the endless meetings of the corporate conference he was attending at a hotel in Cupertino, California. Wilhoit knew iSight by reputation and John Hultquist in particular and made a note to take a closer look at the end of the day. He sensed that discoveries as significant as iSight's tended to cascade. Perhaps it would shake loose new findings for him and Trend Micro.

That night, sitting outside at the hotel bar, Wilhoit and another Trend Micro researcher, Jim Gogolinski, pulled out their laptops and downloaded everything that iSight had made public—the so-called indicators of compromise it had published in the hopes of helping other potential victims of Sandworm detect and block their attackers.

Among those bits of evidence, like the plastic-bagged exhibits from a crime scene, were the IP addresses of the command-and-control servers the BlackEnergy samples had communicated back to. As the night wore on and the bar emptied out, Wilhoit and Gogolinski began to check those IP addresses against Trend Micro's own archive of malware and VirusTotal, to see if they could find any new matches.

After the hotel's bar closed, leaving the two researchers alone on the dark patio, Wilhoit found a match for one of those IP addresses, pointing to a server Sandworm had used in Stockholm. The file he'd found, config.bak, also connected to that Swedish machine. And while it would have looked entirely unremarkable to the average person in the security industry, it immediately snapped Wilhoit's mind to attention.

Wilhoit had an unusual background for a security researcher. Just two years earlier, he'd left a job in St. Louis as manager of IT security for Peabody Energy, America's largest coal company. So he knew his way around so-called industrial control systems, or ICS—also known in some cases as supervisory control and data acquisition, or SCADA, systems. That software doesn't just push bits around, but instead sends commands to and takes in feedback from industrial equipment, a point where the digital and physical worlds meet.

ICS software is used for everything from the ventilators that circulate air in Peabody's mines to the massive washing basins that scrub its coal, to the generators that burn coal in power plants to the circuit breakers at the substations that feed electrical power to consumers. ICS applications run factories, water plants, oil and gas refineries, and transportation systems—in other words, all of the gargantuan, highly complex machinery that forms the backbone of modern civilization and that most of us take for granted.

One common piece of ICS software sold by General Electric is Cimplicity, which includes a kind of application known as a human-machine interface, essentially the control panel for those digital-to-physical command systems. The config.bak file Wilhoit had found was in fact a .cim file, designed to be opened in Cimplicity. Typically, a .cim file loads up an entire custom control panel in Cimplicity's software, like an infinitely reconfigurable dashboard for industrial equipment.

This Cimplicity file didn't do much of anything—except connect back to the Stockholm server iSight had identified as Sandworm's. But for anyone who had dealt with industrial control systems, the notion of that connection alone was deeply troubling. The infrastructure that runs those sensitive systems is meant to be entirely cut off from the internet, to protect it from hackers who might sabotage it and carry out catastrophic attacks.

The companies that run such equipment, particularly the electric utilities that serve as the most fundamental layer on which the rest of the industrialized world is built, constantly offer the public assurances that they have a strict "air gap" between their normal IT network and their industrial control network. But in a disturbing fraction of cases, those industrial control systems still maintain thin connections to the rest of their systems—or even the public internet—allowing engineers to access them remotely, for instance, or update their software.

The link between Sandworm and a Cimplicity file that phoned home to a server in Sweden was enough for Wilhoit to come to a startling conclusion: Sandworm wasn't merely focused on espionage. Intelligence-gathering operations don't break into industrial control systems. Sandworm seemed to be going further, trying to reach into victims' systems that could potentially hijack physical machinery, with physical consequences.

"They're gathering information in preparation to move to a second stage," Wilhoit realized as he sat in the cool night air outside his Cupertino hotel. "They're possibly trying to bridge the gap between digital and kinetic." The hackers' goals seemed to extend beyond spying to industrial sabotage.

Wilhoit and Gogolinski didn't sleep that night. Instead, they settled in at the hotel's outdoor table and started scouring for more clues of what Sandworm might be doing in ICS systems. How was it gaining control of those interfaces? Who were its targets? The answers continued to elude them.

They skipped all their meetings the next day, writing up their findings and posting them on Trend Micro's blog. Wilhoit also shared them with a contact at the FBI who—in typically tight-lipped G-man fashion—accepted the information without offering any in return.

Back in his Chantilly office, John Hultquist read Trend Micro's blog post on the Cimplicity file. He was so excited that he didn't even think to be annoyed that Trend Micro had found an unturned stone in the middle of iSight's major discovery. "It totally opened up a new game," Hultquist said.

Suddenly those misfit infrastructure targets among Sandworm's victims, like the Polish energy firm, made sense. Six weeks earlier, iSight had found the clues that shifted its mental model of the hackers' mission from mere cybercrime to nation-state-level intelligence gathering. Now Hultquist's idea of the threat was shifting again: beyond cyberspying to cyberwar. "This didn't look like classic espionage anymore," Hultquist thought. "We were looking at reconnaissance for attack."

■

Hultquist had, in some sense, been searching for something like Sandworm his entire career, long before iSight stumbled into it, before he even knew what form it would take. Like many others in the cybersecurity industry, and particularly those with a military background, he'd been expecting cyberwar's arrival: a new era that would finally apply hackers' digital abilities to the older, more familiar worlds of war and terrorism. For Hultquist, it would be a return to form. Since his army days a decade and a half earlier, he'd learned to think of adversaries as ruthless people willing to blow things up, to disrupt infrastructure, and to kill him, his friends, and innocent civilians he'd been tasked to protect.

An army reservist from the tiny town of Alcoa in eastern Tennessee, Hultquist had been called up in the midst of college to serve in Afghanistan after September 11. Soon the twenty-year-old found himself in Kandahar province in a Civil Affairs unit. Their job was to roll around the countryside in a six-man team, meeting with the heads of local villages in an effort to win hearts and minds. "We were still armed to the teeth, of course," Hultquist told me, followed by a kind of cackle that punctuates many of his stories. "It was high adventure." He let his black beard grow wild and came to be known within the unit as Teen Wolf.

His Civil Affairs unit's motto, printed across a badge on their uniforms' shoulder, was *vis amplificans vim,* a phrase his superiors had told him roughly translated to "force multiplier." The idea was to build relationships with local civilians that would aid in and expand on the less subtle work of expelling and killing the Taliban; they were the carrot to the infantry and Special Forces' stick. They'd have lunch with a group of village elders, ask them what they needed over a meal of goat and flatbread, and then, say, dig them a well. "Sometimes we'd come back a couple weeks later and they'd tell us where an ammo cache was hidden," Hultquist says.

In those early days of the war, the Taliban had already mostly fled the country, evaporating away from the initial U.S. invasion into the mountains of Pakistan. As they slowly began to slip back into Afghanistan in the months that followed, however, the violence ramped up again. One night, a Taliban guerrilla shot two rockets at the building where Hultquist and his unit were sleeping. One missed, banking skyward. The other, by a stroke of luck, failed to explode and was defused by their explosive-ordnance unit. Just days later, those same bomb technicians were killed when explosives they were defusing in a hidden Taliban rocket cache suddenly detonated. Hultquist and his unit were the first to the scene and spent hours collecting their dismembered body parts.

After the invasion of Iraq in 2003, Hultquist was transferred there, a deployment that was immediately as intense and bloody as Afghanistan had grown to be. In Iraq, the war quickly shifted to a hunt for a largely invisible force of saboteurs planting hidden makeshift bombs, a highly asymmetric guerrilla conflict. Hultquist learned how psychologically devastating those repeated, unpredictable, and lethal explosions could be. He'd eventually earn an army commendation for valor for his quick response when a team of fellow soldiers' Humvee was hit with a roadside bomb, administering first aid and an IV to two men who survived the attack.

The gunner on top of the vehicle, however, had died instantly in the blast. When the bomb had gone off, he'd had grenades strapped to his chest so that he could quickly feed them into the launcher.

Hultquist still remembers the sound of those grenades exploding one by one as the man's body burned.

■

Hultquist completed his tour of duty, returned to the United States, and finished college. After graduating, he got a job teaching a course on psychological operations at Fort Dix in New Jersey and then moved to one of the Information Sharing and Analysis Centers, or ISACs, that had been created around the country in the years after 9/11 to address possible terrorism threats. He was assigned to focus on the problem of highway safety and later the security of water systems and railways, thinking up countermeasures to grim scenarios like attackers plowing large vehicles into crowds or planting bombs in vehicles' cargo holds, as terrorists had done in Sri Lanka in cases he studied.

He was introduced to the digital side of those security threats only in 2006, when he joined the State Department as a junior intelligence analyst contractor, tasked mostly with helping to protect the agency's own networks from hackers. At the time, China's state-sponsored cyberspying campaigns were just coming into focus as a serious problem for America's national security and even its commercial dominance. In the mid-2000s, a series of intrusions known as Titan Rain, believed to be carried out by cyberspies working for China's People's Liberation Army, had broken into Lockheed Martin, Sandia National Labs, and NASA. By the time Hultquist started his job at State, reports were surfacing on an almost weekly basis of Chinese espionage that had breached the networks of targets from defense contractors to tech companies. "They were stealing all of our intellectual property, and all of our attention," Hultquist says of the Chinese hackers.

But from his first years tracking state-sponsored cyberspies in the U.S. government, Hultquist gravitated to a different, less considered form of digital attack. After his experience trying to outthink insurgents and terrorists in the army and then at the ISACs, he naturally focused not on espionage but on the threats capable of inflicting psychological disruption on an enemy, shutting down civilian resources and creating chaos.

In 2007, for instance, Estonia had come under a punishing, unprecedented barrage of DDoS attacks that all seemed to originate in Russia. When Estonian police cracked down on riots incited by the country's Russian-speaking minority, targeted floods of junk traffic knocked Estonia's government, media, and banking sites off-line for days in a networked blitzkrieg like nothing the world had ever seen before. The next year, when war broke out between Russia and Georgia, another of its post-Soviet neighbors, crude cyberattacks pummeled that country's government and media, too. Russia, it seemed to Hultquist, was trying out basic methods of pairing traditional physical attacks with digital weapons of mass disruption.

Back then, Hultquist had mostly watched from the sidelines. He'd studied the Estonian and Georgian attacks, met with researchers who tracked them, and briefed senior officials. But he'd rarely been able to pull their attention away from the massive siphoning of state secrets and intellectual property being carried out by China's hackers, a threat that seemed far more immediate to American interests.

Now, years later, iSight's Sandworm discovery had put Hultquist at the vanguard of what seemed to be a new, far more advanced form of Russian cyberwar. In the midst of Russia's invasion into Ukraine, a team of Russian hackers was using sophisticated penetration tools to gain access to its adversaries' infrastructure, potentially laying the groundwork to attack the underpinnings of civilian society, hundreds of miles beyond the front lines: He imagined sabotaged manufacturing, paralyzed transportation, blackouts.

As Sandworm's mission crystallized in his mind, a phrase from his time in the army's Civil Affairs unit came to him from more than a decade earlier: *vis amplificans vim*.

■

After he read Trend Micro's report, Hultquist's fascination grew: Sandworm had transformed in his mind from a vexing puzzle to a rare and dangerous geopolitical phenomenon. He began to bring it up constantly with iSight's analysts, with any reporter he spoke to, with other members of the security industry, and with the D.C. intelligence community. For iSight's office Halloween party, he even made himself a Sandworm costume out of a green children's play tunnel, an expression of his pet preoccupation that was perhaps only partly a self-mocking joke. "Sandworm was my favorite thing," Hultquist said simply.

He was nonetheless frustrated to find that after the initial hype around iSight's discovery, his Sandworm-watchers club didn't have many other members. The mainstream media seemed to have, for the moment, largely exhausted its interest in the group. Vague hints of a technically convoluted connection to infrastructure attacks weren't enough, it seemed, to attract even a fraction of the attention that iSight had initially brought to Sandworm's zero day and secret *Dune* clues.

But Hultquist didn't know that someone else had been tracking the group's campaign of intrusions, too, and had quietly assembled by far the most disturbing portrait of the group yet.

Thirteen days after Trend Micro had released its findings on Sandworm's connection to industrial control system attacks, the division of the Department of Homeland Security known as the Industrial Control Systems Cyber Emergency Response Team, or ICS-CERT, released its own report. ICS-CERT acts as a specialized infrastructure-focused government cybersecurity watchdog tasked with warning Americans about impending digital security threats. It had deep ties with U.S. utilities like power and water suppliers. And now, perhaps triggered by iSight and Trend Micro's research, it was confirming Hultquist's worst fears about Sandworm's reach.

Sandworm, according to the ICS-CERT report, had built tools for hacking not only the GE Cimplicity human-machine interfaces Trend Micro had noted but also similar software sold by two other major vendors, Siemens and Advantech/Broadwin. The report stated that the intrusions of industrial control system targets had begun as early as 2011 and continued until as recently as September 2014, the month iSight detected Sandworm. And the hackers had successfully penetrated multiple critical infrastructure targets, though none were named in the document. As far as ICS-CERT could tell, the operations had only reached the stage of reconnaissance, not actual sabotage.

iSight's analysts began discreetly following up on the DHS report with their sources in the security industry and quickly confirmed what they'd read between the lines: Some of Sandworm's intrusions had occurred at infrastructure targets that weren't just Ukrainian or Polish. They were American.

Less than two months after iSight had found its first fingerprints, Hultquist's idea of Sandworm had shifted yet again. "This was a foreign actor who had access to zero days making a deliberate attempt on our critical infrastructure," Hultquist says. "We'd detected a group on the other side of the world carrying out espionage. We'd pored over its artifacts. And we'd found it was a threat to the United States."

■

Even the revelation that Sandworm was a fully equipped infrastructure-hacking team with ties to Russia and global attack ambitions never received the attention Hultquist thought it deserved. It was accompanied by no statement from White House officials. The security and utility industry trade press briefly buzzed with the news and then moved on. "It was a sideshow, and no one gave a shit," Hultquist said with a rare hint of bitterness.

But all the attention seemed to have finally reached one audience: Sandworm itself. When iSight looked for the servers connected with the malware again after all of the public reports, the computers had been pulled off-line. The company would find one more BlackEnergy sample in early 2015 that seemed to have been created by the same authors, this time without any *Dune* references in its campaign codes. It would never find that sort of obvious, human fingerprint again; the group had learned from the mistake of revealing its sci-fi preferences.

Sandworm had gone back underground. It wouldn't surface again for another year. When it did, it would no longer be focused on reconnaissance. It would be primed to strike.

5

STARLIGHTMEDIA

On a calm Sunday morning in October 2015, more than a year before Yasinsky would look out of his kitchen window at a blacked-out skyline, he sat near that same window in his family's high-rise apartment in Kiev, sipping tea and eating a bowl of cornflakes. Suddenly his phone buzzed with a call from an IT administrator at work.

Yasinsky was, at the time, employed as the director of information security at StarLightMedia, Ukraine's largest TV broadcasting conglomerate. The night before, his colleague on the phone told him, two of StarLight's servers had inexplicably gone off-line. The admin assured Yasinsky that it wasn't an emergency. The machines had already been restored from backups.

But as Yasinsky quizzed his colleague further about the server outage, one fact immediately made him feel uneasy. The two machines had gone dark at almost the same minute. "One server going down, it happens," Yasinsky thought. "But two servers at the same time? That's suspicious."

Resigned to a lost weekend, he left his apartment and began his commute to StarLight's offices, descending the endless escalator that leads into Kiev's metro, one of the deepest in the world and designed during the Cold War to serve as a series of potential bomb shelter tunnels. After forty minutes underground, Yasinsky emerged into the cool autumn air of central Kiev. He took the scenic route to the office, walking through Taras Shevchenko Park and the university campus next to it. As he passed street musicians, college students on dates, then the botanical gardens, whose leaves were beginning to turn, the dismal war that had broken out in the east of the country felt far away.

Yasinsky arrived at StarLightMedia's office, a five-story building on a quiet street. Inside, he and the company's IT administrators began examining the image they'd kept of one of the corrupted servers, a digital replica of all its data. Yasinsky's hunch that the outage was no accident was immediately confirmed. The server's master boot record—the deep-seated, reptile-brain portion of a computer's hard drive that tells the machine where to find its own operating system—had been precisely overwritten with zeros. And the two victim servers that had suffered that lobotomy weren't randomly chosen. They were domain controllers, computers with powerful privileges that could be used to reach into hundreds of other machines on the corporate network.

Yasinsky quickly discovered the attack had indeed gone far beyond just those two machines. Before they had been wiped, the pair of corrupted servers had themselves planted malware on the laptops of thirteen StarLight employees. The staffers had been preparing a morning TV news bulletin ahead of Kiev's local elections when they suddenly found that their computers had been turned into black-screened, useless bricks. The infection had triggered the same boot-record overwrite technique on each of their hard drives.

Nonetheless, Yasinsky could see that his company had been lucky. When he looked at StarLightMedia's network logs, it appeared the domain controllers had committed suicide prematurely. They'd actually been set to infect and destroy two hundred more of the company's PCs. Someone had carefully planted a logic bomb at the heart of the media firm's network, designed to cause it as much disruption as possible.

Yasinsky managed to pull a copy of the destructive program from the backups, and that night, back at home in the north of the city, he scrutinized its code. He was struck by the layers of obfuscation; the malware had evaded all antivirus scans. It had even impersonated an antivirus scanner itself, Microsoft's Windows Defender. After his family had gone to sleep, Yasinsky printed the code and laid the papers across his kitchen table and floor, crossing out lines of camouflaging characters and highlighting commands to see the malware's true form.

Yasinsky had been working in information security for twenty years. After a stint in the army, he'd spent thirteen years as an IT security analyst for Kyivstar, Ukraine's largest telecommunications firm. He'd managed massive networks and fought off crews of sophisticated cybercriminal hackers. But he'd never analyzed such a well-concealed and highly targeted digital weapon.

As a security researcher, Yasinsky had long prided himself on a dispassionate and scientific approach to the problems of information security, drilling into the practical details of digital defense rather than obsessing over the psychology of his adversary. But as he followed Sandworm's tracks through StarLightMedia's network, he nonetheless could sense he was facing an enemy more sophisticated than he'd ever seen before.

■

Oleksii Yasinsky had understood intuitively from childhood that the digital was no less real than the physical—that life and death could depend as easily on one as on the other.

As a nine-year-old growing up in Soviet Kiev in 1985, he'd sneak a copy of the state-issued magazine *Tekhnika Molodezhi,* or "Technology for the Youth," under his blanket, along with a flashlight and his treasured MK-61 calculator. He'd flip to the pages devoted to the continuing adventures of the two fictional cosmonauts Korshunov and Perepyolkin. The pair, through the vagaries of fate, had found themselves stuck on the moon with only a lunar transport vehicle designed for short trips. Even worse, they were low on fuel, with no electronic guidance system. It was Yasinsky's secret responsibility, in his illicit post-bedtime cocoon, to get those two men home by copying commands from the magazine into his programmable calculator.

"The life of two people helplessly dangling in space depended on this little boy," Yasinsky would later write in a journal, describing the intensity of that first programming experience.

> Back then I did not yet understand the meaning hidden
> in the neat columns of mysterious characters printed on
> yellowed pages of the magazine. Pages seemed to be torn
> from some sort of wizard manuscript, and I was clicking
> on the soft gray keys of the calculator anticipating a new

adventure. But even at the time I knew: this was the key to a completely different world, or, more precisely, the myriad of other worlds I could create myself.

Yasinsky grew up in a two-room home in a typical five-story, Khrushchev-era Soviet apartment complex in Kiev. He was a child of engineers: His father worked in a record-player factory, and his mother was a university researcher in aerospace metals. He had, as he describes it, a very typical Soviet childhood. He proudly wore the red-scarfed uniform of Lenin's Young Pioneers to school every day, played in the building's courtyard with his friends, and occasionally broke neighbors' windows with a soccer ball. He remembers no politics ever being discussed at home, with the exception of a few whispers from his parents in the kitchen about a visit his great-grandparents had received from the secret police, a conversation quickly cut short for fear of eavesdropping neighbors.

School never interested Yasinsky as much as the adventures he unlocked with his MK-61 calculator. It was, after all, his first computer, at a time when the Apple IIs and Nintendo consoles of the West had yet to penetrate the Iron Curtain. But when Yasinsky was around twelve, his father managed to collect and then assemble the components of a Sinclair Spectrum PC. It was, for Yasinsky, a mind-blowing upgrade. He spent hours painstakingly reading manuals he found photocopied at the local radio market, writing code in BASIC and later assembly, filling the screen with pixel art depictions of wire-frame spaceships.

The moment he believes turned his obsession with computers from a hobby to a career, however, was an act not of programming but of reverse engineering. Simply by changing a few bytes in the code of a primitive shooter video game, he discovered he could endow his character with unlimited lives and ammunition. That basic act of hacking, for Yasinsky, wasn't merely a way to cheat in a meaningless game. It was instead as if he'd gained new powers to reshape reality itself. "I had turned the world upside down. I'd gone into the other side of the screen," Yasinsky remembers.

It followed intuitively, for him, that if this power could change the digital world, it could control the physical universe, too. "I realized the world is not what we see," he says. "It wasn't about getting extra lives; it was about changing the world I'd found myself in."

In the late 1980s, however, came Gorbachev's policy of glasnost, or "openness," and with it a flood of Western distractions. For Yasinsky and his young teenage friends, the influx of global media took the form of Jean-Claude Van Damme and Bruce Lee kung fu films. A karate and judo obsession briefly superseded his love for computers. Yasinsky was a talented enough fighter that in 1993 he was selected for the Ukrainian national karate championships. But in one of those tournament matches, he says, an opponent struck him with an illegal kick just below the knee, tearing the ligaments in the back of his leg and ending his brief martial arts career. "Fortunately, I still had Assembly," Yasinsky wrote in his journal.

After two years studying computer science at the Kiev Polytechnic Institute, Yasinsky was drafted into the army. He describes the next year and a half as a long lesson in discipline, organization, self-confidence, and intensely rigorous drudgery. "A soldier's best friend is a shovel, and it's good to be a soldier," he remembers his superiors drumming into him. Aside from that bit of character building, he says that he learned nothing except how to properly make a bed.

When he was released and got back to his university education, he finally returned to computer science. He found that there was an emerging field within the discipline that appealed to his sense of the hidden structure of the world and the levers that moved it: cybersecurity.

Yasinsky learned only its barest basics in his studies. But when he graduated, he landed a job at Kyivstar, then Ukraine's largest telecom provider. That job, he says, gave him his real education. Though most of his career there is protected by a nondisclosure agreement, he hints that he worked on the company's team that fights fraud and crime and served as a consultant to law enforcement. He also says that the job was his first experience learning to sift through massive data sets to fight intelligent, malicious adversaries. "It was like the Matrix," he says. "You look at all these numbers and you can see real human behavior."

After six years, Yasinsky moved on to a purely digital version of the same cat-and-mouse game: Rather than physical-world criminals, he was tasked with tracking the hackers who sought to exploit Kyivstar's systems. In the late 2000s, those hackers were transitioning from opportunistic criminal schemes to highly organized fraud operations. Yasinsky found himself engaged in the same sort of reverse engineering that had captivated him as a teenager. But instead of taking apart the code of a mere video game, he was dissecting elaborate criminal intrusions, deconstructing malware to see the intentions of the devious parasites within Kyivstar's network.

Even as the stakes of that cat-and-mouse game escalated, it had seemed like a fair fight. In cybersecurity, attackers have the advantage: There are always more points of ingress than defenders can protect, and a skilled hacker needs only one. But these were nonetheless mostly small criminal operations facing a well-organized corporate security team capable of identifying their incursions and limiting the damage they could inflict.

Then, not long before the outbreak of Ukraine's war with Russia, Yasinsky took a position as chief information security officer at StarLightMedia. And he found himself facing a new form of conflict— one for which neither his company nor his country nor the world at large was prepared.

■

By the fall of 2015, only the smallest hints of that conflict's scale were visible. For days, Yasinsky worked to determine the basic facts of the mysterious attack on StarLightMedia, reverse engineering the obfuscated code he'd pulled from the company's backups, the digital IED that had nearly devastated its network. Beneath all its cloaking and misdirection, Yasinsky determined, was a piece of malware known as KillDisk, a data-destroying tool that had been circulating among hackers for about a decade.*

Understanding how that destructive program got into StarLight-Media's system would take weeks longer: Along with two colleagues,

---

* Two security researchers, Michael Goedeker and Andrii Bezverkhyi, say they and Bezverkhyi's security firm, SOC Prime, were deeply involved in StarLightMedia's investigation. But Yasinsky disputed the extent of this cooperation, telling me that while he had shared some information with Bezverkhyi and SOC Prime had provided some tools for their work, neither Goedeker nor anyone from SOC Prime had contributed to StarLightMedia's final analysis.

Yasinsky obsessively dug into the company's network logs, combing them again and again, working through nights and weekends to parse the data with ever finer filters, hoping to extract clues.

The team began to find the telltale signs of the hackers' presence—some compromised corporate YouTube accounts, an administrator's network log-in that had remained active even when he was out sick. Slowly, with a sinking dread, they found evidence showing that the intruders had been inside their network for weeks before detonating their attack's payload. Then another clue suggested they'd been inside the system for three months. Then six.

Finally, they identified the piece of malware that had given the hackers their initial foothold, penetrating one of the staff's PCs via an infected attachment: It was again a form of BlackEnergy, the same malware that iSight had tied to Sandworm a year earlier. But now it had been reworked to evade detection by antivirus software and included new modules that allowed the hacker to spread to other machines on the same network and execute the KillDisk data wiper.

As he dug into the forensics of how his company had been sabotaged, Yasinsky began to hear from colleagues at other firms and in the government that they too had been hacked, and in almost exactly the same way. A competing media company, TRK, hadn't gotten off as easily: It had lost more than a hundred computers to the KillDisk attack. Another intrusion had hit Ukrzaliznytsia, Ukraine's biggest railway company. Yasinsky would later learn that Kiev's main airport, Boryspil, had been struck. There were other targets, too, ones that asked Yasinsky to keep their breaches secret. Again and again, the hackers used the all-purpose BlackEnergy malware for access and reconnaissance, then KillDisk for data destruction. Their motives remained an enigma, but their marks were everywhere.

"With every step forward, it became clearer that our *Titanic* had found its iceberg," says Yasinsky. "The deeper we looked, the bigger it was."

6

HOLODOMOR TO CHERNOBYL

Though he didn't know it yet, Yasinsky had found himself in the middle of the sort of event that had defined Ukraine's long and unkind history: a foreign invasion.

To understand how Ukraine would come to serve as the battleground for the world's first full-blown cyberwar, it helps to look back at a millennium of conflict and domination, with Ukraine as the point where the bloodiest edges of two continents meet. Over the last thousand years, incursions into Ukraine have taken the form of Mongol hordes from the east and Lithuanian heathens and Polish imperialists from the west. The nation's name itself, "Ukraina," comes from a Slavic word for "borderland." Ukraine's existence has been defined by its position, caught between powerful neighbors. But the country's most perpetual nemesis has been the one with whom it shares not only the longest border but also the most history and culture—its larger, more aggressive, estranged brother from the same mother.

Russia and Ukraine trace the origins of their two civilizations to a common ancestor, the flourishing medieval state of Kievan Rus. That kingdom, growing around Kiev from the tenth century AD, became an eastern outpost of European culture after its king Volodymyr somewhat arbitrarily decided to convert his people from paganism to Orthodox Christianity. Ukrainians like to point out that his son Yaroslav the Wise built Kiev's iconic St. Sophia Cathedral in 1037, when Moscow was little more than a forest by the Volga River.

But geography was never in Ukraine's favor. Kievan Rus was destroyed in the thirteenth century by brutal Mongols riding southwest from the Urals across the indefensible landscape of the steppe, led by Batu Khan, one of the grandsons of Genghis Khan. After a long siege, the invaders massacred Kiev's population, burned hundreds of churches, and razed its city walls.

In the wake of that massive destruction, as Russians tell it, the refugees of Kievan Rus's early Slavic society migrated to Moscow, where they became Russians. In the Ukrainian version, their culture quietly continued to grow where it was first planted, in the rich black soil of the broad region north of the Black Sea, surviving for centuries despite the successive layers of foreigners who tried to lay claim to it, from Mongols to Poles to Turks to Tatars and finally Russians.

Prior to the last thirty years, however, Ukraine's attempts at actual independence have been painful, hard-fought failures. Over the last millennium, the country's hopes for self-rule rose and fell three times: in the seventeenth-century rebellion of the Ukrainian Cossacks, stubbornly autonomous warrior settlers of the steppes; in the bloody Ukrainian civil war following Russia's Bolshevik Revolution in 1917; and again after a brief, tragically misguided alliance with Nazi occupiers during World War II. As Anna Reid wrote in her history of Ukraine, *Borderland*, Ukraine's rebellions have long been "nasty, brutish, and above all short." By the beginning of the twentieth century, Ukraine—or "the Ukraine," because it was considered little more than a region, not a nation—was a possession of the Russian empire and commonly referred to as "Southwest Russia" or "Little Russia."

As dark as Ukraine's history has been, its greatest litany of horrors arguably came in just the last century or so of Russian hegemony. In World War I, 3.5 million Ukrainians were conscripted to fight for their Russian rulers. Even after Bolshevism swept Russia and pulled the country out of the war, fighting raged for years in Ukraine between the country's own independence fighters, the "Whites," who remained loyal to Russia's czarist regime, and the communist army of Vladimir Lenin.

Even more so than World War I, the civil war spilled into tragic and indiscriminate chaos on Ukrainian soil. Soldiers and bandits on all sides committed atrocities against civilians, including many of the

Jewish-targeted pogroms that have made "Cossack" synonymous with "murderer" in much of the global Jewish diaspora. In total, about 1.5 million Ukrainians died in the violent years between 1914 and 1921.

It was the next decade between the wars, however, that for many Ukrainians still resonates as a memory of deep, even unforgivable oppression. The Soviet regime manufactured a famine in Ukraine that would kill 3.9 million people, a tragedy of unimaginable scope that's known today as the Holodomor, a combination of the Ukrainian words for "hunger" and "extermination."

The starvation began through simple exploitation: Ukraine's fertile black soil offered a tempting breadbasket for Russia. During its own civil war from 1917 to 1922, Russia seized as much grain as it could at gunpoint to alleviate its own wartime food shortages. "For God's sake, use all energy and all revolutionary measures to send grain, grain and more grain!" Lenin wrote in a telegram to Soviet forces in Ukraine in 1918. The secret police force known as the KGB, initially called the Cheka and then the OGPU, was formed in part to find and take grain from Ukrainian peasants by whatever means necessary. When American Relief Administration workers were sent to Russia to help relieve the food crisis, Soviet forces kept them out of Ukraine, obscuring the fact that it was Ukrainians who were experiencing the worst of the shortages.

By 1932, starvation had become a far more purposeful Soviet tool of control. Moscow, now under the rule of Joseph Stalin, had imposed agricultural collectivization, moving peasants off the land they had owned for generations and onto communally held farms. At the same time, the most prosperous peasants, known as *kulaks*, were branded as class traitors and subjected to exile, imprisonment, and massacre. When the result, inevitably, was massive shortfalls in food production, the Soviets only redoubled their efforts to seize every ounce of grain possible from Ukraine's peasants. They searched systematically, using hooked and spiked poles to dig behind walls, under floorboards, and even in the earth outside homes in search of hidden food. When they found it, they piled the confiscated grain in locked warehouses. OGPU guards patrolled fields, shooting scavengers on sight.

Peasants responded with scattered resistance, butchering their live-stock rather than give it to collective farms and taking up arms in guerrilla bands. Those acts of rebellion only stoked Stalin's paranoid fears of a Ukrainian nationalist rebellion, refreshing Bolshevik memories of war with Ukrainian freedom fighters just a few years earlier. So famine soon became not only the cause of Ukrainian subversion but its solution too: The Soviet regime simply starved the country into submission.

The Soviet government restricted travel, preventing hungry peasants from fleeing to other regions or countries. Bodies piled up in railway stations and along roads. The historian Anne Applebaum's book on the Holodomor, *Red Famine,* documents stories of desperate peasants resorting to eating leather and rodents, grass, and, in states of starvation-induced mania, even their own children. All of this occurred in one of the most fertile grain-production regions in the world.

Roughly 13 percent of Ukraine's population at the time died, but no Ukrainian survived the period untouched by the trauma. Raphael Lemkin, the Polish-Jewish lawyer who lost forty-nine relatives in the next decade's Holocaust and went on to coin the term "genocide," later cited the Holodomor in a 1953 speech in New York as a quintessential example of his neologism. "This is not simply a case of mass murder," Lemkin said. "It is a case of genocide, of destruction, not of individuals only, but of a culture and a nation."

■

Ukraine's greatest misfortune, aside from finding itself in Russia's inescapable shadow, was that it was destined to serve as the battlefield between East and West. World War II was no exception. Like a bloody rerun of the country's civil war from two decades earlier, Hitler's war with Russia's Red Army split Ukraine into three warring sides: those supporting the Nazis in an ill-fated hope of a life better than the one under Stalin, those conscripted into the Soviet forces, and a small faction fighting in vain for an independent Ukraine.

In fact, the Soviet atrocities had begun even before the Nazis arrived, during the brief period of German-Russian nonaggression.

When Hitler seized Poland in 1939, the region of western Ukraine known as Galicia that had until then been under Polish control suddenly fell to Moscow. Stalin and his Ukrainian Communist Party subordinate Nikita Khrushchev wasted no time in purging the region of anyone who might possibly fight the Soviet Union's annexation: farmers who resisted collectivization, Poles, Jews, lawyers, priests, and government officials.

Between 800,000 and 1.6 million people were arrested and deported from western Ukraine to labor camps in Kazakhstan and Siberia, as much as a fifth of the region's population. When Hitler did invade two years later, in a surprise attack that shattered the two countries' pact, the Soviets hurriedly massacred the Ukrainian prisoners they hadn't yet deported before fleeing to the east.

In the years that followed, the Nazis took their turn brutalizing Ukraine. As Hitler's army marched east, SS troops followed, murdering as many Jewish civilians as they could find, killing them mostly with firing squads and dumping bodies in mass graves rather than bothering with trains to concentration camps. Ukrainians who had welcomed the Germans and even aided in the Holocaust's slaughter were rewarded with a policy that treated all Slavs, Russians, and Ukrainians alike, as *Untermenschen*. The Nazis rounded up 2.8 million Soviet citizens, more than 2 million of whom where Ukrainian, and shipped them to Germany to work in factories for slave wages.

Even after the Red Army turned the tide of the war with an immensely costly victory in 1943 at Stalingrad—where more than 1 million Soviet soldiers died—the Nazis continued to kill en masse, starving 2 million captured Soviet prisoners as they death-marched them westward. In all, 1 in 6 Ukrainians died in the war, and about 1 in 8 Russians, with a staggering total of 26.6 million deaths across the U.S.S.R., a number unparalleled in the history of war.

In the postwar decades that followed, Moscow's treatment of Ukraine settled into a slower-burning repression of a subjugated state. In the 1950s, through the last years of Stalin's terror and the rise of Khrushchev to take his place, more Ukrainians were sent to the U.S.S.R.'s gulags than any other nationality. Through the 1960s and 1970s, groups like the Sixtiers and the Helsinki Group fought for Ukrainian autonomy and human rights, only to be quickly swept away to a life of destitution and hopelessness in Siberian labor camps.

The 1980s and the rise of Gorbachev would lay the groundwork, after eight hundred years, for Ukrainian independence. But not before giving Ukraine one more lasting keepsake of its Soviet rule.

■

On the night of April 25, 1986, engineers were conducting a test at the Chernobyl nuclear plant near the northern Ukrainian town of Pripyat, population fifty thousand. The experiment was designed to check how long the reactor would continue to function in the case of a total electric failure. Just after midnight, operators turned off the system that would cool the reactor core with water in the case of an emergency and initiated a power shutdown.

Exactly what happened next remains a subject of controversy among scientists, even today. But at 1:23 a.m., a massive eruption—perhaps caused by a sudden buildup of steam or perhaps a nuclear explosion that subsequently triggered that steam blowup—tore through the plant, rupturing the reactor core and killing two engineers. A jet of radioactive material immediately shot more than three thousand feet in the air.

Firemen rushed to the scene to extinguish the plant's burning roofs, many unwittingly receiving fatal doses of radioactivity. But no public warning went out to the citizens of nearby Pripyat, where people went about their Saturday routines unaware of the nuclear fallout spewing from the meltdown just a few miles down the river. Only thirty-six hours later did Communist Party officials enact a limited evacuation, starting with just a small area of a few miles around the plant. In fact, a radioactive plume was already spreading through the atmosphere that would reach as far as Sweden, with an invisible toll on the health of its victims that still eludes measurement.

For weeks after, Moscow-based state news agencies made no mention of the ongoing disaster. Nor did Communist Party General Secretary Mikhail Gorbachev. Six days after the explosion, as nuclear fragments continued to rain down from Chernobyl's toxic cloud, party officials evacuated their own children to safety on the Crimean peninsula, even as they instructed Ukraine's citizens to carry on with their annual May Day parade. Just sixty miles south of Chernobyl's ground zero, thousands of people—including countless children—marched down Kiev's main drag of Khreshchatyk Street. They carried flowers, flags, and portraits of Soviet leaders, unaware that those same leaders had knowingly exposed them to the fallout of one of the worst industrial disasters in history.

7

MAIDAN TO DONBAS

On my first night in Kiev in the spring of 2017, I stepped out of the towering Hotel Ukraine—formerly the Hotel Moscow, a Soviet-era luxury hotel now devolved into a cheap and run-down relic of U.S.S.R. tastes—and into the Maidan below, the central square of Ukraine's capital. Before my jet-lagged brain had even oriented itself, I found myself in a crowd around the steps of the Monument to the Founders of Kiev, where a man dressed in black holding a guitar was belting out the Ukrainian national anthem, his fist across his chest, flanked by soldiers in camouflage fatigues, one wearing sunglasses in the dark.

Behind the singer were pictures of friendly faces wearing balaclavas and helmets. Only later would I make the connection that these were photographs of ordinary Ukrainians who had been killed near that very spot three years earlier. Many had been shot by snipers positioned in the top floors of the Hotel Ukraine I'd just checked into. The hotel's lobby, too, had been conscripted into the revolution, one side turned into a field clinic for wounded protesters, the other into a morgue.

As the Maidan crowd around the singer bellowed out the national anthem along with him, their hands on their hearts and some draped in Ukrainian flags, their voices were charged with an eerie intensity that raised the hair on my skin. "Ukraine's freedom has not yet perished, nor has her glory," they sang. "We will not allow others to rule in our motherland." In my first hour in Ukraine, I felt I had stepped into the buzzing epicenter of a postrevolutionary nation at war.

■

After centuries of bloody fighting for its independence, Ukraine's liberation had originally arrived in 1991, almost by accident. With the U.S.S.R.'s collapse, a stunned Ukrainian parliament voted to become a sovereign nation, with only the far eastern region of Donetsk, the most ethnically Russian slice of the country, opposing the decision.

But for the decades that followed, Moscow maintained a powerful influence over Ukraine, and the two countries transitioned in tandem from communism to kleptocracy. Ukraine's prime minister and then president for its first fourteen years of independence, Leonid Kuchma, became known for siphoning a stream of boondoggle deals and cheap loans to cronies. In the year 2000, a bodyguard released tapes of Kuchma discussing the torture and killing of an investigative journalist who had been found dead in the woods south of Kiev, as well as vote rigging, bribe taking, and selling weapons systems to Saddam Hussein.

For a population inured to corruption and fed lies by state-run news for as long as they could remember, even so-called Kuchmagate failed to oust the president. Instead, he lasted until his chosen successor, Viktor Yanukovich, an oligarch with close ties to the Russian president, Vladimir Putin, ran for president in 2004. His opponent was Viktor Yushchenko, a Ukrainian nationalist, financier, and reformer who promised to finally bring the country out from under Russia's thumb.

Sensing a shift, the Kremlin determined to tighten Ukraine's leash. Russian political operatives began working secretly for Yanukovich, and soon Yushchenko was finding his speaking venues closed and his plane diverted from campaign stops. Then, a month before elections, Yushchenko was mysteriously poisoned with dioxin, falling deathly ill. He barely survived, his skin left scarred and disfigured by the attack. Later, two Russians were arrested in a failed attempt to blow up Yushchenko's campaign headquarters in Kiev.

When Yanukovich was declared the winner of the elections that November, the vote rigging was barely hidden. Yushchenko had, by this time, recovered enough from his poisoning to return to campaigning and was winning by double digits in polls. But the cheating was evident: Putin had gone so far as to send Yanukovich his congratulations before the results were even tallied.

This time, Ukrainians had had enough. Hundreds of thousands of people flooded the streets of Kiev, filling the Maidan and waving orange scarves, the chosen color of Yushchenko's campaign. Facing a mass uprising, Yanukovich stepped down a month later. The Orange Revolution, finally, was Ukraine's first step toward real independence. Yushchenko won a legitimate election the next month and declared a new era of the country's history.

But politics in Ukraine are never so simple. Yushchenko turned out to be an inspiring but disorganized leader, warring with his prime minister, Yulia Tymoshenko. The government deadlocked and the economy foundered. Amazingly, Yanukovich managed to wheedle his way back into the spotlight, thanks in part to his Russian backing and a makeover overseen by the U.S. lobbyist Paul Manafort, the future campaign manager of Donald Trump. From 2006 to 2007, Yanukovich even served as prime minister under his former archrival Yushchenko. In 2010, he defeated Tymoshenko in the presidential election, definitively ending the Orange Revolution five years after it had begun.

Ukraine took four years to simmer to the boiling point again. As president, Yanukovich proved himself to be even more ambitious in his mass theft than Kuchma, openly pillaging state coffers. His group of blatantly corrupt associates, known as the Family, tucked away as much as $100 billion of government funds into their private accounts. Yanukovich's estate north of Kiev, called Mezhyhirya, became a mobster's Xanadu, complete with a menagerie of exotic birds, a bowling alley, a rifle range, a boxing ring, and $46.5 million worth of chandeliers.

The final straw, however, wasn't Yanukovich's corruption but his Russian alliances. Under Yushchenko, Ukraine had started on a long road to membership in NATO, a prospect that no doubt infuriated and terrified Putin. Ukrainians' European hopes had still lingered under Yanukovich in the form of an association agreement with the European Union, trade negotiations that represented the first baby step toward the West. But a week before signing the agreement, under pressure from Putin, Yanukovich killed the deal.

The uprising and crackdown that followed had little of the bloodless idealism of the Orange Revolution. When hundreds of thousands of people again flooded the Maidan in November 2013, police clumsily sought to disperse them with water cannons, rubber bullets, and tear gas. Protesters responded with barricades and Molotov cocktails.

In the midst of that increasing violence, the Maidan movement also began to see the first signs of digital attacks. Calls and SMS messages from mysterious origins flooded the phone lines of pro-Western and pro-revolution government officials. At the telecom provider Kyivstar, engineers like Oleksii Yasinsky found themselves struggling to keep the mobile network intact as the crisis mounted. On one street near the Maidan, devices known as IMSI catchers impersonated cell phone towers to spam out text messages to protesters, telling them to go home. But as the square's physical conflict ramped up, few people registered those first signs of digital meddling.

By the end of that winter, the bullets were no longer rubber. As protesters made a final notorious charge up the slope of the Maidan toward the Hotel Ukraine, snipers fired on them from above, led by a unit of brutal pro-Russian militarized police known as the Berkut—Ukrainian for "eagle." Many Ukrainians believe the Berkut were joined by actual Russian soldiers brought in by Yanukovich. The death toll was 103 protesters, a group now immortalized as the "Heavenly Hundred"—the same martyrs whose lives were being memorialized on the Maidan on my first night in Kiev.

After the revolution's final, tragic bloodletting, Yanukovich could see that the violence had only steeled the movement against him. He fled to Russia.

Putin, not one to let geopolitics turn against him, took a different approach: He promptly invaded.

■

Before the dust had even settled on the Maidan, in late February 2014, a group of militiamen in unmarked uniforms, including Berkut soldiers, entered the parliament of the southern Ukrainian peninsular state of Crimea and installed a pro-Russian government. In a blink, thirty-five thousand Russian troops moved in, swiftly occupying the region with barely a shot fired. Two months later, more unmarked Russian soldiers—they soon came to be known as "little green men"—began to trickle across the border into the Russian-speaking eastern Ukrainian region of Donbas, helping to arm a separatist movement that quickly took control of the cities of Donetsk and Luhansk with Russian tanks and artillery.

Since then, Russia has successfully made Crimea its full-fledged possession as Ukraine's eastern front has settled into a grinding, undeclared war. Two million Ukrainians have become internal refugees, and 10,000 Ukrainians have been killed. In July 2014, the callousness of the Kremlin-backed forces shocked the world when a Russian anti-aircraft unit, under the guise of pro-Russian Ukrainian forces, fired a Buk missile that downed a Malaysian passenger jet over Ukrainian territory, killing all 298 people on board.

But from the early months of the invasion, another kind of front began to form in Ukraine's war. Four days before Ukraine's post-revolution elections in May 2014, a pro-Russian hacker group calling itself CyberBerkut—an allusion to the same police force that had killed protesters during the Maidan revolution—announced on the website cyber-berkut.org its intention to disrupt the coming presidential election to replace the seat vacated by Yanukovich. "The anti-people junta is trying to legalize itself by organizing this show, directed by the West," the message read in Russian. "We will not allow it!"

That night, the group began a devious series of cyberattacks on the country's Central Election Commission: They broke into the commission's network and wiped dozens of computers. "The idea was to destroy the system, to prevent it showing the results, and then to blame Ukraine's so-called junta," says Victor Zhora, a security contractor for the commission at the time. "The goal was to discredit the election process."

The commission's IT administrators managed to rebuild the network in time for the election. But they found on Election Day that hackers had planted an image of fake results on the commission's web server, which seemed to show the ultraright presidential candidate, Dmytro Yarosh, as the winner. Administrators discovered the image file before voting ended and prevented it from ever being publicly displayed. But Russian state television, seemingly coordinating with the hackers, went ahead with a false announcement that Yarosh had won, an apparent attempt to cast doubt on the election of the real winner, the politically moderate chocolate magnate Petro Poroshenko. The next morning, the election commission was hit with a third and final attack, this time a punishing wave of junk traffic designed to keep its servers off-line and prevent them from confirming the legitimate results. (The CyberBerkut hackers would be revealed years later to be linked with the Russian hacker group Fancy Bear that meddled in U.S. elections, too.)

That election trickery was the prelude to a far wider digital barrage, destroying thousands of computers and paralyzing victim organizations. By the time I visited Kiev in early 2017, practically every strata of Ukrainian society was being hit in successive waves of coordinated hacker sabotage: media, energy, transportation, finance, government, and military. "You can't really find a space in Ukraine where there *hasn't* been an attack," Kenneth Geers, a NATO ambassador who focuses on cybersecurity, told me at the time. "Turn over every rock, and you'll find a computer network operation."

When I spoke to former president Yushchenko on the phone later that year, he argued that Russia's tactics, online and off, have one single aim: "to destabilize the situation in Ukraine, to make its government look incompetent and vulnerable." He lumped the cyberattacks together with the Russian disinformation flooding Ukraine's media, the terroristic fighting in the east of the country, and his own poisoning years earlier—all underhanded moves aimed at pulling Ukraine to the east or painting it as a broken nation. "Russia will never accept Ukraine being a sovereign and independent country," he told me. "Twenty-five years since the Soviet collapse, Russia is still sick with this imperialistic syndrome."

Putin's fixation on Ukraine no doubt includes economic jealousy of its position as a lucrative pipeline route to Europe and its access to warm-water ports. But foreign policy analysts argued that Putin wasn't necessarily seeking to somehow reintegrate his Little Russia into the Kremlin's empire. Instead, he hoped to create a "frozen conflict": By taking enough Ukrainian territory to lock it into a permanent war, Russia sought to prevent the country from being welcomed into the European Union or NATO, instead pinning it in place as a strategic buffer between Moscow and the West.

But in my conversation with Yushchenko, he also insisted on another, less explained and more foreboding point: that Russia's attacks on Ukraine, whether they're carried out with destructive malware or Buk missiles, shouldn't be seen as Ukraine's problem alone. Russia's aggression against its neighbor reveals a dark playbook, he insisted, one that would sooner or later spread to the rest of the globe.

"The question is not for whom the bell tolls," Yushchenko warned. "The bell tolls for us all. This is a threat to every country in the world."

■

In late November 2015, as the pace of the digital blitzkrieg against Ukraine was accelerating, John Hultquist was invited to give a briefing at the Pentagon, a rare chance to win contracts and bend the ear of the world's most powerful military. He sat down among intelligence officials at a conference table in the most senior officer's medal-adorned office, deep in the gargantuan building.

When it came to his turn to speak, Hultquist wasted no time introducing his favorite subject. He gave the elevator-pitch version of Sandworm's history: Russian fingerprints, dangerous sophistication, targets stretching from Poland to the United States but clustering in Ukraine, with a disturbing focus on critical infrastructure. He noted that Russia's actual, ongoing war with Ukraine was heating up and that it had increasingly metastasized from physical invasion to disruptive digital attacks on everything from media firms to government agencies. Pro-Ukrainian activists had retaliated against Russia with a lower-tech form of sabotage, tearing down pylons that supplied electricity to the Crimean peninsula, throwing the territory Russia had seized into a mass blackout. Putin, of course, blamed the Ukrainian government for the sabotage.

With all those elements aligning, Hultquist went on to predict that

Russia's hackers were about to carry out a form of attack that had never before occurred in the history of cybersecurity. "I think there's a good chance," he told the Pentagon officials, "that they're going to try to turn out the lights."

The military audience seemed to acknowledge his warning, Hultquist remembers. But there were myriad other trouble spots across an internet crawling with potential threats, and so the meeting moved on. "To be honest," Hultquist says, "I don't think it really sunk in at all."

8

BLACKOUT

At first, Robert Lee blamed the squirrels.

It was Christmas Eve 2015—and also, as it happened, the day before Lee was set to be married in his hometown of Cullman, Alabama. A barrel-chested, bearded, and redheaded twenty-seven-year-old, Lee had recently left a high-level job at the NSA, where he'd led a team of analysts focused on a unique mission: tracking hackers who threatened critical infrastructure. Now he was settling down to launch his own security start-up and marry the Dutch girlfriend he'd met while stationed abroad.

As Lee busied himself with wedding preparations, he saw news reports that immediately distracted him from his matrimonial duties. Hackers had just taken down a power grid in western Ukraine, the headlines on his phone's screen read. A significant swath of the country had apparently gone dark for six hours. After the initial wave of adrenaline passed, Lee's natural skepticism kicked in. He remembered this was probably just more media hype; he had other things on his mind, and he'd heard spurious claims of hacked grids plenty of times before. The cause was usually a rodent or a bird; the notion that squirrels represented a greater threat to the power grid than hackers had become a running joke in the industry.

The next day, however, just before the wedding itself, Lee received a text message that dragged the incident back into his awareness. It came from Mike Assante, the director of industrial control systems security at the SANS Institute, an elite cybersecurity training center where Lee also taught courses. A message from Assante, for Lee, held far more weight than any news outlet: When it comes to digital threats affecting power grids, Assante was one of the most respected experts in the world. And he was telling Lee that the Ukraine blackout hack looked like the real thing.

Lee cleared the messages from his phone and tried to focus on his wedding. But moments after he had said his vows and kissed his bride, a contact in Ukraine pinged him: The blackout hack was real, the man said, and he needed Lee's help.

Lee had spent his career preparing for this moment. At the NSA, he'd devoted years to tracking the rare, sophisticated hacker teams that targeted power grids, pipelines, and water systems, priding himself on protecting the most fundamental underpinnings of civilization. He'd briefed the government's most senior officials on those threats. He'd gone so far as to build mock-ups of industrial control systems for testing in his own basement. Now, with absurdly bad timing, the historic milestone he'd anticipated for years seemed to have finally arrived: the first-known case of an actual hacker-induced blackout.

There was hardly a choice to be made. He skipped out on not only Christmas with his family but also his own wedding reception, found a quiet corner of the room, and began to text with Assante about the details of the Ukrainian power grid attack.

Still in his wedding suit, Lee eventually retreated to his mother's desktop computer in his parents' nearby home. Working in tandem with Assante, who had pulled out his laptop and hidden in the corner of a friend's Christmas party in rural Idaho, they examined maps of Ukraine and a chart of its power grid. The three power companies' substations that had been hit were in different regions of the country, hundreds of miles from one another, and unconnected. "This was not a squirrel," Lee concluded with a dark thrill.

By that night, Lee was busy dissecting the KillDisk malware his Ukrainian contact had sent him from the hacked power companies, much as Yasinsky had done after the StarLightMedia hack months before. "I have a very patient wife," Lee says of his decision to spend his wedding night in front of a computer.

Over the next few days, he received from his Ukrainian contact another sample of code and forensic data from the attacks. Pulling it apart, Lee saw how the intrusion had started. It began with a phishing email impersonating a message from the Ukrainian parliament. A malicious Word attachment had silently run a script known as a macro, a little program hidden inside the document, on the victims' machines.

The effect was the same as the zero-day technique iSight had first found Sandworm using in its infected Microsoft PowerPoint documents in 2014, but with a new trade-off: Without the zero day, the victims had to be tricked into clicking a button to allow the script to run. Until they clicked, the document would appear to be missing content or broken, so most users unthinkingly clicked to load it. But by using a simpler replacement for their zero-day technique, the hackers had been able to operate much less conspicuously, and their attack didn't depend on keeping a rare vulnerability secret from Microsoft.

The Word script had planted an infection of BlackEnergy, the piece of malware that had by now become practically the official national disease of Ukrainian IT networks. From that foothold, it appeared, the hackers had spread through the power companies' systems and eventually compromised a virtual private network, a tool the companies had used for remote access to their systems—including the highly specialized industrial control software that gives operators command over equipment like circuit breakers.

Looking at the attackers' methods and their use of BlackEnergy, Lee began to make connections to iSight's earlier findings and others from his time at NSA. This was the work of Sandworm, he was sure of it. After years of lurking, spying, building their capabilities, and performing reconnaissance work, Sandworm had taken the step that no other hackers had ever dared to: They'd caused an actual blackout, indiscriminately disrupting the physical infrastructure of hundreds of thousands of civilians.

For Lee, the pieces came together: Yes, the Sandworm connection meant the blackout was very likely a Russian attack, targeting Russia's preferred victim, Ukraine. But as he followed the known history of Sandworm to its conclusion, he was reminded that ICS-CERT had blamed the group for BlackEnergy infections on U.S. critical infrastructure networks, too. In other words, the same group that had just snuffed out the lights for nearly a quarter of a million Ukrainians had only a year before infected the computers of American electric utilities with the very same malware.

In Lee's mind, alarms went off. The Ukraine attack represented something more than a faraway foreign case study. "An adversary that had already targeted American energy utilities had crossed the line and taken down a power grid," Lee says. "It was an imminent threat to the United States."

■

Lee had long preached a simple rule. "No one should be messing with civilian industrial control systems," he says. "Never."

Cyberattacks on nonmilitary, physical infrastructure, Lee believed, were a class of weapon that ought to be considered, along with cluster bombs and biological weapons, simply too dangerous and uncontrollable for any ethical nation to wield. After all, not every hacker attack on a power grid could necessarily be remedied in a mere six hours, nor would the attackers know, in some cases, the extent of the damage they were inflicting. Lee had spent years thinking through the potential knock-on effects of cyberattacks on critical infrastructure, and his nightmare scenario was hacker-induced blackouts that lasted weeks or even a month, long enough that their consequences were unpredictable and might include crippling hospitals, manufacturing, or food distribution. "You risk collateral damage that's not even humane," Lee argues. "This is exactly the sort of damage that we've tried through international conventions and norms to do away with in other fields of conflict."

His imagined ban on infrastructure-targeted hacking was a surprisingly dovish take for someone who had practically been born into the military. One of Lee's grandfathers had been a World War II radio operator. The other had been a Green Beret. Both his parents, when he was growing up in Alabama, were U.S. Air Force enlisted personnel; his father had fought in Vietnam, and shortly after Lee was born, his mother and father had both served in Operation Desert Storm, with his mother deployed stateside to take care of Lee and his sisters. When he was a young teenager, she'd deployed again in the wars in Iraq and Afghanistan, coordinating C-17 transport planes from a base in Illinois.

Lee's father, who was ten years older than his mother, had received a Bronze Star in Vietnam, though he'd never told Lee what exactly he'd done to earn it. In Iraq, he worked as an air force loadmaster, responsible for, among other things, arranging all the ordnance that military aircraft would drop onto targets. Lee remembers his father showing him photographs of bombs on which he'd scrawled out a message: "To Saddam, from the Lees."

But Lee himself took a different path. After enrolling in the U.S. Air Force Academy—his father tricked him into it, he says, by telling him he'd never be accepted—he found himself less interested in the endless engineering and physics courses than he was in African studies. He spent one summer on a humanitarian mission to Cameroon, working with an NGO there focused on renewable energy and water supplies. They'd travel across the countryside, sleeping in the locals' villages, eating meals of fish and a starchy cake called *fufu,* and setting up simple water filtration systems and solar energy collectors.

Lee had never been much of a technology nerd. He'd played video games and built computers like other kids but never learned to program. In Cameroon, however, he became fascinated by control systems. A basic programmable logic controller, he found, made the machines he was installing vastly more efficient. The book-sized gray boxes with a few blinking lights, sold by companies like Siemens and Rockwell Automation, would allow him to program the solar-powered water filtration systems he'd place in streams so that they could swap their own filters with no manual intervention. Or the same controllers could be programmed to charge a series of car batteries attached to solar panels or wind turbines. That meant more clean water or more energy to power the LED lamps they'd give the villagers, and thus more hours of light each day, real improvements in human lives.

Lee began to see those programmable logic controllers, digital brains capable of altering the physical world around them, as fundamental building blocks of infrastructure and economic development.

"I thought, I can teach you how to create energy and power your village. That's civilization changing," he says. "I saw control systems as the route to change."

■

When Lee graduated from the U.S. Air Force Academy in 2010, he was sent to Keesler Air Force Base in Biloxi, Mississippi, to train as a communications officer. The air force, at the time, was just beginning to take cybersecurity seriously and lumped the new discipline in with that broader category of education. It was there that Lee learned the hacker basics: network analysis, forensics, exercises in "blue team" defense and "red team" attack.

But when it came to courses on control systems and their security, Lee found that his instructors often knew less about that little-understood computing niche than he had learned from his own hands-on time programming controller devices himself.

Then, during Lee's time at Keesler, he suddenly found that his niche interest was at the center of a buzzing new field of conflict: A mysterious piece of malware called Stuxnet had begun to appear in thousands of computers across the Middle East and South Asia. No one knew what exactly it was designed to do. But the worm seemed to have the ability to meddle with programmable logic controllers, something no one had ever seen before. (Like most of the rest of the world, Lee didn't yet know that Stuxnet was, in fact, an American creation. It had been built by Lee's future employers at the NSA along with Israeli intelligence and aimed directly at destroying equipment in Iranian nuclear enrichment facilities, an act that would mark a new era of cyberwar. But we'll get to that.)

Lee was, at the time, offended by the mere notion of malware capable of attacking physical infrastructure. "Here some asshole had targeted control systems," he remembers thinking. "The path to making the world a better place was control systems. Someone was jeopardizing that, and it pissed me off."

As more information about Stuxnet trickled out to the public, Lee's interest in industrial control system security was elevated to an obsession. He'd spend his time between classes reading every document he could find on the subject. Soon he managed to track down a friendly nuclear scientist at Oak Ridge National Laboratory whom he'd call repeatedly, grilling him over a classified line about the minutiae of programmable logic controllers and the latest findings about the first-ever specimen of malware designed to corrupt them.

Eventually, Lee says, his views of that malware would shift as it became clearer that the code had been designed for a pinpoint strike on a single Iranian complex in Natanz, one that might serve as a key component of Iran's efforts to obtain a nuclear weapon. But in the meantime, he had somehow become the closest thing to an expert on industrial control system security at Keesler Air Force Base. He found himself teaching other students and occasionally even briefing visiting generals.

At the end of his training, Lee took a position with an intelligence unit at Ramstein Air Base in Germany. Exactly what he did in that first real air force job remains obscured by the increasingly secret nature of his classified work. But he hints that the unit was engaged in intelligence missions for the war on terror, carried out by remotely piloted vehicles like the Global Hawk and Predator drones. Lee focused his work on the security of those vehicles' control systems. Within months, however, he was noticed by a different agency that would fundamentally redirect his career: the NSA.

Lee had barely settled in at Ramstein when he was ordered to move to a facility elsewhere in Germany.* The small NSA department in which Lee found himself had a strange and exhilarating mission. Fort Meade, the massive NSA headquarters in Maryland, already had well-resourced teams assigned to practically every known threat to American national security. His field unit of around a hundred people was given the remit to function independently, thinking

---

* Though Lee declined to say more about this base, all signs point to the Dagger Complex in Darmstadt. That NSA outpost resides on a small U.S. Army base in the west of the country whose role as an intelligence operation was at the time secret and would only later be revealed in the classified documents leaked by the NSA whistleblower Edward Snowden.

outside that massive organization's existing patterns of thought—to look where the rest of the NSA wasn't looking. "It was our job to find 'unknown unknowns,'" Lee says.

Naturally, Lee began asking around about who in the NSA was responsible for tracking hackers that threatened the security of industrial control systems. He was shocked to discover there was no devoted group with that mission. The NSA had teams tasked with finding and fixing vulnerabilities in industrial control system equipment. It had, as Stuxnet would expose, its own offensive teams that invented infrastructure exploitation techniques. It didn't, however, have a team assigned exclusively to hunting the enemy's infrastructure-focused hackers.

So Lee offered to build one. He was amazed at how little bureaucracy he confronted; creating the agency's first industrial control system threat intelligence team required filling out one form, he remembers. "So I became the lead of all of industrial control system threat discovery for NSA overnight," Lee says.

He was twenty-two years old. "Pretty fucked-up, isn't it?"

9

THE DELEGATION

Rob Lee describes starting his job at the NSA as something like connecting his brain to a vast, ultra-intelligent hive mind.

Suddenly he had access to not only expert colleagues but the agency's corpus of classified knowledge, as well as its vast intelligence collection abilities. Lee, of course, says little about the details of where that intelligence came from. But thanks in part to Edward Snowden, we know that it included a broad array of secret data-gathering tools, labeled broadly as "signals intelligence," or "sigint," that ranged from the ability to siphon vast quantities of raw internet data from undersea cables to hacking enemy systems administrators and looking over their shoulders at private networks. "When you're given access to essentially the entirety of the U.S. sigint system and then surrounded with the smartest people doing this on the planet, you get spun up pretty quickly," Lee says.

For the next four years, he and a small team of around six analysts spent every working hour tracking the burgeoning, post-Stuxnet world of industrial control system hackers. "Every day was hypothesis-driven hunting. We'd ask ourselves, if I were the adversary, what would I do to break into industrial control systems? Then we'd go search for that out in the world," Lee says. "We quickly went past any human knowledge of how to do this stuff and had to come up with our own models and methods and training." Soon he was writing reports on new critical infrastructure-hacking threats that found their way to the desk of President Obama and briefing the director of the NSA, Keith Alexander.

Lee refuses to talk about the details of his team's findings. But he hints that they'd uncover new, active industrial control system hacking operations being carried out by foreign governments as often as once a week. Only a small fraction of those hacking teams were ever identified in the media. (He's careful, however, to describe the operations his team tracked during that period only as "targeting" industrial control systems. Lee won't say how many—if any—ever followed in Stuxnet's footsteps and crossed the line to disrupting or destroying physical equipment.)

Even as his team built a global view of an internet roiling with threats to critical infrastructure, Lee notes that he remembers Sandworm stood out. He marked it early as a uniquely dangerous actor. "I can confirm that we knew about them and tracked them," he says, choosing his words cautiously. "And I found them to be particularly aggressive compared to the other threats we were seeing."

Then, in 2014, Lee's dream job abruptly ended. As a fast-rising and sometimes brash upstart, he'd never been particularly compliant with the military's strict adherence to rank. The NSA's relatively free-wheeling culture had unshackled him from that system. But he was still frustrated by the treatment of air force recruits, who'd sometimes cycle into his unit at the NSA, show real talent, and then suddenly be pulled out again to perform more menial tasks befitting their low rank.

So Lee spoke out, writing a strongly worded article in the military magazine *Signal* titled "The Failing of Air Force Cyber." His unvarnished opinion piece accused the air force of incompetence in cybersecurity and railed against the bureaucratic dogma of rank that had stifled improvement and wasted intellectual resources.

Lee hadn't bargained for the blowback or fully considered that he was still beholden to the same rank structure that he was attacking. Not long after his *Signal* piece was published, Lee discovered he had been reassigned, pulled out of his hacker-hunting team and back to an air force intelligence unit.

Back in that starched-collar military hierarchy, Lee bristled at his subordination to officers who he felt lacked the expertise he'd gained at the NSA. Worse, he had now been assigned to a team that sat on the other end of the game. He was part of a U.S. Air Force squadron based in Texas, responsible not for cybersecurity but for cyberattack. In other words, he now had orders to engage in exactly the sort of infrastructure hacking that he considered unconscionable. Just four years after first discovering that "some asshole" was targeting industrial control systems, he was that asshole.

He stayed for one unhappy year of highly classified work, then persuaded one of his commanders to let him resign, a nearly unthinkable move in a family of air force lifers. Lee says he wept as he walked out of the base on his last day as an air force officer.

It was 2015. That fall, Lee left Texas and moved to Maryland to attempt to re-create his NSA dream team in the private sector. Not long after, Christmas arrived. And with it, Sandworm reentered his life.

■

Despite his years working in one of the world's most secretive agencies, discretion had never been Lee's strong suit. Shortly after his abbreviated Christmas wedding, he'd linked the Ukrainian blackouts to an active hacker group, one that had already probed U.S. infrastructure, no less. And for the first time in his career, he was no longer bound by security clearances to keep that information hidden. He was immediately determined to warn the world.

In just the days before the New Year, Lee, Mike Assante, and another SANS researcher named Tim Conway had pieced together the broad strokes of the Ukrainian attack. Lee wanted to release it all. "By the twenty-ninth of December, we knew the public needed to know," he says.

Despite the hints that Sandworm was behind the blackout, Assante thought it was too early to start publicly blaming the attack on any particular hacker group—not to mention a government. The three men agreed that Assante should write a blog post delicately addressing the attack without revealing too many details, to get ahead of any media reports that might hype up or misrepresent the story.

The next day, they published a circumspect post on the SANS website, with Assante's byline: "A small number of sources in Russia and Ukraine indicate the electrical outage was caused by a cyber attack, specifically a virus from an outside source," it read. "I am skeptical as the referenced outage has been hard to substantiate."

Just two days later, on New Year's Day, however, Lee went ahead with his own blog post, discussing for the first time the BlackEnergy malware sample he'd obtained. The post still took a cautious approach, but it dropped hints at a conclusion. "The Ukrainian power outage is more likely to have been caused by a cyber attack than previously thought," he wrote. "Early reporting was not conclusive but a sample of malware taken from the network bolsters the claims." Lee says his intention was, in the least alarmist tone he could muster, to make clear to U.S. power companies that they should check their networks immediately for BlackEnergy infections that might be footholds for Sandworm.

For the next week, Lee, Assante, and Conway continued to exchange intelligence about the attack with the Ukrainian government, the Department of Homeland Security, and the Department of Energy. But after eight days, when no U.S. officials had made any public statement about the attack, they published another post under Assante's name that definitively confirmed the blackout had been a cyberattack, naming BlackEnergy and KillDisk as tools used in the attack, though not necessarily as the cause of the power outage. They made plans to release a full report with the blow by blow of the attack based on their analysis.

But at that point, to Lee's immense frustration, a senior DHS official told the SANS researchers to refrain from any further revelations. The request to stand down was directed at Assante, who still had deep government ties from years working at Idaho National Laboratory and the North American Electric Reliability Corporation.

As the Obama administration's cybersecurity coordinator J. Michael Daniel would later describe it to me, the government argued it wanted to give utilities a chance to address the problem discreetly before it revealed anything about those utilities' vulnerabilities in public, where it might tip off opportunistic hackers. But Lee was furious: He instead saw the delay as bureaucratic foot-dragging.

In the days that followed, the SANS researchers and the agency officials came to a compromise over Lee's objections. They'd assemble a fact-finding trip that would travel to Ukraine, meet with the electric utilities that had been victims of the attacks, and put together both classified reports for the government and unclassified reports for the public. Until then, everyone would keep quiet.

Assante and Conway were invited to join the delegation. Lee, whom officials had by then deemed a problematic hothead, was not.

■

A few weeks later, the team of Americans arrived in Kiev on a bright, freezing winter day. They assembled at the Hyatt, a block from the golden dome of the thousand-year-old St. Sophia Cathedral and just down the street from the Maidan. Among them were staff from the FBI, the Department of Energy, the Department of Homeland Security, and the North American Electric Reliability Corporation—the body responsible for the stability of the U.S. grid—as well as SANS's Assante and Conway, all assigned to learn the full truth of the Ukrainian blackout.

On that first day, the group gathered in a sterile hotel conference room with the staff of Kyivoblenergo, Kiev's regional power distribution company and one of the three victims of the power grid attacks. Over the next several hours, the Ukrainian company's stoic execs and engineers laid out the timeline of a ruthless, cunning raid on their network.

As Lee and Assante had noticed, the malware that infected the energy companies hadn't contained any commands capable of actually controlling the circuit breakers. Yet on the afternoon of December 23, Kyivoblenergo employees had watched helplessly as circuit after circuit was opened in dozens of substations across a Massachusetts-sized region of central Ukraine, seemingly commanded by computers on their network that they couldn't see. In fact, Kyivoblenergo's engineers determined that the attackers had set up their own perfectly configured copy of the control software on a PC in a faraway facility and then had used that rogue clone to send the commands that cut the power.

Once the circuit breakers were open and the power for tens of thousands of Ukrainians had gone dead, the hackers launched another phase of the attack. They'd overwritten the obscure code of the substations' serial-to-ethernet converters, tiny boxes in the stations' server closets that translated modern internet communications into a form that could be interpreted by older equipment. By hacking those chunks of hardware, the intruders had permanently bricked the devices, shutting out the legitimate operators from further digital control of the breakers.

The serial-to-ethernet converter trick alone would have taken weeks to devise, Assante thought to himself. Sitting at the conference room table, he marveled at the thoroughness of the operation.

The hackers also left one of their usual calling cards, running Kill-Disk to destroy a handful of the company's PCs. Then came the most vicious element of the attack: When the electricity was cut to the region, the stations themselves also lost power. Control stations have backup batteries for just such an occasion, but the hackers had turned them off, throwing the utility operators into darkness in the midst of their crisis and slowing their recovery efforts. With utmost precision, the hackers had engineered a blackout within a blackout.

"The message was, 'I'm going to make you feel this everywhere.' *Boom boom boom boom boom boom boom,*" Assante says, imagining the attack from the perspective of a bewildered grid operator. "These attackers must have seemed like they were gods."

That night, for the next leg of their trip, the team boarded a flight to the western Ukrainian city of Ivano-Frankivsk, at the foot of the Carpathian Mountains, arriving at its tiny Soviet-era airport in the midst of a snowstorm. The next morning they visited the headquarters of Prykarpattyaoblenergo, the power company that had taken the brunt of the pre-Christmas attack.

The power company executives politely welcomed the Americans into their modern building, which sat under the looming smokestacks of the abandoned coal power plant in the same complex. Then they invited them into their boardroom, seating them at a long wooden table beneath an oil painting of the aftermath of a medieval battle.

The attack the Prykarpattyaoblenergo executives described was almost identical to the one that hit Kyivoblenergo: BlackEnergy, corrupted firmware, disrupted backup power systems, KillDisk. But in this operation, the attackers had taken another step, bombarding the company's call centers with fake phone calls—either to obscure customers' warnings of the power outage or simply to add another layer of chaos and humiliation. It was as if the hackers were determined to impress an audience with the full array of their capabilities or to test the range of their arsenal.

There was another difference from the other utility attacks, too. When the Americans asked whether, as in the Kiev region, cloned control software had sent the commands that shut off the power, the Prykarpattyaoblenergo engineers said no, that their circuit breakers had been opened by another method.

At this point in the meeting, the company's technical director, a tall, serious man with black hair and ice-blue eyes, cut in. Rather than try to explain the hackers' methods to the Americans through a translator, he offered to show them. He clicked "play" on a video he'd recorded himself on his battered iPhone 5s.

The fifty-six-second clip showed a cursor moving around the screen of one of the computers in the company's control room. The pointer glides to the icon for one of the breakers and clicks a command to open it. The video pans from the computer's Samsung monitor to its mouse, which hasn't budged. Then it shows the cursor moving again, seemingly of its own accord, hovering over a breaker and attempting again to cut its flow of power as the engineers in the room ask one another who's controlling it.

The hackers hadn't sent their blackout commands from automated malware, or even a cloned machine, as they'd done at Kyivoblenergo. Instead, they'd exploited the company's IT help-desk tool to take direct control of the mouse movements of the stations' operators. They'd locked the operators out of their own user interface. And before their eyes, phantom hands had clicked through dozens of breakers—each serving power to a different swath of the region—and one by one by one, turned them cold.

PART II
ORIGINS

Once men turned their thinking over to machines in the hope that this would set them free. But that only permitted other men with machines to enslave them.

10

FLASHBACK: AURORA

Nine years before his Ukraine trip, on a piercingly cold and windy morning in March 2007, Mike Assante arrived at an Idaho National Laboratory facility thirty-two miles west of Idaho Falls, a building in the middle of a vast, high desert landscape covered with snow and sagebrush. He walked into an auditorium inside the visitors' center, where a small crowd was gathering. The group included officials from the Department of Homeland Security, the Department of Energy, and the North American Electric Reliability Corporation (NERC), executives from a handful of electric utilities across the country, and other researchers and engineers who, like Assante, were tasked by the national lab to spend their days imagining catastrophic threats to American critical infrastructure.

At the front of the room was an array of video monitors and data feeds, set up to face the room's stadium seating, like mission control at a rocket launch. The screens showed live footage from several angles of a massive diesel generator. The machine was the size of a school bus, a mint green, gargantuan mass of steel weighing twenty-seven tons, about as much as an M3 Bradley tank. It sat a mile away from its audience in an electrical substation, producing enough electricity to power a hospital or a navy ship and emitting a steady roar. Waves of heat coming off its surface rippled the horizon in the video feed's image.

Assante and his fellow INL researchers had bought the generator for $300,000 from an oil field in Alaska. They'd shipped it thousands of miles to the Idaho test site, an 890-square-mile piece of land where the national lab maintained a sizable power grid for testing purposes, complete with sixty-one miles of transmission lines and seven electrical substations.

Now, if Assante had done his job properly, they were going to destroy it. And the assembled researchers planned to kill that very expensive and resilient piece of machinery not with any physical tool or weapon but with about 140 kilobytes of data, a file smaller than the average cat GIF shared today on Twitter.

■

Three years earlier, Assante had been the chief security officer at American Electric Power, a utility with millions of customers in eleven states from Texas to Kentucky. A former navy officer turned cybersecurity engineer, Assante had long been keenly aware of the potential for hackers to attack the power grid. But he was dismayed to see that most of his peers in the electric utility industry had a relatively simplistic view of that still-theoretical and distant threat. If hackers did somehow get deep enough into a utility's network to start opening circuit breakers, the industry's common wisdom at the time was that staff could simply kick the intruders out of the network and flip the power back on. "We could manage it like a storm," Assante remembers his colleagues saying. "The way it was imagined, it would be like an outage and we'd recover from the outage, and that was the limit of thinking around the risk model."

But Assante, who had a rare level of crossover expertise between the architecture of power grids and computer security, was nagged by a more devious thought. What if attackers didn't merely hijack the control systems of grid operators to flip switches and cause short-term blackouts, but instead reprogrammed the automated elements of the grid, components that made their own decisions about grid operations without checking with any human?

In particular, Assante had been thinking about a piece of equipment called a protective relay. Protective relays are designed to function as a safety mechanism to guard against dangerous physical conditions in electric systems. If lines overheat or a generator goes out of sync, it's those protective relays that detect the anomaly and open a circuit breaker, disconnecting the trouble spot, saving precious hardware, even preventing fires. A protective relay functions as a kind of lifeguard for the grid.

But what if that protective relay could be paralyzed—or worse, corrupted so that it became the vehicle for an attacker's payload?

That disturbing question was one Assante had carried over to Idaho National Laboratory from his time at the electric utility. Now, in the visitor center of the lab's test range, he and his fellow engineers were about to put his most malicious idea into practice. The secret experiment was given a code name that would come to be synonymous with the potential for digital attacks to inflict physical consequences: Aurora.

■

The test director read out the time: 11:33 a.m. He checked with a safety engineer that the area around the lab's diesel generator was clear of bystanders. Then he sent a go-ahead to one of the cybersecurity researchers at the national lab's office in Idaho Falls to begin the attack. Like any real digital sabotage, this one would be performed from miles away, over the internet. The test's simulated hacker responded by pushing roughly thirty lines of code from his machine to the protective relay connected to the bus-sized diesel generator.

The inside of that generator, until that exact moment of its sabotage, had been performing a kind of invisible, perfectly harmonized dance with the electric grid to which it was connected. Diesel fuel in its chambers was aerosolized and detonated with inhuman timing to move pistons that rotated a steel rod inside the generator's engine— the full assembly was known as the "prime mover"—roughly 600 times a minute. That rotation was carried through a rubber grommet, designed to reduce any vibration, and then into the electricity-generating components: a rod with arms wrapped in copper wiring, housed between two massive magnets so that each rotation induced electrical current in the wires. Spin that mass of wound copper fast enough, and it produced 60 hertz of alternating current, feeding its power into the vastly larger grid to which it was connected.

A protective relay attached to that generator was designed to prevent it from connecting to the rest of the power system without first syncing to that exact rhythm: 60 hertz. But Assante's hacker in Idaho Falls had just reprogrammed that safeguard device, flipping its logic on its head.

At 11:33 a.m. and 23 seconds, the protective relay observed that the generator was perfectly synced. But then its corrupted brain did the opposite of what it was meant to do: It opened a circuit breaker to disconnect the machine.

When the generator was detached from the larger circuit of Idaho National Laboratory's electrical grid and relieved of the burden of sharing its energy with that vast system, it instantly began to accelerate, spinning faster, like a pack of horses that had been let loose from its carriage. As soon as the protective relay observed that the generator's rotation had sped up to be fully out of sync with the rest of the grid, its maliciously flipped logic immediately reconnected it to the grid's machinery.

The moment the diesel generator was again linked to the larger system, it was hit with the wrenching force of every other rotating generator on the grid. All of that equipment pulled the relatively small mass of the diesel generator's own spinning components back to its original, slower speed to match its neighbors' frequencies.

On the visitor center's screens, the assembled audience watched the giant machine shake with sudden, terrible violence, emitting a sound like a deep crack of a whip. The entire process from the moment the malicious code had been triggered to that first shudder had spanned only a fraction of a second.

Black chunks began to fly out of an access panel on the generator, which the researchers had left open to watch its internals. Inside, the black rubber grommet that linked the two halves of the generator's shaft was tearing itself apart.

A few seconds later, the machine shook again as the protective relay code repeated its sabotage cycle, disconnecting the machine and reconnecting it out of sync. This time a cloud of gray smoke began to spill out of the generator, perhaps the result of the rubber debris burning inside it.

Assante, despite the months of effort and millions of dollars in federal funds he'd spent developing the attack they were witnessing, somehow felt a kind of sympathy for the machine as it was being torn apart from within. "You find yourself rooting for it, like the little engine that could," Assante remembered. "I was thinking, 'You can make it!'"

The machine did not make it. After a third hit, it released a larger cloud of gray smoke. "That prime mover is toast," an engineer standing next to Assante said. After a fourth blow, a plume of black smoke rose from the machine thirty feet into the air in a final death rattle.

The test director ended the experiment and disconnected the ruined generator from the grid one final time, leaving it deathly still. In the forensic analysis that followed, the lab's researchers would find that the engine shaft had collided with the engine's internal wall, leaving deep gouges in both and filling the inside of the machine with metal shavings. On the other side of the generator, its wiring and insulation had melted and burned. The machine was totaled.

In the wake of the demonstration, a silence fell over the visitor center. "It was a sober moment," Assante remembers. The engineers had just proven without a doubt that hackers who attacked an electric utility could go beyond a temporary disruption of the victim's operations: They could damage its most critical equipment beyond repair. "It was so vivid. You could imagine it happening to a machine in an actual plant, and it would be terrible," Assante says. "The implication was that with just a few lines of code, you can create conditions that were physically going to be very damaging to the machines we rely on."

But Assante also remembers feeling something weightier in the moments after the Aurora experiment. It was a sense that, like Robert Oppenheimer watching the first atomic bomb test at another U.S. national lab six decades earlier, he was witnessing the birth of something historic and immensely powerful.

"I had a very real pit in my stomach," Assante says. "It was like a glimpse of the future."

11

FLASHBACK: MOONLIGHT MAZE

The known history of state-sponsored hacking stretches back three decades before Russia's hackers would switch off the power to hundreds of thousands of people and two decades before experiments like the Aurora Generator Test would prove how destructive those attacks could be. It began with a seventy-five-cent accounting error.

In 1986, Cliff Stoll, a thirty-six-year-old astronomer working as the IT administrator at Lawrence Berkeley National Laboratory, was assigned to investigate that financial anomaly: Somehow, someone had remotely used one of the lab's shared machines without paying the usual per-minute fee that was typical for online computers at the time. He quickly realized the unauthorized user was a uniquely sophisticated hacker going by the name "Hunter" who had exploited a zero-day vulnerability in the lab's software. Stoll would spend the next year hunting the hunter, painstakingly tracking the intruder's movements as he stole reams of files from the lab's network.

Eventually, Stoll and his girlfriend, Martha Matthews, created an entire fake collection of files to lure the thief while watching him use the lab's computers as a staging point to attempt to penetrate targets including the Department of Defense's MILNET systems, an Alabama army base, the White Sands Missile Range, a navy data center, air force bases, NASA's Jet Propulsion Laboratory, defense contractors like SRI and BBN, and even the CIA. Meanwhile, Stoll was also tracing the hacker back to his origin: a university in Hannover, Germany.

Thanks in part to Stoll's detective work, which he captured in his seminal cybersecurity book, *The Cuckoo's Egg*, German police arrested Stoll's hacker along with four of his West German associates. Together, they had approached East German agents with an offer to steal secrets from Western government networks and sell them to the KGB.

All five men in the crew were charged with espionage. "Hunter," whose real name was Markus Hess, was given twenty months in prison. Two of the men agreed to cooperate with prosecutors to avoid prison time. The body of one of those cooperators, thirty-year-old Karl Koch, was later found in a forest outside Hannover, burned beyond recognition, a can of gasoline nearby.

■

Ten years after those intrusions, Russia's hackers returned. This time, they were no longer foreign freelancers but organized, professional, and highly persistent spies. They would pillage the secrets of the American government and military for years.

Starting in October 1996, the U.S. Navy, the U.S. Air Force, and agencies including NASA, the Department of Energy, the Environmental Protection Agency, and the National Oceanic and Atmospheric Administration began detecting sporadic intrusions on their networks. Though the interlopers routed their attacks through compromised machines from Colorado to Toronto to London, the first victims of the hacking campaign nonetheless managed to trace the hackers to a Moscow-based internet service provider, Cityline.

By June 1998, the Pentagon's Defense Information Systems Agency was investigating the breaches, along with the FBI and London's Metropolitan Police. They determined that the hackers were stealing an enormous volume of data from U.S. government and military agencies: By one estimate, the total haul was equivalent to a stack of paper files as high as the Washington Monument. As the investigators came to grips with the size of the unprecedented cyberespionage operation they were facing, they gave it a name: Moonlight Maze.

By 1998, it was clear that the Moonlight Maze hackers were almost certainly Russian. The timing of their operations showed that the intruders were working during Moscow daylight hours. Investigators went digging through the records of academic conferences and found that Russian scientists had attended conferences on topics that closely matched the subjects of the files they'd stolen from the U.S. agencies. One former air force forensics expert, Kevin Mandia, even reverse engineered the hackers' tools, stripping away the code's layers of obfuscation and pulling out strings of Russian language. (Decades later, Mandia would be John Hultquist's boss at FireEye, the company that acquired iSight Partners following its similar discovery of Sandworm's Russian origins.)

By all appearances, it looked like a Russian intelligence agency was pilfering the secrets of the U.S. government, in what would soon be recognized as the first state-on-state cyberspying campaign of its kind. But proving that the spies were working for the Russian government itself was far more difficult than proving they were merely located in Russia. It was a fundamental problem that would plague hacker investigations for decades to come. Unless detectives could perform the nearly impossible feat of following the footprints of an intrusion back to an actual building or identify the individuals by name, governments could easily deny all responsibility for their spying, pinning the blame on bored teenagers or criminal gangs.

So in early 1999, after the desperate Moonlight Maze investigators had failed for years to stop the penetrations or prove any definitive connection to the Kremlin, they resorted to a backup plan: They asked Russia for help.

■

In March 1999, FBI agents hosted officials from Russia's Ministry of Internal Affairs at an upscale D.C. restaurant, toasted them with vodka, and formally requested the assistance of Russian law enforcement to track down the hackers who were almost certainly based in Moscow.

The ministry offered a surprisingly friendly response, promising to lend "aggressive investigative support." After all, this was in the post-Soviet, pre-Putin era of the 1990s. America had, ostensibly, won the Cold War. The new, post-perestroika Russia under President Boris

Yeltsin seemed as if it might become an actual democratic ally of the West.

Less than two weeks later, the American investigators flew to Moscow to meet with Russian officials. One, a general, was particularly friendly with the U.S. delegation, inviting the investigators to another vodka-drenched dinner. Too friendly, it turned out: At the end of that second evening of diplomacy, the inebriated general nearly caused an international incident by inserting his tongue uninvited into a female FBI agent's ear.

But the next day, the ministry really did follow through on its offer of cooperation: The hungover general ordered a subordinate to take the Americans to the offices of the internet service providers that had been used by the Moonlight Maze hackers, including Cityline. The investigators soon found that Cityline offered its internet services not just to civilians but to the Russian government, a clue that they hoped might lead to evidence of the Kremlin's involvement.

Then, something unexpected happened. In another meeting at the Russian Defense Ministry, the same general shocked the group by straightforwardly confirming that the Russian government was behind the Moonlight Maze break-ins.

The intrusions had been staged through the Russian Academy of Sciences, the general explained, but the individuals responsible were "those motherfuckers in intelligence." He declared that such behavior toward Russia's newfound friends in the United States would not be tolerated. The U.S. delegation, hardly believing its luck, congratulated each other on the successful trip. Perhaps what had seemed like an intractable problem, this new plague of Russian cyberspying, could be solved with diplomacy.

The Americans' optimism was short-lived. The next day, the delegation learned from their Russian handlers that their schedule had been filled with sightseeing trips around Moscow. When the same thing happened the day after that, the investigators began to grow frustrated. They asked their Russian contacts about the whereabouts of the general they'd been meeting with and received no clear response. After a third day without further meetings, they knew that their brief, unexpected interlude of Russo-American cooperation on cybersecurity was over.

The confused investigators could only guess at what had occurred. Their friendly general, it seemed, had missed the memo on the Kremlin's hacking campaign. He had considered it a rogue aberration instead of what it was: a powerful new capability, and one that the Russian government was honing into a central tool for intelligence gathering in the post-Soviet era. The mistake no doubt carried serious consequences. The Americans never saw the general again.

When the investigators returned to the United States, they found that Moonlight Maze's intrusions had ceased. For a moment, it seemed, their probe might have chastened the Russian government into ordering a stop to the espionage spree. Then, just two months later, in the spring of 1999, military network administrators saw that the same relentless hacking had restarted, now with better stealth and more obfuscation in the code of its tools. A new age of state-sponsored cyberespionage had begun.

Not long after that trip, in June 1999, the Department of Defense officially launched the Joint Task Force–Computer Network Defense, or JTF-CND, a new arm of the Pentagon devoted to the growing threat of digital intrusions. At the ribbon-cutting ceremony to celebrate the unit's creation in August of that year, Deputy Secretary of Defense John Hamre discreetly alluded to the ongoing cybersecurity crisis the military was facing as Moonlight Maze continued to siphon its secrets.

"The Department of Defense has been at cyberwar for the last half year," Hamre told the audience. He didn't name Moonlight Maze; the code name would only leak to the press months later. "Cyberspace isn't just for geeks," Hamre added in his JTF-CND speech. "It's for warriors now."

■

What did Hamre mean by all this talk of warriors in cyberspace and that still unfamiliar word, "cyberwar"?

By the time of Hamre's speech in 1999, the notion had already been tossed around in military studies circles for years. The term "cyberwar" had been coined in a 1987 *Omni* magazine article that

defined it in terms of giant robots and autonomous weapon systems replacing and augmenting human soldiers. It described flying
drones, self-guided tanks, and battlefields covered in the "carcasses
of crippled machines."

But in 1993, another landmark paper scrapped that *Terminator*-
style definition and gave cyberwar a far more influential meaning,
expressing it in terms of military forces' potential exploitation of
information technology. That article by two analysts from the think
tank Rand, John Arquilla and David Ronfeldt, appeared in the journal *Comparative Strategy* with the title "Cyberwar Is Coming!" (The
exclamation point, Arquilla would later say, was intended "to show
everybody how serious this was.")

The two Rand analysts defined cyberwar as any means of warfare
that shifts the balance of knowledge in the attacker's favor. Those
tactics could include reconnaissance and espionage, but also, crucially,
attacking the enemy's command-and-control systems. "It means disrupting if not destroying the information and communications systems, broadly defined to include even military culture, on which an
adversary relies in order to 'know' itself: who it is, where it is, what
it can do when, why it is fighting, which threats to counter first,
etc.," Arquilla and Ronfeldt wrote. "As an innovation in warfare, we
anticipate that cyberwar may be to the 21st century what *blitzkrieg*
was to the 20th century."*

But by the time of Hamre's ribbon-cutting speech half a decade
later, a darker conception of cyberwar had slowly begun to take shape.
Hamre had said in a 1997 congressional hearing that the United
States must prepare for an "electronic Pearl Harbor": a calamitous,

---

* The authors suggested that the sort of cyberwar they described might actually be
a less violent and lethal form of military combat, one in which an attacker might be
able to quickly pierce to the command center of an enemy army rather than fight a
grueling and bloody war of attrition. "It is hard to think of any kind of warfare as
humane, but a fully articulated cyberwar doctrine might allow the development of a
capability to use force not only in ways that minimize the costs to oneself, but which
also allow victory to be achieved without the need to maximize the destruction of the
enemy," they wrote. "If for no other reason, this potential of cyberwar to lessen war's
cruelty demands its careful study and elaboration."

surprise cyberattack designed not just to take out military command-and-control communications but to physically devastate American infrastructure.

That more apocalyptic vision of cyberwar had been brewing in government and military analysis circles, too. What if, the war wonks had only just begun to wonder, hackers could reach out from the internet and into the physical systems that underpin civilization?

Rand's think tankers, three years after Arquilla and Ronfeldt's cyberwar article, had run their own hacker war-game simulations around this exact question in 1996. In that exercise, dramatically titled "The Day After . . . in Cyberspace," Rand's analysts imagined catastrophic, lethal consequences from cyberattacks that affected militaries and civilians alike: the derailment of a train in Germany, the disruption of controls at the Saudi Arabian oil firm Aramco, cutting power to a U.S. air base, crashing an airliner in Chicago, or sparking panic on the New York and London stock exchanges.

This vision of a digital Armageddon took a chilling leap beyond the picture of cyberwar that Arquilla and Ronfeldt had described. Instead of merely using a cyberattack to cut the communicative strings of a military's soldiers and weapons, what if cyberwar meant that hackers themselves would become the soldiers? What if cyberattacks became their weapons, as physically destructive as a bullet or a warhead?

This notion of a physically debilitating attack by digital means, as Rand imagined it, raised troubling questions about the foundations of modern society. "If one quarter of the air traffic control systems were inoperable for 48 hours, could air transportation continue?" the analysts asked themselves in their final report on the exercises. "Would two thirds of banking systems suffice; if so, for how long?"

As they wondered aloud about these unthinkable scenarios, the war gamers came to the consensus that most critical of all was the vulnerability of the electricity supply, upon which all other layers of modern society's technological infrastructure depend. "If the power system is at risk," they wrote, "everything is at risk."

■

In 1999, cyberwar was, more or less, science fiction. By almost any definition, John Hamre was getting ahead of himself in his foreboding speech. Moonlight Maze wasn't cyberwar. It was straightforward cyberespionage.

Even as the Russian hackers stole reams upon reams of data, they weren't using their access to military networks to sabotage or corrupt those systems. There was no sign that they were seeking to disrupt or deceive U.S. command and control to gain the kind of tactical advantage Arquilla and Ronfeldt had described. And they certainly weren't reaching out into the physical world to cause lethal mayhem and blackouts.

But Moonlight Maze did demonstrate that state-sponsored hackers could gain far deeper and broader access than many in the U.S. government had thought possible. And next time, they might not use those abilities for mere spying.

In January 2000, President Bill Clinton himself encapsulated the threat in an ominous speech on the White House's South Lawn. The brief remarks were intended to unveil a plan to kick-start U.S. cybersecurity research and recruiting. Instead, they resonate as a warning from the past. "Today, our critical systems, from power structures to air traffic control, are connected and run by computers," Clinton said.

> There has never been a time like this in which we have the power to create knowledge and the power to create havoc, and both those powers rest in the same hands. We live in an age when one person sitting at one computer can come up with an idea, travel through cyberspace, and take humanity to new heights. Yet, someone can sit at the same computer, hack into a computer system and potentially paralyze a company, a city, or a government.

The day when hackers would inflict that scale of disruption hadn't yet arrived. But Clinton's imagination of that future wasn't wrong. In fact, it was just beyond the horizon.

12

FLASHBACK: ESTONIA

Toomas Hendrik Ilves's internet was down.

Or so it seemed to the fifty-three-year-old president of Estonia when he woke up on his family farm one Saturday in late April 2007. At first, he assumed it must be a problem with the connection at his remote farmhouse, surrounded by acres of rolling hills. Ilves bristled at the latest annoyance. The day before, he'd grudgingly allowed the country's security services to smuggle him out of the presidential palace in the capital of Tallinn and bring him 125 miles south to his family estate, named Ärma, where a perimeter of national guardsmen stood watch.

The last-minute move was designed to protect Ilves from an increasingly volatile situation in Tallinn. Violence had shaken the city for days. Angry rioters, composed largely of the country's Russian-speaking minority, had overturned cars and smashed storefronts, causing millions of dollars in damage. They'd brawled with police and called for the government's resignation—a demand echoed by Russian government statements.

All of that chaos had been triggered by a symbolic slight: Sixteen years after the fall of the Soviet Union, the Estonian government had finally made the decision to relocate from central Tallinn a statue of a Soviet soldier, surrounded by a small collection of graves of World War II casualties. To the country's ethnic Russians, the graves and the six-and-a-half-foot-tall bronze monument served as a remembrance of the Soviet Union's bloody sacrifices to defeat Estonia's Nazi occupiers. To most Estonians, they were instead a reminder of the grim Soviet occupation that followed, marked by mass deportations to Siberia and decades of economic stagnation.

The statue had served for years as a flash point for Estonia's tensions with Russia and its own Russian-speaking population. When government workers exhumed the Soviet war graves and transferred them, along with the statue, to a military cemetery on the edge of town in late April 2007, pro-Russian Estonians flooded into central Tallinn in a seething mass of unrest.

Ilves had left Tallinn reluctantly and remained anxious about the escalating riots. So the first thing he did upon waking up early that morning in his farmhouse's second-floor bedroom was to open his MacBook Pro and visit the website for Estonia's main newspaper, *Postimees,* looking for an update on the riots and Russia's calls for his government's ouster. But the news site mysteriously failed to load. His browser's request timed out and left him with an error message.

He tried other Estonian media sites, and they too were down. Was it his computer's Wi-Fi card? Or his router? But no, he quickly discovered that the British *Financial Times* loaded just fine. Then Ilves tried a few Estonian government websites. They too were unreachable.

Ilves called his IT administrator and asked what might be the problem with the Ärma connection. The confused presidential tech staffer told Ilves that it wasn't unique to him. Estonian sites seemed to be down for everyone. Somehow a significant fraction of Estonia's entire domestic web was crippled.

Estonia had, over the prior decade, sprung out of its Soviet doldrums to become one of the most digitally vibrant countries in the world. The internet had become a pillar of Estonian life: 95 percent of its citizens' banking took place on the web, close to 90 percent of income taxes were filed online, and the country had even become the first in the world to enable internet voting. Ilves himself took significant credit for pushing through many of those initiatives as a minister and later as president. Now it seemed that the uniquely web-friendly society he'd helped to build was experiencing a uniquely web-centric meltdown.

As Ilves clicked through broken sites in his remote farmhouse, he sensed something far worse at play than simple broken technology. It seemed he'd stumbled into the fog of war, a feeling of strategic blindness and isolation in a critical moment of conflict. "Is this a prelude to something?" he asked himself. "What the *hell* is going on?"

∎

The attacks had started the night before. Hillar Aarelaid had been expecting them.

The head of Estonia's Computer Emergency Response Team, or CERT, had been watching on hacker forums for days as pseudonymous figures had planned out an operation to unleash a flood of junk traffic at Estonian websites, in retaliation for the bronze soldier's removal. They asked volunteers to aim a series of repeated pings from their computers at a long list of targets, massing into a brute-force distributed denial-of-service attack that would overwhelm the sites' servers.

When the first waves of that inundation hit, Aarelaid was at a pub in a small town in Ireland, drinking a Guinness after finishing two weeks of forensic training at a nearby police academy. His phone rang with a call from his co-worker at the Estonian CERT. "It's started," the man told him. The two Estonians agreed, with typical brevity, to monitor the attacks and respond with the countermeasures they had planned: work with the sites' administrators to increase bandwidth, bring backup servers online, and filter out the malicious traffic. Aarelaid, a laconic former beat cop with close-cropped hair and perpetual stubble, hung up after no more than ten seconds and went back to drinking his Guinness.

The next morning, as President Ilves was still puzzling over his farmhouse internet connection in the south of Estonia, Aarelaid's CERT colleague picked him up at the Tallinn airport and briefed him on the attackers' progress. The flood of malicious data was growing, and so was the target list. Most of the media and government sites from the Ministry of Defense to the parliament were under bombardment—a barrage big enough that many were now off-line.

Aarelaid remained unmoved. These sorts of distributed denial-of-service attacks were low-hanging fruit for untalented hackers, mostly used for petty extortion. He still believed that the usual response to the annoyance would win out when the attackers got bored of the arms race. "We can handle this," Aarelaid told his CERT co-worker. He considered the attack a mere "cyber riot," the internet extension of the improvised chaos playing out on Tallinn's streets.

By the third day of the attacks, however, it was painfully clear to Aarelaid that these weren't run-of-the-mill website takedowns, and the normal responses weren't going to stop them. With every attempt to block the streams of malicious traffic, the attackers altered their techniques to evade filters and renew their pummeling. More and more computers were being enlisted to add their firepower to the toxic flood. Individual volunteer attackers had given way to massive botnets of tens of thousands of enslaved machines controlled by criminal hackers including the notorious Russian Business Network, a well-known cybercriminal operation responsible for a significant portion of the internet's spam and credit-card-fraud campaigns. That meant malware-infected PCs all over the world, from Vietnam to the United States, were now training fire hoses of data at Estonia.

The attackers' goals shifted, evolving from mere denial-of-service attacks to defacements, replacing the content of websites with swastikas and pictures of the country's prime minister with a Hitler mustache, all in a coordinated effort to paint Estonians as anti-Russian fascists. The target list, too, was growing to absurd proportions, hitting everything from banks to arbitrary e-commerce sites to the community forums of Tallinn's apartment complexes. "Twenty, fifty, a hundred sites, it's not possible anymore with those numbers to respond," says Aarelaid. "By Sunday, we realized the normal response wasn't going to work."

On Monday morning, Aarelaid held a meeting with administrators of key government and commercial target sites at the CERT office in central Tallinn. They agreed that it was time for a draconian new approach. Instead of trying to filter out known sources of malicious traffic, they would simply blacklist every web connection from outside Estonia.

As Estonia's web administrators put that blacklist into effect, one by one, the pressure on their servers was lifted: The small fraction of the attack traffic originating from inside Estonia itself was easily absorbed. But the strategy came at a certain cost: It severed the Estonian media from the rest of the world, preventing it from sharing its stories of riots and digital bombardment. The tiny country had successfully locked out its foreign attackers. But it had also locked itself in.

■

Over the days that followed that lockdown, Estonia's CERT began the slow process of relieving the country's internet isolation. Aarelaid and his colleagues worked with internet service providers around the world to painstakingly identify and filter out the malicious machines hosted by each of those global sources of traffic. The attacks were still growing, mutating, and changing their origins—until finally, a week after the attacks had started, they suddenly stopped.

In the eerie lull that followed, however, Estonia's defenders knew that the attackers would return. On May 9, Russia celebrates Victory Day, a holiday commemorating the Soviet defeat of Hitler after four years of immeasurable losses and sacrifice. Chatter on hacker forums made clear that the next wave of attacks was being saved for that symbolic day, rallying fellow digital protesters to the cause. "You do not agree with the policy of eSStonia???" asked one poster on a Russian forum, using the "SS" to emphasize Estonia's supposed Nazi ties. "You may think you have no influence on the situation??? You CAN have it on the Internet!"

"The action will be massive," wrote another. "It's planned to take Estonnet the fuck down:)."

At almost exactly the stroke of midnight Moscow time on May 8, another barrage hit the Estonian web with close to a million computers conscripted into dozens of botnets, taking down fifty-eight sites simultaneously.

All that night and through the days that followed, Aarelaid coordinated with the internet service providers he'd befriended to filter out new malicious traffic. But in the second wave of the attack, some of the hackers had also moved beyond mere brute-force flooding. He began to see more sophisticated attacks exploiting software vulnerabilities that allowed the hackers to briefly paralyze internet routers, taking down internet-reliant systems that included ATMs and credit card systems. "You go to the shop and want to pay for milk and bread," Aarelaid says. "You cannot pay with a card in the shop. You cannot take cash from the ATM. So you go without milk and bread."

As the escalating attacks wore on, however, they also began to lose their shock-and-awe effect on Estonia's webmasters and its population. As Aarelaid tells it, he and IT administrators around the country developed a typically Estonian stoicism about the attacks. They'd go to sleep each night, giving the attackers free rein to tear down their targets at will. Then the defenders would wake up the next morning and clean up the mess they found, filtering the new traffic and restarting routers to bring the country's digital infrastructure back online before the start of the workday. Even the more sophisticated router attacks had only temporary effects, Aarelaid says, curable with a reboot.

He compares this siege-defense routine to the Estonian ability to tolerate subzero temperatures in winters, with only a few hours of sun a day, collectively honed over thousands of years. "You go into work and it's dark. You come home and it's dark. For a long time, you don't see any light at all, so you're ready for these kinds of things," Aarelaid says. "You prepare your firewood."

■

The attacks ebbed and flowed for the rest of that May until, by the end of the month, they had finally dwindled and then disappeared. They left behind questions that, even a decade later, haven't been answered with certainty: Who was behind the attacks? And what did they intend to achieve?

Estonians who found themselves in the epicenter of the events, like Aarelaid and Ilves, believed from the first that Russia's government—not merely its patriotic hackers—had a hand in planning and executing Estonia's bombardment. After the initial, weak smatterings of malicious traffic, the attacks had come to seem too polished, too professional in their timing and techniques to be the work of rogue hacktivists. Who, after all, was coordinating between dozens of botnets, seemingly controlled by disparate Russian crime syndicates? An analysis by the security firm Arbor Networks also found that a telling subset of the traffic sources overlapped with earlier distributed denial-of-service attacks aimed at the website of Garry Kasparov, an opposition party presidential candidate and outspoken critic of the Kremlin.

"It was a very organized thing, and who can organize this? Criminals? Nope," says Aarelaid. "It was a government. And the Russian government wanted this most."

Other Estonians in the thick of the attacks saw them as a kind of partnership between nongovernment hackers and their government handlers—or in the case of the gangs like the Russian Business Network, cybercriminals directed by Kremlin patrons, in exchange for the country's law enforcement turning a blind eye to their business operations. "It's like feudalism. You can do some kind of business because some boss in your area allows you to, and you pay him some tribute," says Jaan Priisalu, who at the time of the attacks was the head of IT security at Estonia's largest bank, Hansabank. "If your boss is going to war, you're also going to war."

And in early 2007, Russia's boss was indeed going to war, or at least setting the thermostat for a new cold one. Two months before the Estonian attacks, Putin had taken the stage at the Munich Security Conference and given a harsh, history-making speech that excoriated the United States and NATO for creating what he saw as a dangerous imbalance in global geopolitics. He railed against the notion of a post–Cold War "unipolar" world in which no competing force could check the power of the United States and its allies.

Putin clearly felt the direct threat of that rising, singular superpower conglomerate. After all, Estonia had joined NATO's alliance three years earlier, along with the other Baltic states of Lithuania and Latvia, bringing the group for the first time to Russia's doorstep, less than a hundred miles from St. Petersburg.

"NATO has put its frontline forces on our borders," Putin said in his Munich speech. The alliance's expansion, he continued, represents "a serious provocation that reduces the level of mutual trust. And we have the right to ask: against whom is this expansion intended?" Putin's unspoken answer to that question was, of course, Russia—and himself.

When the cyberattacks in Estonia peaked in intensity three months later, Putin didn't hide his approval, even as his government denied responsibility. In a May 9 Victory Day speech, he gave his implicit blessing to the hackers. "Those who desecrate monuments to the heroes of the war are insulting their own people and sowing discord and new distrust," he told a crowd in Moscow's Red Square.

Still, NATO never treated the Estonian cyberattacks as an overt act of aggression by the Russian state against one of NATO's own. Under Article 5 of the Washington Treaty that lays out NATO's rules, an attack against any NATO member is meant to be considered an attack against all of them, with a collective response in kind. But when President Ilves began speaking with his ambassadors in the first week of the cyberattacks, he was told that NATO members were unwilling to remotely consider an Article 5 response to the Russian provocations. This was, after all, a mere attack on the internet, not a life-threatening act of physical warfare.

Ilves says he asked his diplomats to instead inquire about Article 4, which merely convenes NATO leaders for a "consultation" when a member's security is threatened. The liaisons quickly brought back an answer: Even that milder step proved a nonstarter. How could they determine Russia was behind the provocations? After all, NATO's diplomats and leaders hardly understood the mechanics of a distributed denial-of-service attack. The traffic's source appeared to be Russian freelance hackers and criminals or, more confusing still to the lay observer, hijacked computers in countries around the world.

Underlying all of that inaction, Ilves says, was another motivation: what he describes as a kind of fracture between western European NATO countries and eastern Europeans facing Russian threats. "There's a sense that it's 'over there,' that 'they're not like us,'" Ilves says, mocking what he describes as a "haughty, arrogant" tone of western European NATO members. "'Oh, those eastern Europeans, they don't like the Russians, so they have a failure and they blame it on Russia.'"

In the end, NATO did essentially nothing to confront Russia in response to the Estonian attacks. Putin, it seemed, had tested a new method to bloody the nose of a NATO country with plausible deniability, using tools that were virtually impossible to trace to the Kremlin. And he'd correctly judged the lack of political will to defend

NATO's eastern European members from an innovative new form of mass sabotage.

The events of those two months in Estonia would, in some circles, come to be seen as the first cyberwar, or, more creatively, "Web War I." The cyberattacks were, in reality, hardly as catastrophic as any true war; the threat of an "electronic Pearl Harbor" still lay in the future. But the Russian government nonetheless appeared to have demonstrated an indiscriminate, unprecedented form of disruption of an adversary's government and civil society alike. And it had gotten away with it.

13

FLASHBACK: GEORGIA

It was a few hours after nightfall when Khatuna Mshvidobadze learned Russian tanks were rolling toward her location.

Mshvidobadze was, on the night of August 11, 2008, working late in her office at the NATO Information Center in central Tbilisi, the capital of the former Soviet republic of Georgia. She held a position at the time as the deputy director of that organization, a part of Georgia's Ministry of Defense devoted to lobbying for the small Caucasus country to become part of NATO's alliance. Much of the group's work consisted in hosting events and persuading media to make the case for Georgia to join forces with its Western neighbors across the Black Sea. But in the summer of 2008, the NATO Information Center found itself with a new, far more urgent focus: combating the Kremlin's attempts to dominate the media narrative surrounding a Russian invasion.

War had broken out days earlier. Russia had moved troops and artillery into two separatist regions within Georgia's borders, Abkhazia and South Ossetia. In response, the Georgian forces launched a preemptive strike. On August 7, they shelled military targets in the South Ossetian town of Tskhinvali, trying to gain the initiative in what they saw as an inevitable conflict fueled by the Kremlin's aggression. But their plan, by all appearances, hadn't accounted for the overwhelming force of the Russian response.

Proclaiming that it was protecting Abkhazia and South Ossetia from Georgian oppression, Russia flooded the small country with more than twenty-five thousand troops, twelve hundred artillery vehicles, two hundred planes, and forty helicopters. Those numbers dwarfed Georgia's army of fewer than fifteen thousand soldiers and its bare-bones air force of eight planes and twenty-five helicopters. By the second day of the war, the Kremlin had unleashed its Black Sea fleet of warships for the first time since World War II, sending an armada across the water to blockade Georgia's coastline. The country had, in mere days, been outgunned and surrounded.

By August 11, Russian forces were moving out of the separatist regions and into the heart of Georgian territory, taking the city of Gori and splitting the invaded country in two. By that evening, Russian tanks were poised to close the forty-mile stretch from Gori to the capital.

For Mshvidobadze, working in her downtown Tbilisi office, that night of August 11 was the most chaotic of her life. To start, her building's internet was inexplicably down, making her job of combating Russian military propaganda—including false claims that Georgians had been massacring civilians in South Ossetia and Abkhazia—nearly impossible.

In the midst of that rising sense of helplessness, she received a phone call from her boss, the NATO Information Center's director. Days prior, the director had traveled to the South Ossetian front to cover the unfolding conflict as a journalist, leaving her deputy, Mshvidobadze, to run the organization in her absence. Now Mshvidobadze's boss wanted to warn her that the Russians were coming for Tbilisi. Everyone needed to evacuate.

In the hour that followed, Mshvidobadze and her staff prepared for a potential occupation, deleting sensitive files and destroying documents that they feared might fall into Russian hands. Then, in a final injection of chaos, the power across the city suddenly went out—perhaps the result of physical sabotage by the invading forces. It was around midnight when the staff finally hurried out of the blacked-out building and parted ways.

The NATO Information Center was, at the time, housed in a glass structure on a side street of Tbilisi's Vake District, a trendy neighborhood known during Georgia's Soviet era as the home of the city's intelligentsia. Mshvidobadze walked a block to a busier street nearby and found a scene of utter societal breakdown. The power outage had left the streetlights dark, so that only the headlights of cars illuminated sidewalks. Drivers were frantic, ignoring all traffic laws and plowing through intersections with dead traffic signals— preventing her from even crossing the street. As she tried in vain to flag a taxi, other desperate pedestrians ran past her, some screaming in fear or crying.

Mshvidobadze was determined to get home to her younger sister, who lived with her in an apartment across the city. But she couldn't reach her or call a cabdriver to pick her up: Cell phones were working only intermittently, as desperate Tbilisians' phones swamped telecom networks.

It would be half an hour before she could finally get through to a driver who could find her amid the pandemonium. Until then, she remained frozen at the intersection, watching the city panic. "It was a terrible, crazy situation. You have to be in a war zone to understand the feeling," she says. "All these thoughts were running through my head. I thought of my sister, my family, myself. I thought of the future of my country."

■

Jose Nazario had seen Georgia's war coming, nearly a month earlier— not from the front lines of the Caucasus, but from his office in Michigan. Nazario, a security researcher for Arbor Networks, the cyberattack-tracking firm, had come into work that July morning at the company's offices, a block from the south end of the University of Michigan's campus in Ann Arbor, and started the day with his usual routine: checking the aftermath of the previous night's botnet battles.

To analyze the entire internet's digital conflicts in real time, Arbor ran a system called BladeRunner, named for its bot-tracking purpose. It was part of a collection of millions of "honeypots"—virtual computers running on Arbor's servers around the world, each of which was expressly designed to be hacked and conscripted into a botnet's horde of enslaved PCs. Arbor used the computers as a kind of guinea-pig collective, harvesting them for malware samples and, more important for the company's business model, to monitor the instructions the bots received from botnets' command-and-control servers. Those instructions would allow them to determine whom the hackers were targeting and with what sort of firepower.

That morning, the results of Nazario's BladeRunner review turned up something strange. A major botnet was training its toxic torrent of pings at the website for the Georgian president, Mikheil Saakashvili. The site had apparently been punished with enough malicious traffic to knock it off-line. And the queries that had overwhelmed the site's server had included a strange set of characters, what appeared to be a message for its administrators: "win+love+in+Rusia."

That strange and slightly misspelled string immediately hinted to Nazario that the attack wasn't the usual criminal extortion takedown but something with a political bent. It looked more like the work of the botnets that had barraged Estonia the year prior, which he and the rest of Arbor's staff had tracked with fascination.

"It probably sounds better in the original Russian," Nazario says of the message. "But it was pretty unambiguous." He called up one of his favorite contacts for discussing the web's geopolitical conflicts: John Hultquist, then a young analyst at the State Department with a focus on cybersecurity and eastern Europe.

In the months since Hultquist had joined State, he and Nazario had been cultivating a mutually beneficial friendship. Hultquist, eager for access to Arbor Networks' attack data, had initially called Nazario to offer him a ride to the airport during one of Nazario's sales visits to D.C. Nazario was equally interested to hear Hultquist's views on the foreign policy context for the attacks Arbor tracked. Since then, the two men had developed a routine: Hultquist would pick Nazario up at the end of his D.C. trips, and they'd drive to dinner at Jaleo, a tapas restaurant in Crystal City. There they'd talk over the latest attacks waged against targets ranging from Estonia to Ingushetia to Chechnya and then rush to the airport for Nazario's flight home.

After Nazario discovered the attack on Georgia's president's website, he and Hultquist quickly pieced together the larger picture: Tensions between Russia and Georgia were approaching a breaking point. Much like Ukraine, Georgia's newly re-elected, pro-Western president was pushing the country toward NATO. If the country joined that alliance, it would represent NATO's farthest expansion yet into Russia's sphere of influence. That very idea, of course, infuriated the Kremlin.

In response, Russia was slowly ramping up its military presence in Abkhazia and South Ossetia as part of a so-called peacekeeping force. When Georgia protested to NATO that Russia was quietly threatening its sovereignty, it was mostly dismissed, warned not to provoke a conflict with its massive, powerful neighbor. In the meantime, skirmishes and flashes of violence were breaking out in Georgia's Russia-backed separatist regions, with bombings and intermittent firefights killing or wounding handfuls of separatists, as well as Georgian police and soldiers.

Now it seemed to Nazario and Hultquist that the Russian government—or at least patriotic Russian hackers aligned with its goals—was using new tools to tighten the screws against Georgia, the same ones it had experimented with in its fracas with Estonia. Only this time the cyberattacks might be a prelude to an actual shooting war.

That war arrived on August 7. A day later, a nearly simultaneous wave of distributed denial-of-service attacks hit thirty-eight websites, including the Ministry of Foreign Affairs, Georgia's National Bank, its parliament, its supreme court, the U.S. and U.K. embassies in Tbilisi, and again, President Saakashvili's website. As in Estonia, hackers defaced some sites to post pictures of Saakashvili alongside pictures of Hitler. And the attacks appeared to be centrally coordinated: They began within half an hour of one another and would continue unabated until shortly after noon on August 11, just as Russia was beginning to negotiate a cease-fire.

As in Estonia, the attacks were impossible to tie directly to Moscow. They came, as all botnet attacks do, from all directions at once. But the security firm Secureworks and researchers at the nonprofit Shadowserver Foundation were able to connect the attacks with the Russian Business Network, the same cybercriminals whose botnets had contributed to the Estonian attacks, as well as more grassroots hackers organized through sites like StopGeorgia.ru.

In some cases, the digital and physical attacks seemed uncannily coordinated. The hackers hit official sites and news outlets in the city of Gori, for instance, just before Russian planes began bombing it.

"How did they know that they were going to drop bombs on Gori and not the capital?" asked Secureworks researcher Don Jackson. "From what I've seen firsthand, there was at some level actual coordination and/or direction."

Khatuna Mshvidobadze, who after the Georgian war went on to get a doctorate in political science and cybersecurity policy and now works as a security researcher and consultant, argues that there can be little doubt today that the Kremlin had a direct hand in the cyberattacks. "How many signs do you need?" she asks, her voice tinged with anger. "This is how the Russian government behaves. They use proxies, oligarchs, criminals to make attribution harder, to give Russia deniability. This kind of game doesn't work anymore. We know who you are and what you're up to."

For John Hultquist, there was a detail of the attacks that stayed with him, a clue that he would file away in his memory, only to have it resurface six years later as he was tracking Sandworm. Many of the hackers bombarding Georgia were using a certain piece of malware to control and direct their digital armies, one that was still in an earlier incarnation but would develop over time into a far more sophisticated tool of cyberwar: BlackEnergy.

■

Russia and Georgia agreed to a cease-fire on August 12, 2008. In the days that followed, Russia's tanks continued to advance into Georgian territory—a final provocation before they ultimately turned around and withdrew. They never entered the capital. The shelling ceased, and the Russian fleet dismantled its Black Sea blockade.

Russia's gains from its brief war with Georgia, however, were tangible. It had consolidated pro-Russian separatist control of Abkhazia and South Ossetia, granting Russia a permanent foothold on roughly 20 percent of Georgia's territory. Just as in Ukraine in 2014, Russia hadn't sought to conquer or occupy its smaller neighbor, but instead to lock it into a "frozen conflict," a permanent state of low-level war on its own soil. The dream of many Georgians, like Mshvidobadze, that their country would become part of NATO, and thus protected from Russian aggression, had been put on indefinite hold.

And what role did Russia's cyberattacks play in that war? Practically none, Mshvidobadze says. "No one was even thinking about cyber back then, no one knew anything about it," she says. At the time, after all, Georgia was hardly Estonia. Only seven in a hundred Georgians even used the internet. And they had much more immediate concerns than inaccessible websites—like the mortar shells exploding around their cities and villages and the tanks lumbering toward their homes.

But the cyberattacks contributed to a broader confusion, both internally and internationally. They disabled a key avenue for Georgians to reach the West and share their own narrative about their war with Russia. Mshvidobadze still fumes at the commonly held idea, for instance, that the Georgian shelling of Tskhinvali sparked the war and not Russia's quietly amassing troops and matériel inside Georgian territory for weeks prior.

But perhaps more important than the cyberattacks' practical effects were the historical precedent they set. No country had ever before so openly combined hacker disruption tactics with traditional warfare. The Russians had sought to dominate their enemy in every domain of war: land, sea, air, and now the internet. Georgia was the first crude experiment in a new flavor of hybrid warfare that bridged the digital and the physical.

Reflecting on both the Georgian and the Estonian conflicts today, Hultquist sees primitive prototypes for what was to come. The Russian hackers behind them were nowhere near Sandworm in their skill or resources. But they hinted at an era of unrestricted, indiscriminate digital attacks, with little regard for the line between military and civilian.

"Hackers turning off the power? We weren't there yet," says Hultquist. "But whatever cyberwar would become, there's no doubt, this is where it began."

14

FLASHBACK: STUXNET

In January 2009, just days before Barack Obama would be inaugurated, he met with President George W. Bush to discuss a subject shrouded under the highest echelon of executive secrecy. On most matters of national security, even on topics as sensitive as the command sequence to initiate nuclear missile launches, Bush had let his subordinates brief the incoming president. But on this, he felt the need to speak with Obama himself. Bush wanted his successor's commitment to continue an unprecedented project. It was an operation the Bush-era NSA had developed for years but that was only just beginning to come to fruition: the deployment of a piece of code that would come to be known as Stuxnet, the most sophisticated cyberweapon in history.

Stuxnet's conception, more than two years earlier, had been the result of a desperate dilemma. When Iran's hard-liner president Mahmoud Ahmadinejad had taken power in 2005, he'd publicly flaunted his intention to develop the country's nuclear capabilities. That included enriching uranium to a grade that could be used for nuclear power. But international watchdog groups noted that Iran had only a single nuclear power plant, and it was already supplied with enriched uranium from Russia. They suspected a far less innocent motive: Ahmadinejad wanted nuclear weapons—a desire that Israel would likely consider an existential threat and a potential match that could ignite the entire Middle East.

Iran's government had sought to obtain nukes since as early as the

1980s, when it was locked in a brutal war with Iraq and suspected that the Iraqi leader, Saddam Hussein, was seeking to build nuclear bombs of his own. But neither country had actually succeeded in its atomic ambitions, and in the decades that followed, Iran had made only stuttering progress toward joining the world's nuclear superpowers.

Within two months of Ahmadinejad's election in the summer of 2005, however, he had thrown out an agreement Iran had made with the International Atomic Energy Agency, or IAEA, suspending the country's nuclear evolution. The country had, for years prior to that agreement, been building two 270,000-square-foot, largely subterranean facilities, twenty-five feet beneath the desert surface in Natanz, a central Iranian city. The purpose of those vast bunkers had been to enrich uranium to a weapons-grade purity. Under Ahmadinejad, Natanz was pitched back into high gear.

In 2005, U.S. intelligence agencies had estimated it would take six to ten years for Iran to develop a nuclear bomb. Israeli intelligence had put their estimate closer to five. But after Iran restarted its nuclear enrichment program at Natanz, Israeli intelligence shrank that estimate to as little as two years. Privately, the Israelis told U.S. officials a bomb might be ready in six months. A crisis was looming.

As that deadline grew ever closer, Bush's national security team had laid out two options, neither remotely appealing. Either the United States could allow Iran's unpredictable and highly aggressive government to obtain a devastating weapon, or it could launch a missile strike on Natanz—an act of war. In fact, war seemed inevitable on either horn of the dilemma. If Iran ventured too close to the cusp of fulfilling its nuclear ambitions, Israel's hard-line government was poised to launch its own strike against the country. "I need a third option," Bush had repeatedly told his advisers.

That option would be Stuxnet. It was a tantalizing notion: a piece of code designed to kneecap Iran's nuclear program as effectively as an act of physical sabotage, carried out deep in the heart of Natanz, and without the risks or collateral damage of a full-blown military attack. Together with the NSA's elite offensive hacking team, then known as Tailored Access Operations, or TAO, and the Israeli cybersecurity team known as Unit 8200, the Pentagon's Strategic Command began developing a piece of malware unlike any before. It would be capable of not simply disrupting critical equipment in Natanz but destroying it.

By 2007, a collection of Department of Energy national labs had obtained the same P1 centrifuges the Iranians were using, gleaming cylinders as thick as a telephone pole and nearly six and a half feet tall. For months, the labs would quietly test the physical properties of those machines, experimenting with how they might be destroyed purely via digital commands. (Some of those tests occurred at Idaho National Laboratory, during roughly the same period the lab's researchers were working on the Aurora hacking demonstration that showed they could destroy a massive diesel generator with a few lines of code. Mike Assante, who masterminded the Aurora work, declined to answer any questions about Stuxnet.)

Not long after the tests began, Bush's intelligence advisers laid out for him on a table the metal detritus of a centrifuge destroyed by code alone. The president was impressed. He green-lighted a plan to deploy that brilliant, malicious piece of software, an operation code-named Olympic Games. It would prove to be a tool of cyberwar so sophisticated that it made the cyberattacks in Estonia and Georgia look like medieval catapults by comparison.

Olympic Games was still in its early stages when the Bush presidency came to a close in early 2009. Stuxnet had only just begun to demonstrate its potential to infiltrate and degrade Iran's enrichment processes. So Bush held an urgent transition meeting with Obama, where the outgoing president explained firsthand to his successor the geopolitical importance and delicacy of their cyberwarfare mission, the likes of which had never before been attempted.

Obama was listening. He wouldn't simply choose to continue the Stuxnet operation. He would vastly expand it.

■

Fortunately for the continued existence of the human race, enriching uranium to the purity necessary to power the world's most destructive weapon is an absurdly intricate process. Uranium ore, when it's dug out of the earth, is mostly made up of an isotope called uranium-238. It contains less than 1 percent uranium-235, the slightly lighter form of the silvery metal that can be used for nuclear fission, unleashing the energy necessary to power or destroy entire cities. Nuclear power requires uranium that's about 3 to 5 percent uranium-235, but nuclear weapons require a core of uranium that's as much as 95 percent composed of that rarer isotope.

This is where centrifuges come in. To enrich uranium into bomb-worthy material, it has to be turned into a gas and pumped into a centrifuge's long, aluminum cylinder. A chamber inside the length of that cylinder is spun by a motor at one end, revolving at tens of thousands of rotations per minute, such that the outer edge of the chamber is moving beyond the speed of sound. The centrifugal force pushing from the center toward the walls of that spinning chamber reaches as much as a million times the force of gravity, separating out the heavier uranium-238 so that the uranium-235 can be siphoned off. To reach weapons-grade concentrations, the process has to be repeated again and again through a "cascade" of centrifuges. That's why a nuclear enrichment facility such as the one hidden deep beneath Natanz requires a vast forest of thousands of those tall, fragile, and highly engineered whirling machines.

Stuxnet was designed to be the perfect, invisible wrench thrown into those works.

Sometime in 2008, Natanz's engineers began to face a mysterious problem: At seemingly random times, one of their centrifuges would begin to spin out of control, its internal chamber moving faster than even its carefully crafted bearings were designed to handle. In other cases, pressure inside the chamber would increase until it was pushed out of its orbit. The spinning cylinder would then crash into its housing at supersonic speed, tearing the machine apart from the inside—just as Idaho National Laboratory's diesel generator had eviscerated itself in the Aurora test a year earlier.

Natanz's operators could see no sign or warning in their digital monitoring of the centrifuges to explain the machines' sudden suicides. Yet they kept happening. Eventually, the plant's administrators would assign staff to sit and physically watch the centrifuges for any indication that might explain the mystery. They resorted to decommissioning entire cascades of 164 centrifuges in an attempt to isolate the problem. Nothing worked.

"The intent was that the failures should make them feel they were stupid, which is what happened," one of the participants in the secret Olympic Games operation would later tell the *New York Times* reporter David Sanger. U.S. and Israeli intelligence saw signs of internal disputes among Iran's scientists as they sought to place the blame for the repeated disasters. Some were fired.

As time wore on—and as the Obama administration began to shepherd the operation—Natanz's centrifuge problems only grew more acute. In late 2009 and early 2010, officials at the International Atomic Energy Agency who were tensely monitoring Iran's nuclear progress saw evidence that the Iranians were carting decommissioned centrifuges out of their enrichment facility at a pace well beyond the usual failure rate. Out of the 8,700 centrifuges in Natanz at the time, as many as 2,000 were damaged, according to one IAEA official.

Olympic Games, in other words, was working. American and Israeli hackers had planted their digital sabotage code into the exact heart of the mechanical process that had brought the Middle East to the brink of war, and they were disrupting it with uncanny precision. Stuxnet had allowed them to pull off that coup without even tipping off their targets that they were under attack. Everything was going according to plan—until the summer of 2010, when the hackers behind Stuxnet would lose control of their creation, exposing it to the world.

■

The discovery of Stuxnet began the same way as the discovery of Sandworm would years later: a zero day.

In June 2010, VirusBlokAda, an obscure antivirus firm based in Minsk, Belarus, found that a computer of one of its customers in Iran had been stuck in a loop of repeated crashes and restarts. The company's researchers investigated the source of those crashes and found something far more sophisticated than they had imagined. An ultra-stealthy form of malware known as a "rootkit" had buried itself deep within the computer's operating system. And as they analyzed that rootkit, they found something far more shocking: It had infected the machine via a powerful zero day that took advantage of the way Windows displays the contents of a USB drive. As soon as an infected USB stick was inserted into the computer's port, the malware had sprung out to install itself on the machine with no indication to the user whatsoever.

After VirusBlokAda published an announcement about the malware on a security forum, researchers at the security giant Symantec picked up the thread. They would pull on it for months to come, a detective story detailed in Kim Zetter's definitive book on Stuxnet, *Countdown to Zero Day.* The malware's size and complexity alone were remarkable: It consisted of five hundred kilobytes of code, twenty to fifty times as large as the typical malware they dealt with on a daily basis. And as the researchers reverse engineered that code's contents, they found it contained *three* more zero days, allowing it to effortlessly spread among Windows machines—an entire built-in, automated arsenal of masterful hacker tricks.

No one in the security community could remember seeing a piece of malware that used four zero days in a single attack. Stuxnet, as Microsoft eventually dubbed the malware based on file names in its code, was easily the most sophisticated cyberattack ever seen in the wild.

By the end of that summer, Symantec's researchers had assembled more pieces of the puzzle: They'd found that the malware had spread to thirty-eight thousand computers around the world but that twenty-two thousand of those infections were in Iran. And they'd determined that the malware interacted with Siemens's STEP 7 software. That application was one form of the software that allows industrial control system operators to monitor and send commands to equipment. Somehow, the analysts determined, Stuxnet's goal seemed to be linked to physical machines—and probably in Iran. It was only in September 2010 that the German researcher Ralph Langner dove into the minutiae of that Siemens-targeted code and came to the conclusion that Stuxnet's goal was to destroy a very specific piece of equipment: nuclear enrichment centrifuges.

With that final discovery, the researchers could put together all of the links in Stuxnet's intricate kill chain. First, the malware had been designed to jump across air gaps: Iran's engineers had been careful enough to cut off Natanz's network entirely from the internet. So, like a highly evolved parasite, the malware instead piggybacked on human connections, infecting and traveling on USB sticks. There it would lie dormant and unnoticed until one of the drives happened to be plugged into the enrichment facility's isolated systems. (Siemens software engineers might have been the carriers for that malware, or the USB malware might have been more purposefully planted by a human spy working in Natanz.)

Once it had penetrated that air-gapped network, Stuxnet would unfold like a ship in a bottle, requiring no interaction with its creators. It would silently spread via its panoply of zero-day techniques, hunting for a computer running Siemens STEP 7 software. When it found one, it would lie in wait, then unleash its payload. Stuxnet would inject its commands into so-called programmable logic controllers, or PLCs—the small computers that attach to equipment and serve as the interfaces between physical machines and digital signals. Once infected, the centrifuge that a PLC controlled would violently tear itself apart. In a final touch of brilliance, the malware would, before its attack, pre-record feedback from the equipment. It would then play that recording to the plant's operators while it committed its violence so that to an operator observing the Siemens display, nothing would appear amiss until it was far too late.

Stuxnet's only flaw was that it was *too* effective. Among computer security researchers, it's practically a maxim that worms spread beyond their creators' control. This one was no exception. Stuxnet had propagated far beyond its Natanz target to infect computers in more than a hundred countries across the world. Other than in the centrifuge caverns of Natanz, those collateral infections hadn't caused physical destruction. But they had blown the ultrasecret malware's cover, along with an operation that had been millions of dollars and years in the making.

Once Stuxnet's purpose became clear, the United States and Israel quickly became the prime suspects for its creation. (It would be two more years, however, before a front-page story in *The New York Times* confirmed the two countries' involvement.)

When Stuxnet's existence went public, the Obama administration held a series of tense meetings to decide how to proceed. Should they pull the plug on the program before it was definitively tied back to the United States? It was only a matter of time, they figured, before Iran's engineers would learn the true source of their problems and patch their software vulnerabilities, shutting Stuxnet out for good.

Instead, the Americans and Israelis behind the worm decided they had nothing to lose. So in a go-for-broke initiative, they released another, final series of Stuxnet versions that were designed to be even more aggressive than the original. Before Iran's engineers had repaired their vulnerabilities, the malware destroyed nearly a thousand more of their centrifuges, offering one last master class in cybersabotage.

■

Stuxnet would change the way the world saw state-sponsored hacking forever. Inside Natanz's haywire centrifuges, the leading edge of cyberwarfare had taken a giant leap forward, from Russia's now primitive-looking web disruptions of 2007 and 2008 to virtuosic, automated physical destruction.

Today, history is still weighing whether Bush's and Obama's executive decisions to carry out that cyberattack were worth their cost. According to some U.S. intelligence analysts, Stuxnet set back the Iranian nuclear program by a year or even two, giving the Obama administration crucial time to bring Iran to the bargaining table, culminating in a nuclear deal in 2015.

But in fact, those long-term wins against Natanz's operation weren't so definitive. Even in spite of its confusion and mangled centrifuges, the facility actually increased its rate of uranium enrichment over the course of 2010, at times progressing toward bomb-worthy material at a rate 50 percent faster than it had in 2008. Stuxnet might have, if anything, only slowed the acceleration of Ahmadinejad's program.

And what was Stuxnet's price? Most notably, it exposed to the world for the first time the full prowess and aggression of America's— and to a lesser extent Israel's—most elite state hackers. It also revealed to the American people something new about their government and its cybersecurity priorities. After all, the hackers who had dug up the four zero-day vulnerabilities used in Stuxnet hadn't reported them to Microsoft so that they could be patched for other users. Instead, they had exploited them in secret and left Windows machines around the world vulnerable to the same techniques that had allowed them to infiltrate Natanz. When the NSA chose to let its Tailored Access Operations hackers abuse those software flaws, it prioritized military offense over civilian defense.

Who can say how many equally powerful zero days the U.S. government has squirreled away in its secret collection? Despite assurances from both the Obama and the Trump administrations that the U.S. government helps to patch more vulnerabilities than it hoards in secret, the specter of its hidden digital weapons cache has nonetheless haunted defenders in the cybersecurity community for years. (Just a few years later, in fact, that collection of zero days would backfire in an absurd, self-destructive fiasco.)

But in a broader and more abstract sense, Stuxnet also allowed the world to better imagine malware's potential to wreak havoc. In darkened rooms all over the globe, state-sponsored hackers took notice of America's creation, looked back at their own lackluster work, and determined that they would someday meet the new bar Stuxnet had set.

At the same time, political leaders and diplomats around the world recognized in Stuxnet the creation of a new norm, not only in its technical advancements, but in geopolitics. America had dared to use a form of weaponry no country had before. If that weapon were later turned on the United States or its allies, how could it object on principle?

Had physical destruction via code become an acceptable rule of the global game? Even the former NSA and CIA director Michael Hayden seemed shaken by the new precedent. "Somebody crossed the Rubicon," Hayden said in an interview with *The New York Times*. The attack that the West's prophets of cyberwar had always feared, one capable of shutting down or destroying physical equipment from anywhere in the world, had come to pass. And Americans had been the first to do it. "No matter what you think of the effects—and I think destroying a cascade of Iranian centrifuges is an unalloyed good—you can't help but describe it as an attack on critical infra-structure," Hayden concluded.

Stuxnet was no "cyber 9/11" or "electronic Pearl Harbor." It was a highly targeted operation whose damage was precisely limited to its pinpoint victim even when the worm spread out of its creators' control. But the fact remained: In an attempt to prevent Iran from joining the nuclear arms race America had itself started with the bombings of Hiroshima and Nagasaki sixty-five years earlier, it had sparked another form of arms race—one with severe, unforeseeable consequences.

"This has a whiff of August 1945," Hayden would say later in a speech. "Somebody just used a new weapon, and this weapon will not be put back in the box."

PART III
EVOLUTION

*The power to destroy a thing is the
absolute control over it.*

15

WARNINGS

In late 2015, half a decade after Stuxnet opened a Pandora's box of digital threats to the physical world, the first monster had finally emerged from it. That monster was Sandworm.

The Christmas blackout attack on Ukraine made clear that Russia's hackers were indeed waging cyberwar—perhaps the first true, wide-scale cyberwar in history. They had crossed the same line as Stuxnet's creators, from digital hacking to tangible sabotage. And they had also crossed a line from military to civilian, combining the unrestricted hybrid-warfare tactics of Estonia and Georgia with vastly more sophisticated and dangerous hacking techniques.

But even in late January 2016, only a handful of people in the world were aware of that ongoing threat. Two of them were Mike Assante and Rob Lee. When Assante had returned from the U.S. delegation's fact-finding trip to Ukraine, he couldn't share what he'd learned with Lee, since the agencies involved had put a firewall around the information as "for official use only." But Lee, working from the network logs his Ukrainian contacts had shared with him and other forensic evidence, had already pieced together the anatomy of an extraordinary, multipart intrusion: BlackEnergy, KillDisk, rewritten firmware to lock out defenders, the telephone DDoS attack, disabling on-site electrical backups, and finally the phantom mouse attack that had hijacked the controls of the utility operators.

There was nothing to stop Sandworm from attacking again. Lee and Assante agreed they had played the government's bureaucratic games long enough. It was time to publish a full report and warn the world.

But as Lee and Assante assembled their findings, they learned that the White House was *still* insisting on keeping the details of Ukraine's blackout out of the public eye until the Department of Homeland Security's Industrial Control Systems Cyber Emergency Readiness Team, or ICS-CERT, could publish a warning to electric utilities. When that report finally came in late February—two months after Sandworm's attack—it included a statement that left Lee furious: "Public reports indicate that the BlackEnergy (BE) malware was discovered on the companies' computer networks, however it is important to note that the role of BE in this event remains unknown pending further technical analysis."

Lee and Assante knew perfectly well how BlackEnergy had been used in the attack: It was the remote-access Trojan planted on victim machines that had begun the long, devious chain of intrusions, leading up to the hackers opening the utilities' circuit breakers.

Lee saw that ICS-CERT statement as practically a cover-up. By questioning BlackEnergy's role in the attack, or even its existence on the utilities' network, the DHS was obscuring a key fact: that the hackers who'd planted that malware had used the same tool to target American utilities just a year earlier—that Americans, too, were at risk.

"The message was: 'This doesn't map to us; this is a Ukrainian thing,'" says Lee. "They misled the entire community."

■

Over the next weeks, Lee says he protested in meetings and phone calls with contacts in the Department of Homeland Security, the Department of Energy, the NSA, and even the CIA, arguing that the White House and CERT were downplaying a serious, unprecedented new hacker threat that loomed over not just Ukraine but western Europe and the United States. He went so far as to publish an angry blog post on the SANS website. The gist of that entry, as Lee summarizes it today, was this: "This is bullshit. People need to know." The actual text is lost to history; Assante asked Lee to delete the post out of political discretion.

Meanwhile, Lee and Assante fought with the White House for weeks over what they could publicly reveal about the blackout attacks as White House officials insisted on one revision after another to remove details they considered classified. After a month, the SANS researchers resorted to publishing their report through the Electricity Information Sharing and Analysis Center, or E-ISAC, a part of the North American Electric Reliability Corporation that answered to Congress, not the executive branch. The Obama administration had objected to the release until the last minute.

Even then, through that spring, Lee says he found himself combating misinformed or Pollyannaish government officials who had told energy utilities the Ukrainian attacks couldn't have occurred in the United States. Representatives from the Department of Energy and NERC had comforted grid operators that the Ukrainians had used pirated software, had left their networks unsecured, and hadn't even run antivirus software. None of that was true, according to Lee and Assante.

But above all, Lee argued that the U.S. government had made an even greater, irreparable mistake: not simply being slow to warn the public and potential targets about Sandworm, or downplaying its dangers, but failing to send a message to Sandworm itself—or anyone else who might follow its path.

For years, since the first warnings of cyberwar in the late 1990s, hacker-induced blackouts had been the nightmare scenario that kept generals, grid operators, and security wonks awake at night. They had imagined and war-gamed military cyberattacks on the power grid for decades. Even President Clinton had spoken about the need to be prepared for that most fundamental form of digital sabotage, nearly fifteen years before Ukraine's blackout.

Now, as Lee saw it, the moment had finally come, and the U.S. government had done little more than sweep the incident under the rug. Perhaps most dangerous of all, it hadn't issued a single public statement condemning the attack. "We talk and talk and talk about this red line for years, and then, when someone crosses it, we say nothing," Lee said. "Someone in government needed to stand up and say a cyberattack on civilian infrastructure is something we won't stand for."

In fact, just a year before, the federal government *had* offered exactly the sort of response Lee had called for, though for a less novel form of attack. In December 2014, North Korean hackers posing as a hacktivist group known as the Guardians of Peace revealed they had broken into the servers of Sony Pictures in retaliation for its comedy film *The Interview,* which depicted the assassination of the North Korean dictator Kim Jong Un. The intruders destroyed the contents of thousands of computers and stole reams of confidential information that they later leaked onto the web, trickling the files out for weeks, including four unreleased feature films.

In the weeks following Sony's breach, the FBI issued a public statement swiftly identifying North Korea as the culprit, cutting through its hacktivism false flag. The FBI director, James Comey, went so far as to give a public speech laying out the evidence for North Korea's involvement, including how the hackers had failed on multiple occasions to use proxy computers as they'd intended to, and thus revealed IP addresses linked to their previous hacking operations—bread crumbs that led back to the Kim regime. President Obama himself spoke about the attack in a White House press conference, warning the world that the United States wouldn't tolerate North Korea's digital aggression.

"They caused a lot of damage, and we will respond. We will respond proportionally, and we'll respond in a place and time and manner that we choose," President Obama said. (The exact nature of that response has never been confirmed, but North Korea did experience a nationwide internet outage just days later, and the administration announced new financial sanctions against the Kim regime the next month.)

"This points to the need for us to work with the international community," Obama continued, "to start setting up some very clear rules of the road in terms of how the internet and cyber operates."

And yet a year later, when Russian hackers had launched a far broader and more dangerous attack deep inside civil infrastructure, no government official offered statements about proportional responses or international "rules of the road." No U.S. agency even named Russia as the offender, despite the numerous clues available to any researcher who looked. The Obama administration was virtually silent.

America and the world had lost a once-in-history chance, Lee argues, to definitively establish a set of norms to protect civilians in a new age of cyberwar. "It was a missed opportunity," he says. "If you say you won't allow something and then it happens and there's crickets, you're effectively condoning it."

■

In fact, Obama's most senior cybersecurity-focused official never doubted the gravity of Sandworm's blackout attack. In late January, not long after the delegation to Ukraine had flown back to Washington, J. Michael Daniel sat in a highly secured situation room in the Eisenhower Executive Office Building, just beyond the grounds of the West Wing, receiving a briefing from Department of Homeland Security officials on the results of that fact-finding trip. Daniel, a soft-spoken career civil servant with a kind, nervous face and slightly thinning hair, listened carefully. Then he walked back down the hall to his office to meet with his own staff, who would assemble a report for the national security advisor and, in turn, President Obama.

As he spoke with the White House aides about what the president should know, Daniel found himself marveling aloud at the brazenness of the attackers. "We've clearly crossed the Rubicon," he remembers saying, echoing Michael Hayden's comments on Stuxnet three years earlier. "This is something new."

Daniel had prided himself on the Obama administration's work to set clear boundaries on state-sponsored hacker provocations. Working together with Obama administration officials from the Department of Justice to the Pentagon to the Departments of State and Commerce, his team had answered misbehavior by foreign hackers with rigorous retaliation. In 2014, for instance, after Chinese cyberspies had for years pillaged American intellectual property, the Obama Justice Department had identified and levied criminal charges against five members of a Chinese People's Liberation Army hacking unit by name. The next year, the State Department threatened China with sanctions if the economic espionage continued. China's president, Xi Jinping, more or less capitulated, signing an agreement that neither country would hack the other's private sector targets. Security companies such as CrowdStrike and FireEye reported an almost immediate drop-off in Chinese intrusions—90 percent according to CrowdStrike—an unprecedented victory for cybersecurity diplomacy.

North Korea's Sony attack had received almost as forceful a response. And the administration would later indict a group of Iranian state hackers, too, accusing them of DDoS attacks against American banks and of probing the computer systems of a U.S. dam in upstate New York. (The Bowman Avenue Dam they'd targeted was only about twenty feet tall. The hackers might have intended to hit the far larger and more critical Bowman Dam in Oregon.) The message of all those hard-line disciplinary actions was this: No foreign state gets away with hacking American companies or digitally disrupting U.S. infrastructure.

Then came an actual, full-blown act of cyberwar against Ukraine, and all the same diplomats and security officials went silent. Why?

Michael Daniel's immediate train of thought when he first learned of the blackout may offer an answer: When a phone call from the DHS alerted him to Sandworm's attack the day after Christmas, his first reaction was alarm. "The thing we've been worried about has actually happened," he thought. But moments later, he remembers having a very different feeling: "My second reaction was a little bit of relief that it wasn't domestic to the U.S."

Daniel was deeply troubled by the notion that Russian hackers were willing to attack civilian infrastructure. Worse, these seemed to be the same hackers who'd been probing U.S. infrastructure only a year earlier. He had no illusions that the techniques used in the blackout attacks were limited to Ukrainian targets. "We have those systems in the United States, and we can't claim those systems to be any more secure than what Ukraine is running," he later told me. In fact, the greater automation in the American grid might mean that it provided even more points of attack. "We were equally if not more vulnerable." (By the time the U.S. delegation had returned from Ukraine, Daniel also had few doubts that the Russian government was indeed behind the attacks. "If it walks like a duck and quacks like a duck . . . ," he said.)

But even so, when Sandworm had finally pulled the trigger, it had carried out its attack in Ukraine, four thousand miles away from U.S. borders. This was the source of Daniel's relief: Ukraine was not America. It wasn't even a member of NATO. As a result, for the U.S. government, it was officially someone else's problem.

16

FANCY BEAR

Perhaps the Obama administration, given enough time, would have gotten around to calling out Sandworm's acts of cyberwar and making an example of the attackers with speeches, indictments, or sanctions. But by June 2016, its attention had been entirely hijacked by another hacker provocation—one that hit far closer to home.

On June 14, *The Washington Post* revealed that the Democratic National Committee had been penetrated for months by not one but two teams of state-sponsored Russian hackers. The security firm CrowdStrike, which the DNC had brought in to analyze its breach two months earlier, published a blog post identifying the pair of intrusion crews inside the Democrats' network as Cozy Bear and Fancy Bear, teams it had watched carry out spying campaigns for years, hitting everyone from the U.S. State Department and the White House to aerospace and defense contractors.

Based on past years of detective work, CrowdStrike tied Fancy Bear to the Russian military intelligence agency known as the GRU. Cozy Bear, it would later be revealed, worked within Russia's SVR foreign intelligence agency. (The two "bear" names derived from CrowdStrike's system of labeling hacker teams with different animals based on their country of origin—bears for Russia, pandas for China, tigers for India, and so on.) "Both adversaries engage in extensive political and economic espionage for the benefit of the government of the Russian Federation and are believed to be closely linked to the Russian government's powerful and highly capable intelligence services," CrowdStrike's analysis read.

In other words, these were teams that seemed to be focused on silent cyberespionage of the kind Russia had carried out since the days of Moonlight Maze, not the louder, more disruptive cyberwar tactics Sandworm had only just begun to demonstrate. (CrowdStrike had in fact tracked Sandworm's attacks too. Its own code name for the group was Voodoo Bear.)

But while the DNC hack wasn't an act of disruptive cyberwar, neither would it prove to be an ordinary espionage operation. Just twenty-four hours after news of the breach broke, a figure calling himself Guccifer 2.0 appeared on Twitter, posting links to a blog that introduced him to the world. The post was titled "DNC Servers Hacked by a Lone Hacker."

"Worldwide known cyber security company CrowdStrike announced that the Democratic National Committee (DNC) servers had been hacked by 'sophisticated' hacker groups," Guccifer 2.0 wrote glibly. "I'm very pleased the company appreciated my skills so highly))) But in fact, it was easy, very easy."

What came next in the post shocked the world: a sample of actual stolen documents from the DNC's servers. They included a file of opposition research on the Republican presidential front-runner, Donald Trump, policy documents, and a list of donors by name and amount. "The main part of the papers, thousands of files and mails, I gave to WikiLeaks. They will publish them soon," Guccifer 2.0 wrote. "Fuck the Illuminati and their conspiracies!!!!!!!!!"

That "Illuminati" reference and Guccifer 2.0's name were meant to convey a kind of rogue hacktivist, stealing and leaking the documents of the powerful to upend the corrupt social order. The original Guccifer had been a Romanian amateur hacker named Marcel Lehel Lazăr who had broken into the email accounts of high-profile figures like Colin Powell, the Rockefeller family, and the sister of former president George W. Bush.

Guccifer 2.0 took on the persona of a cocky eastern European cyberpunk who idolized figures like the original Guccifer, Edward Snowden, and Julian Assange. "Personally I think that I'm among the best hackers in the world," he would write in a FAQ.

When CrowdStrike maintained that Guccifer 2.0 was a thin disguise meant to obscure the Russian state hackers behind the DNC intrusion, Guccifer 2.0 shot back with vague denials. "They just fucked up! They can prove nothing!" he wrote. "All I hear is blah-blah-blah, unfounded theories and somebody's estimates."

But in reality, the Russians' mask almost immediately showed cracks. A former staffer for the British intelligence service GCHQ, Matt Tait, found that the very first document the Russians released, the Trump opposition file, contained Russian-language formatting-error messages. Moreover, the metadata from the file showed that it had been opened on a computer with the username "Feliks Dzer-zhinsky." That clue was almost comically revealing: Dzerzhinsky was the founder of the Soviet secret police, whose bronze statue had once stood in front of the KGB headquarters.

When the tech news site *Motherboard* reached out to Guccifer 2.0 via Twitter and the hacker agreed to an instant-message interview, *Motherboard*'s reporter Lorenzo Franceschi-Bicchierai cleverly threw him off guard with a series of questions in English, Romanian, and Russian. Guccifer 2.0 answered those questions in broken English and Romanian and protested that he couldn't understand the Russian. Franceschi-Bicchierai then showed the chat logs to Romanians and language experts who pointed out small linguistic clues that Guccifer wrote like a Russian and appeared to be pulling his Romanian answers from Google Translate. The Russian hackers seemingly hadn't even bothered to recruit a real Romanian for their cover story.

■

The flimsiness of the Guccifer 2.0 lie hardly mattered. The hackers sent the news site *Gawker* the Trump opposition research document, and it published a story on the file that received half a million clicks, robbing the Democrats of the ability to time the release of their Trump dirt. Soon, as promised, WikiLeaks began to publish a steady trickle of the hackers' stolen data, too; after all, Julian Assange's secret-spilling group had never been very particular about whether its "leaks" came from whistle-blowers or hackers.

The documents, now with WikiLeaks' stamp of credibility, began to be picked up by news outlets including *The New York Times,*

The Washington Post, The Guardian, Politico, BuzzFeed, and *The Inter-cept.* The revelations were very real: It turned out the DNC had secretly favored the candidate Hillary Clinton over her opponent Bernie Sanders as the presumptive Democratic nominee for president, despite the committee's purported role as a neutral arbiter for the party. DNC officials had furtively discussed how to discredit Sanders, including staging public confrontations about his religious beliefs and an incident in which his campaign's staff allegedly accessed the Clinton campaign's voter data.

The DNC chairwoman, Debbie Wasserman Schultz, was hit the hardest. The stolen emails revealed that she had privately written that Sanders's campaign manager was a "damn liar" and that Sanders "isn't going to be president." A little over a month after the hacked emails first began to appear, she resigned.

But the hackers weren't content to rely on WikiLeaks, nor was the DNC their only victim. Over the next several months, Gucci-fer 2.0's stolen DNC emails also began to appear on a new site called DCLeaks, along with emails stolen from other targets ranging from Republican and Democratic lawmakers to General Philip Breedlove, an air force official who had pushed for a more aggressive response to Russia's invasion of Ukraine. Despite DCLeaks' attempt to appear as another whistle-blowing "leak" site, the security firm ThreatConnect quickly identified it as a cover for Russia's Fancy Bear hackers, based on overlapping target data with known Fancy Bear intrusion opera-tions and clues in DCLeaks' registration data.

If anyone still doubted that Fancy Bear was behind the serial data dumps, that uncertainty lifted in September 2016, when the group launched a new attack on the World Anti-Doping Agency. Putin's government had been furious at the agency's recommendation that all Russian athletes be banned from that year's Summer Olympics after multiple athletic teams from the country were found to be part of widespread programs of performance-enhancing drug use. In retali-ation, Fancy Bear published the stolen medical records of the ten-nis stars Venus and Serena Williams and the gymnast Simone Biles, showing they too had used medications that could be interpreted—at a stretch—as offering athletic advantages. This time, in a blatant mockery of critics, the leaks were published on Fancybears.net, a website covered with clip art and animated GIFs of bears.

Fancy Bear had emerged as brash practitioners of what intelligence analysts call "influence operations." More specifically, they were using an old Russian intelligence practice known as *kompromat:* the tradition, stretching back to Soviet times, of obtaining compromising information about political opponents and using it to leverage public opinion with tactical leaks and smears.

Sandworm's hackers were stealthy, professional saboteurs. Fancy Bear, by contrast, seemed to be shameless, profane propagandists. And now, in the service of Vladimir Putin, they were tasked with helping Donald Trump to win the presidency.

The 2016 presidential race wasn't Fancy Bear's first time using its skills to influence elections. In May 2017, a group of security researchers at the University of Toronto called the Citizen Lab would find forensic evidence that the group was also behind CyberBerkut, the pro-Putin hacktivist group that had in 2014 hacked Ukraine's Central Election Commission. Like Guccifer 2.0 and DCLeaks, CyberBerkut was just another cover story.

Most of the group's techniques were simple. Next to an operation like Sandworm's 2015 Christmas blackout, they were practically primitive. But one of Fancy Bear's crudest tactics turned out to be its most effective of all: a rudimentary spoofed log-in page.

On October 7, WikiLeaks began publishing a new series of leaks, this time stolen directly from the email account of Hillary Clinton's campaign chair, John Podesta. The previous March, Podesta had fallen prey to a basic phishing email, directing him to a fake Gmail site that asked for his username and password, which he handed over. The site, of course, was a Fancy Bear trap.

WikiLeaks would trickle out its resulting stash of Clinton campaign *kompromat* for weeks to come. The revelations included eighty pages of closely guarded speeches Clinton had given to private Wall Street audiences. One included a reference to politicians' need to have separate "public" and "private" positions, which her critics interpreted as an admission of deception. Another seemed to call for "open borders," enraging immigration hard-liners. The daily media bombs would keep the campaign off balance through its final days.*

The Podesta hack also eradicated any last doubts about Fancy Bear's role: The security firm Secureworks found the link to the fake Gmail site that had tricked Podesta was created with an account on the URL-shortening service Bitly that had also been used to target hundreds of other Fancy Bear victims, from Ukrainian officials to Russia-focused academics and journalists.

Trump, of course, brushed aside the evidence of Russia's involvement and reveled in the flood of scandals. "I love WikiLeaks!" he declared at one rally. At another point, he quipped that he hoped the Russian hackers had also breached the controversial private email server Clinton had set up in her home, and asked the hackers to release thousands more of her emails. But for the most part, Trump nihilistically denied that those leaks had been enabled by the Kremlin, instead suggesting that the hackers might just as easily be Chinese or a "400-pound" loner or that the Democrats had hacked themselves. Trump's obfuscation served Fancy Bear well: Even months later, in December 2016, only about a third of Americans believed Russia had meddled in the U.S. election, while 44 percent doubted it, and a quarter were unsure.†

Whether the Kremlin actually expected to swing the 2016 race with its influence operation has never been clear. Putin, whose hatred of Hillary Clinton since her days as secretary of state under Obama

---

* The most powerful effect of those leaks may have been to distract from a shocking video released by *The Washington Post* on October 7, in which Trump bragged on the set of the TV show *Access Hollywood* that he had grabbed women's genitals without their consent. WikiLeaks published the first Podesta leaks just hours after that tape surfaced.

† When this book went to press, the extent of Trump's collaboration with the Russian government in its election interference remained unclear. But the investigation of independent counsel Robert Mueller had revealed that multiple members of Trump's staff as well as Donald Trump Jr. had met with Kremlin officials and other Russian nationals who had offered compromising information on Clinton, which Trump Jr. was eager to accept. As a candidate, Trump had also weakened the Republican Party position on defending Ukraine from Russia, all while pursuing a billion-dollar deal to establish a Trump Tower in Moscow.

could barely be concealed, might have simply wished to saddle her presidency with crippling political baggage. Russian officials, of course, repeatedly denied any hand in the attacks. But regardless of what outcome they imagined, they had successfully thrown the core of American democracy into chaos.

When I met up with CrowdStrike's chief technology officer, Dmitri Alperovitch, at a park in Manhattan's financial district in October 2016, with the election just weeks away, he seemed to almost grudgingly admire the effectiveness of the hackers whose operation his firm had first uncovered four months earlier.

"I think they've gotten medals already," he said ruefully. "They've had success beyond their wildest dreams."

In fact, Fancy Bear's real moment of glory came three weeks later: Donald Trump won the U.S. presidential election.

■

When J. Michael Daniel had become Obama's most senior official concerned solely with cybersecurity in 2012, one of his first big moves had been to fly to Moscow in 2013 to finalize a "cyber hotline." Using a protocol first established to prevent nuclear Armageddon half a century earlier, the hotline was intended to serve as an open channel between the White House and the Kremlin for sending messages about cyberattacks, a kind of safety valve to avoid misunderstandings that might lead to unnecessary escalation and war. Daniel describes the setup as a "glorified, dedicated email system."

On October 7, 2016, Daniel used that hotline for the first and only time in his tenure, to send a message to Putin in response to Russia's blatant election interference. He paraphrases the message: "We know that you are carrying out these kinds of activities. And stop. Knock it off." The same day, the Department of Homeland Security and the Office of the Director of National Intelligence released a public statement that U.S. intelligence agencies had officially come to a consensus that the Russian government was the source of the stolen emails, as cybersecurity researchers had been pointing out for four months.

Eventually, in the waning days of Obama's presidency, the administration would escalate its response to include new economic sanctions against Russian intelligence agencies as punishment for their election hacking, effectively preventing them from doing any business with American citizens and companies. The order would eject thirty-five Russian diplomats from the United States and seize control of two Russian government compounds on U.S. soil. James Lewis, a cybersecurity-focused fellow at the Center for Strategic and International Studies, would describe the reaction as "the biggest retaliatory move against Russian espionage since the Cold War."

But on the subject of Russia's blackout attacks, the hotline from the White House to the Kremlin remained silent. Sandworm had been sent an implicit signal. It could now proceed with impunity.

17

FSOCIETY

On election night, Michael Matonis had gone to bed early. He'd seen the increasing likelihood of Trump's win. But he'd chosen, rather than biting his nails all evening, to just assume Clinton would prevail as expected and sleep through the drama until then.

At 5:00 a.m., he was woken up by the shortwave radio next to his bed, immediately heard the news, and emitted a long, heartfelt moan of profanity.

Matonis, a twenty-seven-year-old security researcher with a mass of curly black hair, lived at the time in Albany, New York, but had been planning a party that night in his hometown of Brooklyn—not so much to celebrate Clinton's victory as to herald an end to seeing Trump's face on television every day. After learning the shocking election results, Matonis and his friends quickly reconceived the party as a kind of emotional support group. So he nonetheless boarded an Amtrak train south, then made his way from Penn Station through a New York City that was visibly grieving, with signs of protest and condolences posted on subway platforms and in shopwindows.

When he arrived in the city, Matonis had planned to wander around Williamsburg and find some good Turkish or Brazilian food. But he soon found that he was too depressed to leave his Airbnb. So instead, despite officially being on vacation, he opened his laptop to distract himself with work.

Matonis was a member of the team of researchers that reported to John Hultquist, who by then had become director of cyberespionage analysis at FireEye, the security firm that had acquired iSight earlier in 2016. As part of his daily hunting, Matonis had created his own software tools that automatically scanned malware feeds like VirusTotal for interesting tidbits that might serve as footprints of state-sponsored hackers—what he calls "cyber gold panning."

Early that morning, one of his filter tools had pinged him with results that he'd been too distracted to read. Now he dug into its origin: Someone had uploaded to VirusTotal a piece of malicious code that used a Microsoft Office script to install itself on the victim's machine, just as BlackEnergy had done in the late 2015 attacks. The new malware appeared to be a fresh backdoor for remote access to victim machines, one that curiously used the encrypted instant-messaging software Telegram to communicate with its command-and-control servers. But Matonis had tracked the BlackEnergy attacks closely enough to see that they shared a similar encoding.

The backdoor program was packaged in a Word document written in Cyrillic characters. When Matonis put the file through Google Translate, he found that it was a list of prices of storage hardware and servers written in Ukrainian, what appeared to be bait for Ukrainian IT systems administrators. "I could think of only one group that would do this thing, in this particular way," he says.

Since the Ukrainian blackouts nearly a year earlier, Sandworm had gone entirely silent. After its grid-hacking tour de force, it seemed as if the group might even have disappeared. Aside from a few die-hard obsessives including Matonis, his boss, Hultquist, and Rob Lee, much of the American security community's attention to Russian hacking had shifted almost entirely to Fancy Bear's election meddling.

Now Matonis was seeing the first sign that Russia's blackout hackers had surfaced again. "Holy shit," Matonis thought to himself as he sat at the kitchen table of his Brooklyn rental. "I think I've found Sandworm version two."

■

By August 2016, eight months after the first Christmas blackout, Yasinsky had left his job at StarLightMedia. It wasn't enough, he decided, to defend a single company from an onslaught that seemed to be targeting every stratum of Ukrainian society. Despite Sandworm's silence since the blackout, Yasinsky knew that the group spent long months advancing its intrusions and that the next wave of attacks was likely already in motion. He needed a more holistic view of the hackers' work, and Ukraine needed a more coherent response to the brazen, callous organization of attackers that Sandworm was becoming. "The light side remains divided," he told me of the balkanized reaction to the hackers among their victims. "The dark side is united."

So Yasinsky took a position as the head of research and forensics for a Kiev firm called Information Systems Security Partners, or ISSP. The company was hardly a big name in the security industry. But Yasinsky joined with the intention of using his position to make ISSP the go-to first responder for victims of Ukraine's digital siege.

Not long after he switched jobs, as if on cue, the country came under another, even broader, more punishing wave of attacks. Starting in December, a month after FireEye's Michael Matonis and other researchers around the world were seeing the first signs of Sandworm's reemergence, Yasinsky began to learn of other Ukrainian agencies and infrastructure companies targeted by the same destructive hackers as in 2015. Those victims would eventually include Ukraine's pension fund, Treasury, seaport authority, and Ministries of Infrastructure, Defense, and Finance. In each case, as in the year before, the attacks culminated with a KillDisk-style detonation on the target's hard drives.

The hackers again hit Ukraine's railway company, Ukrzaliznytsia, this time knocking out its online booking system for days, right in the midst of the holiday travel season. In the case of the Finance Ministry, the logic bomb deleted terabytes of data, destroying the contents of 80 percent of the agency's computers, deleting its draft of the national budget for the next year, and leaving its network entirely off-line for the next two weeks.

In other words, the hackers' new winter onslaught matched and exceeded the previous year's in both its scale and the calculated pain of its targeting. But as security researchers delved into the companies' logs in those first weeks of December, they could see their tormentors were trying out new forms of deception, too. In one round of attacks, for instance, the hackers had altered their KillDisk code to not merely cripple victims' machines but also to display a haunting image on their screens.

The picture—first published by researchers at the Slovakian security firm ESET, who were also closely tracking the second wave of Ukrainian attacks—wasn't merely a file planted on the victims' computers. Instead, with a kind of hacker flourish, it had been painstakingly programmed into the malware to be drawn by Windows's graphics interface every time the code ran. The resulting image was a neon-green and black low-resolution mustachioed mask, over a background of multicolored ones and zeros. Above and below the mask were the words "WE ARE FSOCIETY" and "JOIN US."

The hackers had co-opted the symbology of the fictional anarchist hackers in the television show *Mr. Robot,* perhaps to create a veneer of freewheeling, grassroots nihilism over what was clearly a well-organized, state-sponsored disruption campaign. (With the benefit of hindsight, they might have also been revealing something about their intentions: In *Mr. Robot,* FSociety's hackers permanently destroy the records of a massive banking conglomerate, erasing the debt of thousands of people and throwing the world economy into chaos—a story line that, within a year, would feel prescient.)

In the second round of attacks, the hackers switched up their ruse: Instead of a hacktivist front, they adopted a cybercriminal one, plastering victims' corrupted machines with a ransom message demanding a Bitcoin payment: "We are sorry, but the encryption of your data has been successfully completed, so you can lose your data or pay 222 btc."

Sandworm seemed to have adapted its cover story to mimic an increasingly trendy tactic among hacker profiteers: Rather than try to steal credit cards or other data that had to be resold to be monetized, cybercriminals had discovered they could extort money directly from victims by encrypting their hard drives and demanding payment to unlock them. Only once the victims forked over the ransom—within a prescribed time limit—would the extortionists send a key to decrypt their data. Some ransomware schemes had become so professional that they even included live customer support, increasing the likelihood of payment by reassuring victims that they would actually receive their data back.

But most of those moneymaking schemes, as cruel as they were, asked for just a few hundred or thousand dollars from victims. This one demanded, at late 2016 Bitcoin exchange rates, more than $150,000. No one, it seemed, was foolish enough to pay. And ESET's researchers found that even if they had, there was no decryption mechanism in the malware. Instead, the ransom demand only added another layer of confusion to the same KillDisk-style data destruction that Sandworm had been carrying out since the year before.

Yasinsky could see that the hackers were not only evolving but experimenting. After a year underground, they had reemerged more dangerous and deceptive than ever. Ukraine's cyberwar was ramping up. And then, on a Saturday night two weeks into that growing plague, not long after Yasinsky sat down on the couch of his Kiev apartment to watch the movie *Snowden* with his family, Sandworm put its full capabilities on display.

■

On December 17, 2016, a young engineer named Oleg Zaychenko was four hours into his twelve-hour night shift at Ukrenergo's transmission station just north of Kiev's city limits. He sat in an old Soviet-era control room, its walls covered in beige and red floor-to-ceiling analog control panels. The station's tabby cat, Aza, was out hunting; all that kept Zaychenko company was a television in the corner playing pop music videos.

He was filling out a paper-and-pencil log, documenting another uneventful Saturday evening, when the station's alarm suddenly sounded, a deafening continuous ringing. To his right, Zaychenko saw that two of the lights indicating the state of the transmission system's circuits had switched from red to green—in the counterintuitive, universal language of electrical engineers, a sign that they had turned off.

The technician picked up the black desk phone to his left and called an operator at Ukrenergo's headquarters to alert him to the routine mishap. As he did, another light turned green. Then another. Zaychenko's adrenaline began to kick in. While he hurriedly explained the situation to the remote operator, the lights kept flipping: red to green, red to green. Eight, then ten, then twelve.

As the crisis escalated, the operator on the phone ordered Zaychenko to run outside and check the equipment for physical damage. At that moment, the twentieth and final circuit switched off, and the lights in the control room went out, along with the computer and TV. Zaychenko was already throwing a coat over his blue-and-yellow uniform and sprinting for the door.

Ukrenergo's northern Kiev transmission station is normally a vast, buzzing jungle of electrical equipment stretching over twenty acres, the size of more than a dozen football fields. But as Zaychenko came out of the building into the freezing night air, the atmosphere was eerier than ever before: The three tank-sized transformers arrayed alongside the building, responsible for about a fifth of the capital's electrical capacity, had gone entirely silent.

Until then, Zaychenko had been mechanically ticking through an emergency mental checklist. As he ran past the paralyzed machines, the thought entered his mind for the first time: The blackout hackers had struck again.

18

POLIGON

This time the attack had moved up the circulatory system of Ukraine's grid. Instead of taking down the distribution substations that branch off into capillaries of power lines, the saboteurs had hit an artery. That single northern Kiev transmission station carried two hundred megawatts, more total electric load than all the fifty-plus distribution stations knocked out in the 2015 attack combined.

Luckily, the system was down for just an hour—hardly long enough for pipes to freeze or for locals to start panicking—before Ukrenergo's engineers began manually closing circuits and bringing everything back online. Even so, when that hour-long midnight blackout enveloped Yasinsky's home in northern Kiev, it unnerved him like no cyberattack he'd ever experienced in his years as a security professional.

Yasinsky told me he's always tried to maintain a dispassionate perspective on the intruders who were ransacking his country. He seeks to avoid entirely, for instance, the topic of the attackers' identities, arguing that their names or nationalities don't figure into the analysis of their intrusions or strategies for defending against them. (That refusal to wade into questions of attribution is common in the cybersecurity industry. But Yasinsky takes it to an extreme, going so far as to wag his finger with a mock-scolding grin when I refer to the attackers as Russian.)

Yasinsky has always preferred to see his job as a game of chess, logically analyzing the adversary's moves on an abstract plane free from any personal psychology. Become too emotionally invested, he argued, let your thinking be corrupted by your own anger or obsession or self-interest, and you begin to make mistakes. "You need a cold, clear mind," Yasinsky said. "If you want to play well, you can't afford to hate your opponent."

But when the blackout extended to his own home, he admitted that it crossed a new boundary. It was "like being robbed," he told me. "It was a kind of violation, a moment when you realize your own private space is just an illusion."

Within twenty-four hours of the blackout, Ukrenergo staffers had publicly confirmed that it had indeed been caused by another cyberattack, just as Yasinsky had immediately suspected. Ukrenergo and the SBU—the Ukrainian security service that partly functions as the country's equivalent of the NSA—determined that Ukraine would handle the response itself. This time, there would be no American delegation. And so naturally, when ISSP called up Ukrenergo and offered its services, the job was handed to Yasinsky.

■

In early 2017, at a meeting in Ukrenergo's central Kiev headquarters, the company gave ISSP a hard drive filled with the terabytes of log files that Yasinsky would need to begin his forensic analysis. Just as he had at StarLightMedia, he pored over the logs for weeks, combing them for any anomaly that might reveal the traces of hackers who had sought at every point in their intrusion to perfectly mimic the normal behavior of the victims they had infiltrated—what Yasinsky calls "finding needles among needles."

After tracking the same hackers for more than a year, Yasinsky knew where to find their footprints. By the end of January, ISSP had assembled nearly the entire anatomy of the intrusion. He presented it in a briefing for Ukrenergo's IT administrators, rolling out in front of them a six-foot-long printed paper timeline of the hackers' work. Though the company had given him six months of logs, it appeared the hackers had likely obtained their access far earlier: In January 2016, nearly a year before the second blackout, Ukrenergo had discovered an infection of the same BlackEnergy malware that had hit

StarLightMedia, TRK, and Boryspil airport. Yasinsky guessed that despite the utility's cleanup efforts the intruders had maintained a stealthy foothold somewhere inside Ukrenergo's systems, patiently biding their time.

To move between computers within Ukrenergo's network, they had deployed a common hacker tool called Mimikatz, designed to take advantage of a security oversight in older versions of Windows that leaves passwords accessible in a computer's memory. Mimikatz plucks credentials out of that ephemeral murk so that hackers can use them to gain repeated access to a computer, or to any others that a victim's account could access on the same network. The hackers had also exploited a more obscure trick, one that allows them to dig through memory when an application unexpectedly crashed, with sensitive credentials lingering in the "crashdump" of data that borked programs leave behind—a bit like grabbing and instantly copying the keys from a stalled car.

With those stolen credentials, the hackers eventually gained access to a kind of all-seeing database server in Ukrenergo's network, what's sometimes known as a "historian." That database acted as a record keeper for the utility's operations, collecting data from physical equipment and making it available to the business network. For the intruders, it offered a crucial bridge between the traditional IT side of Ukrenergo's network and the industrial control system side, including workstations with access to circuit breakers.

That historian database didn't merely collect data from the utility's computers. It also, more dangerously, had the ability to send certain commands to them. As Yasinsky describes it, the hackers hijacked that functionality to turn the database into a "Swiss Army knife," capable of running any code the hackers chose. Ultimately, that included planting the payload of their attack at the doorstep of Ukrenergo's actual transmission station equipment and, as in 2015, callously flipping those switches to cut power to hundreds of thousands of people.

The attackers seemed to have shifted their focus from the 2015 attack, when they had ransacked the three regional power utilities with a broad arsenal of humiliations, attacking everything from the utilities' own backup generators to their phone systems. Instead, this time they had penetrated directly into the transmission systems with single-minded professionalism. "In 2015, they were like a group of brutal street fighters," says Marina Krotofil, a Ukraine-born German industrial control systems expert who then worked at Honeywell and who advised Yasinsky during ISSP's analysis. "In 2016, they were ninjas."

But the final payload those saboteurs had planted, to Yasinsky, was a kind of black box. He could see that the hackers had, ahead of their midnight strike, installed a collection of dynamic-link library, or .dll files, essentially collections of instructions they could call upon. But industrial control systems are their own arcane discipline within cybersecurity, and Yasinsky, despite his knowledge of the forensics of traditional IT systems, couldn't interpret the .dll files himself. Krotofil, his friend and go-to industrial control systems expert, had helped to guide him through that side of the Ukrenergo investigation. But thanks to the nondisclosure agreement he'd signed with the utility, he couldn't share the .dlls with her.

Yasinsky showed the files to Ukrenergo's engineers, and they told him that the code included commands written in a particular protocol— a kind of computer vocabulary understood by their circuit breaker equipment. Somehow, those files had triggered the final, disruptive step of the hackers' blackout operation. Exactly how would remain a mystery for months to come.

■

In the United States, meanwhile, the second Ukrainian blackout resonated momentarily through the cybersecurity community, stealing back a modicum of attention from the frenzy around Russia's election-focused attacks. For the first time in history, as Lee described it to me, a group of hackers had shown it was willing and able to repeatedly attack critical infrastructure. They'd refined their techniques over multiple, evolving assaults. And they'd planted their malware on the U.S. grid once before.

All of that meant, Lee argued, that American utilities and government officials needed to see Russia's escalating cyberwar operations not only as Ukraine's problem but as their own. "The people who understand the U.S. power grid know that it can happen here," he told me.

When I'd run that notion by NERC's chief security officer, Marcus Sachs, in a phone call, he'd downplayed the threat. American power companies have already learned from Ukraine's victimization, he argued. Sachs pointed to the road show of briefings he and others had performed for U.S. utilities to educate them about the attacks, hammering into them that they need to shore up their basic cybersecurity practices and turn off remote access to their critical systems whenever possible. And for all the sophistication of the Ukraine grid hacks, he pointed out, even they didn't really constitute a catastrophe; the lights did, after all, come back on.

"It would be hard to say we're not vulnerable. Anything connected to something else is vulnerable," Sachs said. "To make the leap and suggest that the grid is milliseconds away from collapse is irresponsible."

But to hackers like Sandworm, Lee countered, the United States could present an even more convenient set of targets. U.S. power firms are more attuned to cybersecurity, but they're also more automated and modern than those in Ukraine, with more computer-controlled equipment. In other words, they present more of a digital "attack surface" to hackers than some older systems.

American engineers, he argued, also have less experience with manual recovery from frequent blackouts than a country like Ukraine. Regional utilities in Ukraine, and even Ukrenergo in Kiev, are all far more accustomed to blackouts from the usual equipment failures than American utilities. They have fleets of trucks ready to drive out to substations and manually switch the power back on, as Ukrainian utilities did in 2015 when the hackers first hit them. Not every hyper-automated American utility is prepared for that all-hands, on-the-ground manual override. "Taking down the American grid would be harder than Ukraine," Lee said. "*Keeping* it down might be easier."

As Sandworm's power and brashness grew, the question remained: Would it ever dare hit the United States the way it had Ukraine? An attack on American utilities, after all, would almost certainly result in immediate, serious retaliation from the U.S. government, even if the same attacks in a regional war of Russian aggression had barely elicited a murmur from U.S. officials.

Some cybersecurity analysts at the time of Sandworm's second grid attack argued that Russia's goal was simply to hem in America's own cyberwar strategy: By turning the lights out in Kiev—and by showing that it's capable of penetrating the American grid—Moscow had sent a message warning the United States not to try a Stuxnet-style attack on Russia or its allies, such as the Syrian dictator, Bashar al-Assad, whose revolutionary opponents the United States was supporting in the Syrian civil war.

In that view, it was all a game of deterrence. As one influential pseudonymous hacker and security analyst known as the Grugq had written in a blog post after the second Ukraine blackout, "This expensive light flicking makes more sense when viewed as an influence operation to signal the West that Russia has what the West itself believes are 'real cyberwar cyberweapons.'

"Russia has flicked Ukraine's lights twice now," he wrote. "There is no reason to run two tests of an offensive operation if the first is successful. They want to make sure the West gets the signal."

But Lee, who was involved in plenty of war-game scenarios during his time at the NSA, could imagine Russia striking American utilities as a retaliatory measure if it ever saw itself as backed into a corner—if the United States, say, threatened to interfere with Moscow's military interests in Ukraine or Syria. "When you deny a state's ability to project power," he argued, "it has to lash out."

Lee and his ilk, of course, had been war-gaming these nightmares for well over a decade. And as yet, cyber doomsday had never come to U.S. soil. But in the wake of Fancy Bear's election interference, there seemed to be no limits to Russia's brazenness. The Kremlin had meddled in the Ukrainian election and faced no real repercussions; then it applied similar tactics to the United States. Russian hackers turned off the power in Ukraine with impunity; the syllogism wasn't hard to complete.

For John Hultquist, who had now watched Sandworm's attacks escalate for more than two years, that next step was clear enough. Three weeks after the 2016 Kiev attack, he wrote a prediction on

Twitter and pinned it to his profile for posterity: "I swear, when Sand-worm Team finally nails Western critical infrastructure, and folks react like this was a huge surprise, I'm gonna lose it."

■

On a gray day in March 2017, a taxi dropped me off in a parking lot in front of the headquarters of ISSP in Kiev. The company at the time occupied a low-lying building in an industrial neighborhood of the Ukrainian capital, surrounded by muddy sports fields and crumbling high-rises—a few of the country's many lingering souvenirs from the Soviet Union.

When I found Oleksii Yasinsky inside, we sat down in the company's "Cyber Lab," a darkened room with a round table that's covered in the same sort of network maps he'd developed for the Ukrenergo operation, long scrolls of paper showing nodes and connections of Borgesian complexity. Each map represented the timeline of an intrusion by Sandworm. By then, the hacker group had been the consuming focus of Yasinsky's work for nearly two years, going back to its first attack on StarLightMedia. He told me there was still no way to know exactly how many Ukrainian institutions had been hit in the escalating campaign of cyberattacks; any count was liable to be an underestimate. For every publicly known target, there was at least one secret victim that hadn't admitted to being breached, and still other targets that hadn't yet discovered the intruders in their systems.

In fact, Yasinsky said, the next wave of the digital invasion might have already been under way even then. Behind him, two younger, bearded ISSP staffers were locked into their keyboards and screens, pulling apart malware that the company had obtained just the day before from a new round of phishing emails. The attacks, Yasinsky had come to believe, took on a seasonal cycle: During the first months of the year, the hackers laid their groundwork, silently penetrating targets and spreading their presence. At the end of the year, they unleashed their payload. Yasinsky suggested that even as he was analyzing last year's power grid attack, the seeds had already been sown for 2017's December surprises.

Bracing for the next round, Yasinsky told me, was like "studying for an approaching final exam." He maintained that what he and Ukraine had faced so far was likely just a series of practice tests.

He summed up the attackers' intentions in a single Russian word: *poligon.* A training ground. Even in their most damaging attacks, Yasinsky said, the hackers could have gone further. They could have destroyed not just the Ministry of Finance's stored data but its backups too. They probably could have knocked out Ukrenergo's transmission station for longer or caused permanent, physical harm to the grid—a restraint that American analysts like Assante and Lee had also noted in my conversations with them. "They're still playing with us," Yasinsky said. Each time, the hackers retreated before accomplishing the maximum possible damage, as if reserving their true capabilities for some future operation. "We can only hope that they're not done playing yet."

Yasinsky wasn't alone in forming that new, foreboding theory around Ukraine's cyberwar: International observers began to posit that Russia was turning the country into a test lab, trying out digital tactics that it might later unleash on the West. Where better to train an army of Kremlin hackers than in the no-holds-barred atmosphere of a hot war inside Putin's own sphere of influence? "The gloves are off. This is a place where you can do your worst without retaliation or prosecution," Kenneth Geers, the NATO ambassador, told me. "Ukraine is not France or Germany. A lot of Americans can't find it on a map. So you can practice there."

In that shadow of neglect, Russia wasn't only pushing the limits of its technical abilities, said Thomas Rid, a professor of strategic and military studies at Johns Hopkins. It was also feeling out the edges of what the international community would tolerate. "They're testing out red lines, what they can get away with," Rid told me. "You push and see if you're pushed back. If not, you try the next step."

And what would it look like when the hackers ceased to play those exhibition games and unleashed their full powers? In the dim back room at ISSP's office in Kiev during my spring 2017 visit, Yasinsky admitted to me that he didn't know what form the next attack would take. Perhaps another, more severe blackout. Or maybe a targeted attack on a water facility. Regardless, he said, he believed it would reach out, like the blackout that he felt in his own home, well beyond the internet as we've long understood it, into the infrastructure of the physical world.

Behind him, the fading afternoon light glowed through the blinds, rendering his face a dark silhouette. "Cyberspace is not a target in itself. It's a medium," Yasinsky said. "Use your imagination."

19

INDUSTROYER/CRASH OVERRIDE

Yasinsky, it turned out, hadn't been the only one delving into the forensic evidence of the Ukrenergo blackout. Six hundred miles to the west, another security researcher, Anton Cherepanov, wasn't merely tracing those same footprints inside the utility's network; he was, though neither man yet knew it, filling in the missing pieces of Yasinsky's puzzle.

Five days after Sandworm's December 17 blackout attack, Cherepanov opened on his computer the same set of .dll files that had represented the final, unsolved mystery in ISSP's analysis of the Ukrenergo intrusion. Cherepanov was working in the main operations center of the headquarters of the Slovakian security firm ESET, an open-plan office with rows of workstations all facing a wall covered in screens showing visualizations of malware data feeds pulled from ESET's antivirus software. The company, in an homage to NASA, called the room "Houston."

ESET's office is situated on the sixteenth floor of Aupark Tower, a corporate building that stands on the south bank of the Slovakian capital of Bratislava. The building offers a stunning view of the Danube River and, across it, Bratislava Castle looming over the city's historic quarter. But on that day in December, Cherepanov was entirely fixated on the code unfolding on the two screens in front of him. He was working alone; "Houston" was otherwise empty. Almost all of ESET's other employees had already begun their Christmas holidays.

Only Cherepanov, as a Russian, celebrated not Western Christmas in December but Orthodox Christmas in early January.

Cherepanov had moved to Slovakia from the Russian city of Chelyabinsk in 2012 after solving a five-part reverse-engineering and cryptography challenge ESET used for recruitment. Now, looking at the .dll files at the heart of Ukrenergo's blackout, he found an enigma as confounding as anything he'd faced in the five years since. After a combination of painstaking scrolling through the code for recognizable strings and intensive googling, he could see that the files weren't, in fact, one payload but four distinct ones, each designed to send commands in a different industrial control system protocol—the digital lingo understood by certain pieces of electric equipment.

The code was like nothing he'd ever seen before in his years at ESET, analyzing thousands of criminal and state-sponsored hacker creations. "It was something I couldn't understand. Most malware is simple: It steals some passwords, encrypts the drive, wipes the data. This was something different," Cherepanov says. "I realized it's going to be a long Christmas."

ESET and Cherepanov had been watching the late 2016 malware bombardment of their Ukrainian neighbors from a front-row seat: The company had long sold one of the most popular antivirus programs in Ukraine, and its collection of antivirus installations had given it early access to the malware samples plaguing the country. (In fact, even as ISSP and FireEye analyzed the attacks privately, ESET had been the first to publish many of the details of Sandworm's second Ukrainian blitz. While John Hultquist's researchers at FireEye had classified the intrusions as the second coming of Sandworm, ESET gave the hackers behind the attack wave its own name: TeleBots, based on the Telegram-based backdoor it had first installed on victims' machines.) So when that wave of attacks culminated in the sabotage of Ukrenergo's transmission station a week before Christmas, ESET immediately began its own analysis of the second-ever hacker blackout.

Cherepanov refused to reveal how ESET obtained the code at the heart of Ukrenergo's intrusion. But when he looked at the collection of .dll files it contained, they were at first as inscrutable to him as they would be to Yasinsky when the Ukrainian researcher gained access to the same code a few weeks later. Still, he could already sense their significance. He inspected the payload programs for hours that winter day, remaining in front of his screens in ESET's silent office even after the sun had set behind the hills west of Bratislava, over the Austrian border.

Cherepanov told his wife they'd need to cancel a Serbian vacation they'd planned. When New Year's Day arrived, he was still reverse engineering the code, digging up manuals for the obscure industrial control system protocols it used, and analyzing its functions step-by-step.

ESET's staff returned to the office in early January, and he finally explained to them the remarkable tool of sabotage he'd uncovered: The malware was something like a self-propelled blackout bot. Once installed on a computer connected to equipment such as circuit breakers, it was designed to locate those physical machines, performing its own automatic discovery and sending configuration data back to its operators. Then, when the time came to attack, it could "speak" directly to the victim's equipment in any of the four industrial control system protocols the .dlls contained.

In Ukrenergo's case, only one of those four protocols had actually been used, and it had apparently opened every circuit breaker at Ukrenergo's northern Kiev transmission station. For as long as the machine running the malware remained connected, it would keep repeating those "open" commands, in a kind of rapid-fire barrage. Even if an operator tried to close a breaker and restore the power, it would be instantly, digitally jackhammered open again.

The hackers had, in other words, created an automated cyber-weapon that performed the same task they'd carried out the year before, but now with inhuman speed. Instead of manually clicking through circuit breakers with phantom hands, they'd created a piece of malware that carried out that attack with cruel, machine-quick efficiency.

"Holy shit," Robert Lipovsky, Cherepanov's boss at ESET, remembers thinking when Cherepanov outlined his findings. "This is the biggest thing we've worked on since Stuxnet."

In fact, the inevitable had come to pass. One of America's adversaries had finally built a Stuxnet of its own: the second-ever specimen of code that directly attacked the physical world.

■

ESET named the malware Industroyer, a play on its rare ability to disrupt industrial control systems. The firm knew it was sitting on a history-making discovery. But even after Cherepanov had burned through his holiday to fully reverse engineer the malware, ESET would inexplicably keep his findings a closely held secret for nearly another six months.

ESET's staff cited a need to confirm and reconfirm their findings, a nondisclosure agreement they'd signed, and the complexities of sharing their research with Ukrainian authorities via intermediaries. It was only in June 2017 that ESET was ready to finally publish a report on the code it had found at the heart of Ukrenergo's blackout.

On a Thursday, four days before it planned to finally reveal Industroyer in a public report, ESET's researchers contacted Rob Lee. They wanted to give him a preview of their discovery so that the former NSA critical infrastructure security expert, who'd contributed to the most detailed write-up on the first Ukrainian blackout, could act as a credible voice to support their analysis. They cautiously sent him a portion of the Industroyer code and a draft of the blog post they planned to release.

Lee was immediately floored by the gravity of what he saw. The code before him crystallized everything he already believed about Sandworm's escalating cyberwar tactics into a single, concrete piece of programming. "This was the first piece of malware to cause disruption to civilian infrastructure," he marveled, pointing out that even Stuxnet limited itself to a military target. "It was a huge deal."

Lee asked for the complete code, but ESET refused. Unfortunately for ESET, they had underestimated Lee's dogged curiosity and naked ambition, not to mention his willingness to piss off his security industry peers.

So Lee tasked the staff at Dragos, his young industrial control system security start-up, with finding the malware on their own. The company began combing through its own sources of malware samples, using ESET's code snippet as a fingerprint. Within hours, Lee says, they had found a match on a computer that had been turned into a so-called staging server for Sandworm's operations.

A staging server acts as a kind of field outpost for hackers, a hop point where they can store and then launch their hacking tools against a target without revealing their own point of origin. Somehow, Lee told me—and he refused to explain further—Dragos had accessed that server and pulled from it the same code that ESET had found.

With less than seventy-two hours before ESET planned to release its findings, the researchers at Dragos began racing to produce their own report. The company's six main reverse engineers, who all worked remotely, set up an open videoconference channel. From their home offices in six states across three time zones, they began to tear apart the payload code, working in tandem and barely sleeping. Lee himself, in his home office in suburban Maryland, powered through the entire seventy-two-hour sprint, drinking from a bottle of Nikka Coffey Grain Japanese whiskey and a twenty-four-pack of Red Bulls. Only when Dragos's own report was complete on Monday morning at 6:00 did he allow himself a two-hour nap.

Hours later, both companies published their reports. Dragos had taken the controversial step of giving the program its own name: Crash Override. That moniker combined the name of a launcher component of the malware called "crash.dll" that activated its malicious modules and the fact that it was designed to repeatedly open circuit breakers faster than an operator could close them, overriding those manual commands. It was also an allusion to the pseudonym of the protagonist of the 1995 film *Hackers*. (When Microsoft and US-CERT issued warnings that Monday about the code, they called it Crash Override, *not* Industroyer. Cherepanov and the shocked ESET team have yet to forgive Lee for the slight.)

Industry backbiting aside, Dragos's and ESET's reports agreed on many of the most troubling findings about the blackout payload. Crash Override or Industroyer, whatever it was to be called, had no easy remedy. If hackers could plant this automated malware as deeply into a utility's network as Sandworm had into Ukrenergo's, it would exploit the intended features of industrial control systems, sending commands that were indistinguishable from the ones sent by legitimate operators. "There's nothing to patch away, nothing to address," Lee said. "It's an unfixable attack."

Even worse, the automated nature of the disruption meant that the kind of blackout operation Sandworm had now performed twice in Ukraine could be scaled up to multiple simultaneous targets across a country or region. Lee estimated that the 2015 attack had required as many as twenty hackers manually hijacking computers and clicking through circuit breakers. Now, he pointed out, a team of that same size could plant their self-propelled malware on ten or fifteen utility targets simultaneously and set the code to activate at a certain time, like a ticking bomb. From the hacker's point of view, he explained, "you can be confident it will cause disruption without your interaction."

Finally, the malware payload also included its own wiper tool labeled haslo.dat—Ukrainian for "torch"—designed to destroy all the data from target systems. Marina Krotofil, who would follow up with her own analysis of the code months later, described that function as both an attempt to prolong the blackout and a cleanup stage, intended to prevent forensic analysts from finding the malware afterward. In this case, by a fateful stroke of luck, that wiping functionality had somehow failed. "They didn't mean to burn this tool," she told me, using the hacker jargon "burn" to mean that the program was exposed, eliminating its element of surprise. "We were never meant to see it."

One of the most disturbing aspects of the malware had been just briefly mentioned in ESET's report: Yes, it was designed to send commands in four different electrical transmission systems protocols, only one of which had actually been in use at Ukrenergo. But the code was also highly modular. The protocols could just as easily be swapped out for others—including those used in the United States. "I salute the author of this malware, because it will work anywhere," as Krotofil would later put it. "The beauty of this is that you can launch it in any country, in any substation."

The notion that Sandworm was using Ukraine to test out techniques that it might someday repeat in western Europe or the United States was now more than an abstract theory: It had been borne out in the actual mechanics of the tool the researchers had uncovered. The malware seemed designed not as a onetime-use grenade but as a reusable and adaptable weapons system.

No one would build such a unique piece of malicious software and spend a year burrowing into a victim's network to plant it, only to inflict a one-off, one-hour blackout. "This is a piece of malware that looks like it's built to target *other* sites," Lee told me. "Nothing about this attack looks like it's singular. The way it's built and designed and run makes it look like it was meant to be used multiple times. And not just in Ukraine."

■

The same week that Lee and his Dragos researchers published their report on the Crash Override malware, Lee was invited to brief members of the White House's National Security Council. Sitting in a large conference room with representatives of the Department of Homeland Security, Department of Energy, CIA, and NSA, he explained how the discovery of this code represented a unique, scalable, and versatile threat to power grids around the world.

At first, Lee thought the Trump administration might be preparing to launch the sort of response to the second Ukraine blackout that had been so noticeably absent from the first. "Everyone got on the same page. No one was confused. Everyone knew it was important," Lee said.

But as the days and weeks after the briefing passed, Lee heard nothing more. Finally, when he got through to a White House staffer, he was told that the information he'd presented about Russian grid malware had made its way to Director of National Intelligence Dan Coats, who'd passed on a snippet to President Trump. And the answer, as Lee tells it, had been "We're not interested in talking about that."

Trump, whose understanding of computers and digital security was notoriously thin, might have ignored the news simply because he tuned out all things "cyber." But as Lee describes it, the message passed to him, filtered through several layers from the president, had been that the Crash Override news was "bad timing" and "too political." In other words, as the controversy around Russia's role in his election victory began to grow, it seemed that Trump had no interest in discussing any sentence that contained the words "Russian" and "hacker," no matter the context. (The White House never answered my multiple requests for comment on Lee's description of those events.)

If Trump sensed the news could be used against him politically, he was right. In late June 2017, eighteen Democratic senators and Independent Bernie Sanders signed a letter to the president, citing Dragos's work and demanding Trump direct the Department of Energy to conduct a new analysis of the Russian government's capabilities to disrupt America's power grid. They also asked for an exploration of any attempts the Kremlin had already made to compromise America's electric utilities, pipelines, or other energy infrastructure.

"We are deeply concerned that your administration has not backed up a verbal commitment prioritizing cybersecurity of energy networks and fighting cyber aggression with any meaningful action," the legislators wrote. The White House never responded.

Lee quickly regretted that the Crash Override news had become a partisan football. But he was far more frustrated still that history was replaying itself from a year before: Another White House seemed to be pushing another Ukrainian blackout under the rug. "When a cyberattack takes down electric power for the first time with a capability that's scalable and impactful to people around the world, it doesn't even get a sound bite," Lee said. "And that's ridiculous."

∎

In the Dragos researchers' mad seventy-two-hour rush to dissect Crash Override, a.k.a. Industroyer, they had missed something. In fact, Rob Lee would tell me that one element of the code that ESET described in its report was lacking from the version of the malware Dragos found. It hadn't, apparently, been used in the Ukrenergo attack. It's not clear if it even worked. But it was, in some ways, the most foreboding clue of all.

At one point as he was combing the Industroyer code, Cherepanov had spotted that it was programmed to send out a strange eighteen-byte string of numbers. When he googled that string, he found an advisory about a known vulnerability in Siemens Siprotec devices—protective relays designed to function as safety kill switches for electrical equipment. Send that one packet of eighteen bytes to a Siemens Siprotec box, and it would become unresponsive. Only manually rebooting it would wake it up again.

When Mike Assante read ESET's report on Industroyer at his home in Wyoming, that Siprotec trick immediately stuck out to him. Protective relays were, after all, the devices he'd always worried might be hacked to not simply disrupt but *destroy* physical equipment. It had been just over ten years since he'd led the Aurora demonstration, showcasing exactly the scale of disaster that might be possible when protective relays are maliciously altered.

The vulnerability exploited by Sandworm's malware, unlike his Aurora attack, didn't actually change the logic of a protective relay to cause dangerous effects. It simply put the relay to sleep. But if that technique had been combined with other kinds of transmission station sabotage, it could still have caused far more permanent damage: Disable protective relays while messing with the electric load on certain components, and hackers might melt lines or burn transformers, outcomes that would make a one-hour blackout look like an innocent game of tag by comparison. "If you ever see a transformer fire, they're massive," Assante says. "Big black smoke that all of a sudden turns into a fireball."

In 2007, he had first warned the world about hackers unleashing physical destruction on power systems. Now someone seemed to be taking the first steps toward a very literal Aurora-style attack. As he looked out the windows of his second-story home office at the distant Teton mountain range, Assante felt a strange mix of pride and bitter dread. "There was the satisfaction of not having had a failure of imagination," he says. "But also the fear: They're developing these capabilities now."

His Aurora nightmare was now on the verge of coming true. "This is real," he thought to himself. "It's happening." The future he'd glimpsed a full decade earlier had arrived.

PART IV

APOTHEOSIS

*Out of the sand haze came an orderly mass of flashing shapes—
great rising curves with crystal spokes that resolved into the gaping
mouths of sandworms, a massed wall of them, each with troops of
Fremen riding to the attack. They came in a hissing wedge, robes
whipping in the wind as they cut through the melee on the plain.*

20

MAERSK

It was a perfect, sunny summer afternoon in Copenhagen when the world's largest shipping conglomerate began to lose its mind.

The headquarters of A.P. Møller-Maersk sit beside the breezy, cobblestoned esplanade of Copenhagen's harbor. A ship's mast carrying the Danish flag is planted by the building's northeastern corner, and six stories of blue-tinted windows look out over the water, facing a dock where the Danish royal family parks its yacht. In the building's basement, employees can browse a corporate gift shop, stocked with Maersk-branded bags and ties, and even a rare Lego model of the company's gargantuan Triple-E container ship, a vessel roughly as large as the Empire State Building laid on its side, capable of carrying another Empire State Building–sized load of cargo stacked on top of it.

That gift shop also houses a technology help center, a single desk manned by IT troubleshooters next to the shop's cashier. And on the afternoon of June 27, 2017, confused Maersk staffers began to gather at that help desk in twos and threes, almost all of them carrying laptops. On some of the machines' screens were messages that read "repairing file system on C:" with a stark warning not to turn off the computer. Others, more surreally, read "oops, your important files are encrypted" and demanded a payment of $300 worth of bitcoin to decrypt them.

Across the street, an IT administrator named Henrik Jensen was working in another part of the Maersk compound, an ornate white stone building that in previous centuries had served as the royal archive of maritime maps and charts.* Jensen was busy preparing a software update for Maersk's nearly eighty thousand employees when his computer spontaneously restarted.

He quietly swore under his breath. Jensen assumed the unplanned reboot was a typically brusque move by Maersk's central IT department, a little-loved entity in England that oversaw most of the corporate empire, whose eight business units ranged from ports to logistics to oil drilling, in 574 offices in 130 countries around the globe.

Jensen looked up to ask if anyone else in his open-plan office of IT staffers had been so rudely interrupted. And as he craned his neck, he watched every other computer screen around the room blink out in rapid succession.

"I saw a wave of screens turning black. Black, black, black. *Black black black black black,*" he says. The PCs, Jensen and his neighbors quickly discovered, were irreversibly locked. Restarting them only caused them to display the Bitcoin ransom message other Maersk staffers had been seeing.

All across Maersk headquarters, the full scale of the crisis was starting to become clear. Within half an hour, Maersk employees were running down hallways, yelling to their colleagues to turn off computers or disconnect them from Maersk's network before the malicious software could infect them as it dawned on them that every minute could mean dozens or hundreds more corrupted PCs. Tech workers ran into conference rooms and unplugged machines in the middle of meetings. Soon staffers were hurdling over locked key-card gates, which had been paralyzed by the still-mysterious malware, to spread the warning to other sections of the building.

Disconnecting Maersk's entire global network took the company's IT staff more than two panicky hours. By the end of that process, all employees had been ordered to turn off their computers and leave them at their desks. The digital phones at every cubicle, too, had been rendered useless in the emergency network shutdown.

---

* Henrik Jensen is not his real name. Like almost every Maersk employee, customer, or partner I interviewed, Jensen feared the consequences of speaking publicly about this story.

Around 3:00 p.m., a Maersk executive walked into the room where Jensen and a dozen or so of his colleagues were anxiously awaiting news and told them to go home. Maersk's network was so deeply corrupted that even IT staffers were helpless. A few of the company's more old-school managers told their teams to remain at the office. But many employees—rendered entirely idle without computers, servers, routers, or desk phones—simply left.

Jensen walked out of the building and into the warm air of a late June afternoon. Like the vast majority of Maersk staffers, he had no idea when he might return to work. The maritime giant that employed him, responsible for seventy-six ports on all sides of the earth and nearly eight hundred seafaring vessels, including container ships carrying tens of millions of tons of cargo, representing close to a fifth of the entire world's shipping capacity, was dead in the water.

21

SHADOW BROKERS

The worst cyberattack in history, like any perfect storm, came together from a rare confluence of elements. One of the most powerful and volatile precursors was provided, indirectly, by none other than the U.S. government.

For Jake Williams, the fiasco that served up the key element to Sandworm began on an early morning in August 2016—ten months before Maersk's screens would go dark—in a conference room somewhere in Ohio. Williams, the thirty-nine-year-old founder of the security firm Rendition Infosec, was embedded with four of his staffers inside the offices of a corporate client whose computer network had been deeply violated by a team of cybercriminals. This was business as usual: Williams's team had set up laptops and monitors to turn one of the customer's meeting spaces into a war room. They'd worked late the night before, combing the victim's network logs and talking endlessly with the company's lawyers before catching a few hours of sleep and then diving back into the crime scene that morning before 7:00.

On one of the screens Williams had set up in that war room, he'd opened Twitter and created a running feed of all messages that mentioned the client company. He was monitoring for any chatter that might mean news of the breach, which hadn't yet been announced by the company or reported by the media, had leaked out to the public. That's when he saw a trickle of tweets mentioning a different sort of leak, not from his client, but from one of the most secretive organizations on the planet: the NSA.

The tweets linked back to a Twitter account called "@shadow brokerss," which in turn linked to a post on the website Pastebin, a favorite publishing tool of anonymous hackers. There Williams found a rant written in what appeared to be a kind of mock-broken English.

"!!! Attention government sponsors of cyber warfare and those who profit from it !!!!" the message began. "How much you pay for enemies cyber weapons?"

The post went on to present an extraordinary offer. The hackers claimed to have pulled off something almost no one had achieved before—at least not publicly: They had breached the NSA and stolen some of its most sensitive files. Specifically, they wrote that they'd hacked "Equation Group," using the name the Russian security firm Kaspersky had given to the creators of Stuxnet. The Shadow Brokers, whoever they were, were claiming not simply to have hacked the NSA but to have hacked the NSA's top hackers, the most elite team of American government cyberspies, known as Tailored Access Operations. And now they were selling their stolen loot to the highest bidder:

> We follow Equation Group traffic. We find Equation Group source range. We hack Equation Group. We find many many Equation Group cyber weapons. You see pictures. We give you some Equation Group files free, you see. This is good proof no? You enjoy!!! You break many things. You find many intrusions. You write many words. But not all, we are auction the best files.

Below that message, the post included links to download sites where they had uploaded free "proof" files as samples, along with another encrypted file that supposedly contained a collection of secret hacking tools that they bragged were "better than Stuxnet." The Shadow Brokers demanded that anyone who wanted to see the contents of that file send bitcoin bids to a certain address. None of those bids, they stipulated, would be refunded. And only the highest bidder would be given the key to decrypt this purported holy grail of hacking. In another bizarre note, the Shadow Brokers said that if bidding reached one million bitcoins—at the time well over half a billion dollars—they'd release all the secret files to the public.

Finally, the message ended with a strange paragraph about "wealthy elites" whom the Shadow Brokers seemed to be simultaneously threatening with their stolen NSA hacking tools and targeting with a hard-sell pitch. "Let us spell out for Elites. Your wealth and control depends on electronic data," they wrote. "If electronic data go bye bye where leave Wealthy Elites? Maybe with dumb cattle? 'Do you feel in charge?' Wealthy Elites, you send bitcoins, you bid in auction, maybe big advantage for you?"

On its face, nothing about the post looked like the work of hackers skilled enough to have actually hacked the NSA. The almost deliberately shoddy English, the sloppy auction system, even the name "the Shadow Brokers"—apparently a reference to a character from the video game *Mass Effect*—seemed more like the work of bored teenagers than the likes of a state-sponsored group such as Sandworm or even Fancy Bear.

But Jake Williams downloaded the sample files anyway. And when he opened them on his PC, he was surprised to see they included a set of tools capable of silently breaking into a handful of common firewalls, including some sold by Cisco and Fortinet.

In fact, these were not just any firewall-hacking programs. For Williams, they had special significance. Four years earlier, Williams had left the NSA, where he had himself served as a hacker on its Tailored Access Operations team. Even now, the highly classified nature of that work means he couldn't explicitly tell me whether he recognized the hacking tools from his own time inside the agency. But suffice it to say, Williams knew they were as powerful as the Shadow Brokers claimed. "I did not doubt their authenticity," he said.

The tools the Shadow Brokers had offered up as mere free samples were not just any crude hacking programs but the rarest commodities of the cybersecurity world: Many had been designed to exploit zero-day vulnerabilities. Though the files appeared to be dated to 2013, some of the software flaws they targeted had remained secret for all those years until the Shadow Brokers' release. Cisco, for instance, would eventually warn its customers that they needed to change the configuration of eleven different Cisco products to protect them from one of the leaked hacking tools, which might otherwise give intruders full control over those devices. In some cases, that could mean the ability to fully intercept or tamper with the traffic going into and out of networks used by millions of people around the world.

Each of the leaked sample tools, Williams could immediately see, was appallingly dangerous in its own right, and they were being cast out together onto the public internet, where any miscreant could use them to inflict mayhem. If the Shadow Brokers were to be believed, they had far more in store.

As the Rendition team examined the files inside their makeshift war room, temporarily distracted from the work of dissecting the client's breach, Williams exchanged a look with one of his staffers, a man who had also worked with him at the NSA and who seemed equally dismayed at what they were watching unfold.

For the better part of a decade, as the world's state-sponsored hackers slowly progressed toward cyberwar, the apex of that arms race had been Stuxnet. That specimen of rarefied malware had proved the promise of digital dark arts to achieve the impossible in U.S. intelligence and military operations, as well as the peril posed by America's adversaries, like Sandworm, should they employ those same weapons.

But the disaster taking shape that August morning would be expressed in far more literal form. Instead of an abstract fear that U.S. cyberweapons would inspire adversaries to develop their own, America's hacking arsenal had fallen, suddenly and directly, into enemy hands.

■

In the early days after the Shadow Brokers' post, it appeared that the group's operation might be a bust. They did not get their one-million-bitcoin jackpot. Instead, in the first twenty-four hours of their auction, they received a grand total of $937.15, according to the Bitcoin blockchain's public record of transactions.

But the auction nonetheless served to create buzz around the NSA's security breach. Experts largely agreed the profit motive was likely a cover story, that the Shadow Brokers were probably state-sponsored hackers, not cybercriminals, and they were seeking above all to embarrass the NSA. Jake Williams, for his part, immediately suspected Russia. "There's only one government capable of doing this," he said flatly.

Another, less expected former NSA figure offered a similar suggestion. Edward Snowden, the NSA whistle-blower who'd leaked a top secret trove of the agency's documents three years earlier, posted a series of messages on Twitter outlining a larger theory. He guessed that the Shadow Brokers were indeed Russian, that they'd stolen the NSA tools from a "staging server" used as a kind of field outpost for the agency's hacking operations, and that the thieves' primary motive was to shame the NSA and broadcast a specific message: We know what you're up to. "Circumstantial evidence and conventional wisdom indicates Russian responsibility," Snowden wrote. "This may be an effort to influence the calculus of decision-makers wondering how sharply to respond to the DNC hacks."

The Shadow Brokers' first appearance, after all, came just two months after the news that Russia had hacked the Democratic National Committee. Snowden posited that Russia was using its breach of the NSA to put a mirror up to American accusations of reckless hacking, to warn the United States that Russia, too, could call out its adversary's intrusion operations.

That this theory was first articulated by the man behind the *other* largest violation of the NSA's secrets in recent memory—and one who had taken refuge from American law enforcement in Moscow—might have seemed ironic. But for all the damage the NSA had claimed resulted from Snowden's disclosures, he had never released actual zero-day vulnerabilities or hacking tools. In the coming months, the Shadow Brokers' data dumps would prove to be vastly more damaging than anything Snowden had revealed—not just to U.S. intelligence agencies, but to the world.

■

The hackers seemed to savor their torture of the NSA. Over the following months, the Shadow Brokers would disappear for long stretches and then reappear spontaneously to promote new leaks, prolonging the chaos and anxiety they were creating as they disemboweled the agency and threw its radioactive entrails across the internet.

The second of their leaks was, in some senses, a smaller one—perhaps a mere reminder to the NSA that its problem was not going away. Two months after their splashy debut, the Shadow Brokers published another sample of their stolen data the day before Halloween, titling their blog post "Trick or Treat?" This time they offered up a collection of IP addresses representing computers that, they said, the NSA had used as staging servers, exposing a broad map of the agency's secret hacking operations across the world.

The new leak was presented along with a message responding to statements Vice President Joe Biden had made days earlier, naming Russia as the source of the Democratic National Committee hack and promising some sort of retaliatory measures to be carried out by the CIA. "We're sending a message," Biden told the NBC show *Meet the Press*. "It will be at the time of our choosing—and under the circumstances that have the greatest impact."

"Why is DirtyGrandpa threating CIA cyberwar with Russia?" the Shadow Brokers responded. "Oldest control trick in book, yes? Waving flag, blaming problems on external sources, not taking responsibility for failures. But neverminding, hacking DNC is way way most important than EquationGroup losing capabilities." The barbed sarcasm couldn't hide the Shadow Brokers' defensiveness about Russia's meddling in the U.S. election.

After another six weeks, the Shadow Brokers seemed to be losing patience. "TheShadowBrokers is trying auction. Peoples no like," they wrote. "Now TheShadowBrokers is trying direct sales." They had decided to sell their pilfered zero-day hacking techniques à la carte. This time their post included screenshots of a collection of files, giving a glimpse at a broad catalog of secret hacking wares they still held.

Perhaps the Shadow Brokers' sketchy auction setup had scared off buyers. Or perhaps their entire moneymaking venture had been elaborate theater. Either way, by January, they suddenly declared that their sales routine had failed and that they were calling it quits.

"So long, farewell peoples. TheShadowBrokers is going dark, making exit: Continuing is being much risk and bullshit, not many bitcoins," they wrote. "Despite theories, it always being about bitcoins for TheShadowBrokers. Free dumps and bullshit political talk was being for marketing attention."

For another three months, the group seemed to have vanished. Some in the security industry speculated that the group's work had always been designed as a distraction from Russia's hacking of election-related targets and with the inauguration of Donald Trump as president in early 2017 their work was done. "The fun is over," wrote the tech news site *Motherboard*.

But if NSA officials felt any relief that the bleeding had stopped, it was premature. In April 2017, three months later, the Shadow Brokers appeared yet again, posting the thirty-two-character password to the original encrypted file they'd first released, the one they'd originally claimed was "better than Stuxnet."

When hackers around the world decrypted that file, they found a vast collection of hacking tools, all targeting operating systems like Linux, Unix, and Solaris rather than Windows. Many were more than a decade old. The secret programs were not, it seemed, better than Stuxnet. But they meant that the NSA's nightmare continued, with no clear end in sight.

Along with that release, the Shadow Brokers this time posted a fifteen-hundred-word rambling open letter pleading with Trump to stay in touch with his far-right nationalist base, and not to give in to the "deep state" and "globalists." The hackers criticized Trump's decision to launch air strikes in Syria in retaliation for chemical weapons used by the country's Russia-backed dictator, Bashar al-Assad. They now claimed that despite theories of their Russian origin they were actually former U.S. intelligence officers who had become conscientious objectors. They railed against Goldman Sachs, Zionists, socialists, and Russia critics:

> We recognize Americans' having more in common with Russians than Chinese or Globalist or Socialist. Russia and Putin are nationalist and enemies of the Globalist, examples: NATO encroachment and Ukraine conflict.

Therefore Russia and Putin are being best allies until the common enemies are defeated and America is great again.

Jake Williams, like almost anyone with ties to the NSA, had continued to watch the Shadow Brokers fiasco with a mixture of fascination and deep anxiety. After the group resurfaced, he posted a quick analysis to the security industry social media site Peerlyst, stating what he by then considered obvious: The Shadow Brokers were, among other things, clearly another Kremlin influence operation. "Russia is likely using the latest Shadow Brokers release to attempt to control the news cycle and take coverage away from the Syria conflict," he wrote.

The next morning, he woke up in a hotel room in Orlando, where he was scheduled to teach a training course, and looked at Twitter. He immediately discovered that the Shadow Brokers had responded to his blog post. Now they were calling out *him*, Jake Williams, by name. "@malwarejake You having big mouth for former #equationgroup member," they wrote on Twitter, using his handle. "The Shadow Brokers ISNOT in habit of outing #equationgroup members but had make exception for big mouth."

Williams had never publicly revealed that he was a former NSA staffer, no less a member of the Tailored Access Operations team that the Shadow Brokers called Equation Group. He had carefully quarantined that part of his career and described his background to associates and clients only as having worked for the Department of Defense.

He had just been outed. His breath stopped. "It was like being punched in the gut," he said.

The message was accompanied by vague references to code names like "OddJob," "CCI," "Windows BITS persistence," and an investigation involving "Q Group," the NSA's counterintelligence arm. Williams declined to say what all of that meant. But he explained that by including those references, the Shadow Brokers were signaling to him that they were aware not just of his NSA affiliation but of highly specific details of his career inside the agency. "The message was, 'This is not a guess,'" he said. "'We know.'"

That leak of Williams's secrets would change his life. Now that he's a known former TAO hacker, he no longer travels to places where he might be vulnerable to legal or personal attacks from a country like Russia or China. In the months after his outing by the Shadow Brokers, he canceled work trips to the Czech Republic, Singapore, and Hong Kong. Even today, he lives in fear of foreign indictments for his past hacking, just as the United States has sought to sow fear in foreign hackers, from Iran to North Korea, with its own criminal charges.

But in that first moment of seeing his secrets spilled, Williams had a less rational and more visceral reaction: He felt the same kind of violation that the NSA had been undergoing for eight months, only now on a personal level. He sensed that the Shadow Brokers knew vastly more about him than he knew about them and that he was entirely at their mercy. They could release the rest of his private history at any time.

The same, of course, was true of the rest of the NSA's secrets. The worst was yet to come.

22

ETERNALBLUE

When the Shadow Brokers finally decided to unleash the most damaging leak of their short, strange career, they explained their actions with neither political manifestos nor profiteering but pure nihilism.

"Last week theshadowbrokers be trying to help peoples," they wrote in a new message on April 14, 2017, referring back to their political rant from the week before. "This week theshadowbrokers be thinking fuck peoples."

Per usual, they posted a link to a download. "Theshadowbrokers not wanting going there. Is being too bad nobody deciding to be paying theshadowbrokers for just to shutup and going away," they concluded. "Maybe if all suviving WWIII theshadowbrokers be seeing you next week."

Perhaps the World War III quip related to escalating tensions between the United States and North Korea; the latter had revealed that it would soon have the capability to launch a nuclear missile that could strike anywhere in the United States. Or perhaps it was referring to the contents of the file they had just leaked, which offered, in essence, the digital equivalent.

The new collection of files was the mother lode of immensely powerful hacking tools that the Shadow Brokers had promised from the start. After eight months of taunts and games, they had finally dropped an assortment of the NSA's crown jewels. Cybersecurity analysts who downloaded the files counted more than twenty distinct hacking tools, all polished, professional, and ready to cause mayhem in the hands of even unskilled hackers.

But it was one program in particular, which the NSA had code-named EternalBlue, that sent the cybersecurity community into an immediate frenzy. EternalBlue was designed to exploit a zero-day vulnerability in practically every version of Windows prior to Windows 8, a flaw in an old, obscure feature of Windows known as Server Message Block, or SMB. SMB allowed computers to share information, such as files and access to printers, directly from one to the next. And it contained multiple critical bugs that let anyone send SMB messages to a computer and gain full remote code execution on the target machine.

With EternalBlue, the NSA's hackers had coded that exploitation into a simple program capable of penetrating millions upon millions of computers around the world. Then they'd lost control of it.

"This is as big as it gets," Matthew Hickey, a British security analyst who had been analyzing the Shadow Broker leaks for months, told me at the time. "It's internet God mode." Or, as my *Wired* colleague Lily Hay Newman described it, "a sophisticated, top-secret US cyber espionage tool is now the people's crowbar."

Within hours of the Shadow Brokers' release, however, Microsoft put out an unexpected announcement: The zero-day vulnerability EternalBlue exploited wasn't technically a zero day after all. In March, the company had, with no explanation at the time, released a patch for its Server Message Block flaw that neutered the NSA's hacking technique, a full month before the Shadow Brokers had leaked it. *The Washington Post* would later confirm that the NSA had quietly warned Microsoft of the flaw when it learned that EternalBlue was among the tools the Shadow Brokers had stolen.

With the news that a security patch was available, a new question arose: How many people had actually installed that patch? Updating software protections around the world has never been a simple fix so much as a complex epidemiological problem. Systems administrators neglect patches, or don't account for all their computers, or skip patches for fear they'll break features of software they need, or run pirated software that doesn't receive patches at all. All of that means getting a security update out to vulnerable machines is often as involved and imperfect a process as getting humans around the world vaccinated, long after a vaccine is discovered.

Over the next days, hints of the population of machines still unpatched against EternalBlue began to emerge. Security researchers had no way to determine the number of EternalBlue attacks directly, but they could scan the internet for another complementary piece of NSA malware called DoublePulsar, a backdoor program that had also been released by the Shadow Brokers and that was designed to be installed by EternalBlue on target machines. When anyone sent a computer infected with DoublePulsar a certain kind of network ping, it would respond with a recognizable, distinct acknowledgment.

Curious researchers sent out those pings en masse to the entire internet. They immediately received tens of thousands of unique responses, each of which likely signaled a computer that had been hacked with the NSA's skeleton key. Within a week of the Shadow Brokers' release, that number was above 100,000. After two weeks, the count of potential victims had topped 400,000. The internet's EternalBlue nightmare wasn't over. And its full scale was about to become clear.

■

Around 2:30 on a Friday afternoon, Marcus Hutchins returned from lunch at his local fish-and-chips shop in the small English seaside town of Ilfracombe, sat down in front of a computer in his bedroom, and discovered that the internet was on fire.

Hutchins, a soft-spoken English twenty-two-year-old with a semi-controlled explosion of brown curly hair, was supposed to have the day off from his job as a malware analyst for the cybersecurity firm Kryptos Logic. But Hutchins was not one to draw neat boundaries in his life: He worked from home, and his home office was also his first-floor bedroom in his parents' house. That bedroom was set up with three powerful desktop computers—each equipped with multiple monitors and water-cooling radiators to accommodate high-performance processing—as well as two laptops and a full rack of blinking servers.

Hutchins used this elaborate bedroom rig to operate his own self-contained malware research center. On his server setup, he ran virtual machines that could simulate all manner of computers to test out new malware and safely watch it in action. One screen displayed a constant feed of spam and phishing emails he was collecting to analyze their sources and the evil programs often laced into their attachments.

On another of his screens, Hutchins opened a U.K. cybersecurity research forum where he'd been trying to learn more about a certain piece of bank-fraud malware. He found a crisis unfolding. The British National Health Service was being ambushed with a ransomware outbreak. And this wasn't the normal criminal ransomware that was increasingly targeting critical institutions like hospitals and police departments, encrypting their data and holding it hostage. This was something else: Thousands of the agency's computers were being infected, and the number was growing with inhuman speed.

The victim computers were locked, with a red screen demanding they pay $300 in bitcoin. "Your important files are encrypted," the message read. "Maybe you are busy looking for a way to recover your files, but do not waste your time. Nobody can recover your files without our decryption service." On the left of the screen, a countdown timer ticked down the hours over seven days until the hackers would delete the files' decryption keys, leaving the computers' data permanently, irrevocably scrambled.

Researchers were calling the new ransomware WannaCry—an evocative name based on the .wncry extension it added to the file names after encrypting them. And soon it became clear exactly why the code was so virulent: It was using EternalBlue to spread. Each infected machine would scan local networks and the internet for machines that were still unpatched against that leaked NSA tool, use it to break into as many other computers as possible, and repeat.

As WannaCry proliferated, chaos ensued. Thousands of people had their doctors' appointments canceled in regions across the U.K. Some emergency rooms were temporarily closed, forcing patients to travel farther to hospitals lucky enough to have been spared by the attack. Hutchins could see that Britain's woes were only a slice of a global disaster. The Spanish telecommunications firm Telefónica had been hit, too. So had Sberbank in Russia, the German railway firm Deutsche Bahn, and the French carmaker Renault, along with other victims as far-flung as universities in China and police departments in India.

The United States had, by sheer luck, largely been spared so far. But as the ransomware wave swelled, it was a matter of hours or even minutes until America would be engulfed, too.

The nightmare of an uncontrolled NSA-zero-day-propelled worm wreaking havoc across the world had come to pass. And the result was the worst ransomware outbreak anyone had ever seen. "I picked a hell of a fucking week to take off work," Hutchins wrote on Twitter.

■

A hacker friend who went by the name "Kafeine" sent Hutchins a copy of WannaCry's code, and Hutchins quickly began trying to dissect it. First, he spun up a simulated computer on his server, complete with fake files for the ransomware to encrypt, and ran the program in that quarantined test environment. He immediately noticed that before encrypting the fake files, the malware sent out a query to a certain very random-looking web address: iuqerfsodp9ifjaposdfjhgosurijfaewrwergwea.com. That struck Hutchins as significant, if not unusual: A piece of malware pinging back to a domain like that usually represented communications with a command-and-control server somewhere that might be giving the infected computer instructions.

Hutchins copied that long website string into his web browser and found, to his surprise, that no such site existed. So he visited the domain registrar Namecheap and bought that unattractive web address for $10.69. Hutchins hoped that in doing so, he might be able to steal control of some part of WannaCry's horde of victim computers away from the malware's creators. At least he might gain a tool to monitor the number and location of infected machines, a move that malware analysts call "sinkholing."

Sure enough, as soon as Hutchins set up that domain on a cluster of servers hosted by his employer, Kryptos Logic, it was bombarded with thousands of connections from every new computer that was being infected by WannaCry around the world. Hutchins could now see the enormous scale of the attack firsthand. And as he tweeted about his work, he began to be flooded with hundreds of emails from other researchers, journalists, and systems administrators trying to learn more about the plague devouring global networks. With his sinkhole domain, Hutchins was now suddenly pulling in information about those infections that no one else on the planet possessed.

For the next four hours, he responded to those emails and worked frantically to debug a map he was building to track the new infections popping up across the world. It was only at 6:30 p.m., around four hours after registering the domain, that his hacker friend Kafeine sent him a tweet posted by another security researcher, Darien Huss. It put forward a simple statement that shocked Hutchins: "Execution fails now that domain has been sinkholed." In other words, since Hutchins's domain had first appeared online, WannaCry's new infections had continued to spread, but they hadn't actually done any new damage. The worm seemed to be neutralized.

Huss's tweet included a snippet of WannaCry's code that he'd reverse engineered. The code's logic showed that before encrypting any files, the malware first checked if it could reach Hutchins's web address. If not, it went ahead with corrupting the computer's contents. If it *did* reach that address, it simply stopped in its tracks.

Hutchins hadn't found the malware's command-and-control address. He'd found its kill switch. The domain he'd registered was a way to simply, instantly turn off WannaCry's mayhem around the world. It was as if he had fired his proton torpedoes through the Death Star's exhaust port and into its reactor core, blown it up, and saved the galaxy, but without understanding what he was doing or even noticing his action's effects for four hours.

When he saw Huss's tweet, Hutchins's heart started racing. Could it be true? He needed to try his own test for confirmation. He ran a simulation on his server of a WannaCry infection and allowed it to reach out to his domain. Sure enough, it ceased its evil behavior the instant it connected. Then he ran the test again, this time blocking the malware's connection to his sinkhole. In that second test, the computer's files were immediately encrypted, and WannaCry's menacing ransom message popped up on his screen. The test had confirmed that his kill switch worked.

Hutchins reacted in a way that perhaps no one ever before in history has reacted to seeing his computer paralyzed with ransomware: He leaped up from his chair and jumped around his bedroom, overtaken with joy.

■

The goal of WannaCry's creators remains a mystery. Were they seeking to make as much money as possible from their supercharged ransomware scheme? Or merely to inflict maximal global chaos? Either way, building a kill switch into their malware seemed like a strangely sloppy act of self-sabotage.*

The WannaCry programmers had been careless in other ways, too. The payment mechanism built into their code was, effectively, useless: Unlike better-designed ransomware, WannaCry had no automated

---

* Just why that kill switch existed is another mystery. But as Hutchins and other malware researchers puzzled over that flaw, they came to believe that it might have been intended as a sort of anti-forensic technique, designed to make it harder for defenders to decipher WannaCry's behavior. In that theory, the malware's attempt to communicate out to a nonexistent domain was a test of whether the malware was running on a real victim's machine or on some security researcher's simulated one.

In the sort of virtual machine Hutchins ran on his server for malware observation, the researcher wants the malware to think it's running in the wild, but without ever letting it interact with the actual internet; otherwise it might start doing nasty things like sending spam or attacking other computers. So every attempt to connect with a web domain is answered with some arbitrary response, even if the website doesn't actually exist. If the malware reaches out to an address its author knows doesn't exist and still gets a response, it can cleverly deduce that it's running in a simulation, like Neo in *The Matrix* after he's taken the red pill. In that case, when the malware realizes it's under the researcher's microscope, it turns off its malicious features and behaves entirely innocently.

Of course, if that was in fact the ransomware programmers' thinking, they'd been far too clever for their own good. The result was that the mechanism designed to make their feature appear harmless could actually be used to render it ineffectual, as Hutchins did.

system for distributing decryption keys to victims who had paid, or even keeping track of who had paid and who hadn't. When that became clear to victims, they stopped paying. The entire scheme generated a total of less than $200,000, a smaller sum than the annual salary of many of the individual malware analysts tracking it.

Some researchers came to the conclusion that WannaCry must have been released prematurely: Perhaps its creators had been testing their worm, and then, as worms tend to do—as Stuxnet had done seven years earlier—it spread beyond its creators' control, before it was truly ready.

Finally, in another critical act of carelessness, WannaCry's coders had left clues about their identity, too. Within days, security researchers at Google and the Russian cybersecurity firm Kaspersky had noticed that code used in WannaCry overlapped with a favorite backdoor program of a group of North Korean government hackers known as Lazarus. By December 2017, the Trump White House would announce that it had determined North Korea was behind the attack. The same group of hackers who had devastated Sony three years earlier had now unleashed that same destruction on every network in the world, and only an accidental kill switch had prevented utter disaster.*

■

By the end of 2017, theories of how the Shadow Brokers had pulled off their shocking theft of NSA secrets would begin to come to light, too. In December of that year, a sixty-seven-year-old former NSA staffer and developer for the agency's Tailored Access Operations hacking team named Nghia Hoang Pho pleaded guilty to violating his security clearances. He'd taken home enormous troves of classified

---

* Hutchins's role as the hero of the WannaCry story would be complicated just three months later, when he was arrested by the FBI after attending the DEF CON hacker conference. Hutchins was charged with computer fraud and abuse related to his alleged creation and sale of banking malware years earlier. In July 2019, however, a judge sentenced him to no jail time, in part due to his WannaCry work.

5555555555

materials. He'd later tell a Maryland court that after bad performance reviews he'd merely sought to study the materials as a way to get ahead in his work. Pho was sentenced to sixty-six months in prison.

That case connected with another piece of the narrative reported by *The Wall Street Journal* from months earlier, claiming that Russian government hackers had used their access to the antivirus software of Moscow-based Kaspersky Labs to steal a vast collection of NSA files from the home computer of a contract employee of the agency. The contractor, the report stated, had been foolish enough to not only violate his clearances and bring the top secret material home but also to run Kaspersky's software, which—like most antivirus programs—included a capability that allowed the program to upload files to the company's remote servers for analysis.

Kaspersky responded in a statement, denying that it had any "inappropriate ties" to the Russian government that might have let Kremlin hackers exploit its antivirus code. A few weeks later, the company followed up with the results of an internal investigation: It had, the company admitted, uploaded a collection of NSA hacking tools in 2014. But it claimed to have immediately deleted them upon discovering what the files represented.*

Even as those clues added to the circumstantial evidence of Russia's responsibility for the leak of the NSA's secret armory, nothing suggested that either the Shadow Brokers or WannaCry was connected to Sandworm. But just as artists inspire one another, Sandworm was no doubt watching and learning from its hacker peers. The Shadow

---

* Aside from Nghia Hoang Pho, another NSA staffer named Hal Martin remains a suspect in the Shadow Brokers case as of this writing. Martin, a contractor for the agency's TAO group, was arrested in late 2016 for taking home terabytes of classified materials from the agency, much like Pho. In a court filing two years later, the judge presiding over his case revealed that Martin had sent suspicious private Twitter messages to two security researchers at Kaspersky in August 2016 asking for a meeting, which investigators believed might have been intended to sell or share classified information. Martin's messages were sent just hours before the Shadow Brokers' first leaks were announced. Kaspersky reported Martin to U.S. government contacts, leading to a subsequent raid on his house and his arrest.

Brokers had made available a powerful hacking tool that a team of hyper-bellicose cyberwarriors could hardly ignore.

The WannaCry worm that followed offered Sandworm a chance to observe a weapon of mass disruption in action—and, it would turn out, a few ideas about how to build an even more explosive one.

23

MIMIKATZ

In May 2012, Benjamin Delpy walked into his room at the President Hotel in Moscow and found a man dressed in a dark suit with his hands on Delpy's laptop.

Just a few minutes earlier, the twenty-five-year-old French programmer had made a quick trip to the front desk to complain about the room's internet connection. He had arrived two days ahead of a talk he was scheduled to give at the nearby security conference Positive Hack Days, only to discover that his room had no Wi-Fi connection. Nor was the ethernet jack working. Downstairs, one of the hotel's staff insisted he sit in the lobby while a technician was sent up to fix it. Delpy refused and went back to wait in the room instead.

When he returned, as Delpy tells it, he was shocked to find the stranger standing at the room's desk, a small black roller-board suitcase by his side, his fingers hurriedly retracting from Delpy's keyboard. The laptop still showed a locked Windows log-in screen.

The man mumbled an apology about his key card working on the wrong room, brushed past Delpy, and was out the door before Delpy could even react. "It was all very strange for me," Delpy said. "Like being in a spy film."

It didn't take Delpy long to guess why his laptop had been the target of a literal black-bag job. That computer contained the subject of his presentation at the Moscow conference, an early version of a program he'd written called Mimikatz.

Mimikatz had been a kind of hobby for Delpy. He worked as an IT

manager at a French government institution—which one he declined
to tell me—and had observed that Windows had a subtle flaw: Microsoft had created a feature called WDigest, designed to allow corporate
and government Windows users to more conveniently prove their
identity to different applications on their networks or on the web.
WDigest would hold users' authentication credentials like usernames
and passwords in a computer's memory so they would only have to
be entered once and could then be effortlessly reused to unlock other
sensitive programs.

Delpy noticed that while Windows encrypted that copy of the
user's password in the computer's memory, it kept a copy of the secret
key to decrypt it handy in memory, too. "It's like storing a password-
protected secret in an email with the password in the same email,"
Delpy explained to me.

What if a hacker could get a foothold on that computer, pull the
encrypted credentials out of memory along with the decryption key,
decrypt them, and then run amok with the user's stolen identity and
password? Delpy pointed out that potential security lapse to Microsoft in a message submitted on the company's support page in 2011.
But the company brushed off his warning, responding that it wasn't a
real problem. After all, a hacker would already have to possess access
to a victim's computer in the first place before he or she could reach
that password in memory. (When I asked Microsoft about the same
issue, they said as much to me six years later. "It's important to note
that for this tool to be deployed it requires that a system already be
compromised," the company wrote in a statement. "To help stay
protected, we recommend customers follow security best practices
and apply the latest updates.")

But Delpy saw that in practice the Windows authentication system's flaw would still provide a powerful stepping-stone for hackers
trying to expand their infection from one machine to many on a
network. If a hacker could manage to obtain deep enough access
to a target machine—whether with a simple phishing scheme or a
rare zero-day vulnerability—he or she could exploit Delpy's trick to
scoop those credentials out of memory and then use them to access
other computers on the network. The danger was especially acute in
networks with multiuser computers: If another user was logged in to

the second machine the hacker accessed with a stolen password, he or she could run the same program on the second computer to steal that *other* user's password, too—and on and on.

So, with no real response from Microsoft, Delpy did what well-meaning hackers often do when faced with a company that's skeptical of the security bug they've uncovered: He made a proof of concept. Delpy said he'd been meaning to learn the C programming language anyway. So he wrote an application in C to demonstrate the attack he'd warned Microsoft about. He called it Mimikatz—the name used the French slang prefix *mimi,* meaning "cute," thus "cute cats"—and released it publicly in May 2011.

"Because you don't want to fix it, I'll show it to the world to make people aware of it," Delpy said of his attitude at the time. "It turns out it takes years to make changes at Microsoft. The bad guys didn't wait."

Before long, Delpy saw Chinese users in hacker forums discussing Mimikatz and trying to reverse engineer it. Then, in mid-2011, he learned for the first time—he declines to say from whom—that Mimikatz had been used in an intrusion of a foreign government network. Delpy hadn't released the tool's source code, making it harder for anyone else to adapt or tweak the program, but some hackers had apparently been motivated enough to painstakingly disassemble it and create their own working version of Delpy's tool. "The first time I felt very, very bad about it," he said.

Then, that September, Mimikatz was used again, in the landmark hack of the company DigiNotar. That firm was one of the so-called certificate authorities that assures that websites are who they claim to be when their address appears in a user's browser. Certificate authorities serve as the ground truth of trust online, and DigiNotar's compromise corrupted that trust to its core. The intrusion let the unidentified hackers—likely working for the Iranian government—issue fraudulent certificates so that they could perfectly spoof whatever website they chose. They ultimately used their DigiNotar takeover to spy on thousands of Iranians, according to security researchers at the firm Fox-IT, who analyzed the incident. DigiNotar was blacklisted by web browsers, and the company subsequently went bankrupt.

DigiNotar's demise was a telling demonstration of the lock-picking device Delpy had released to the world—more powerful than perhaps even he understood at the time. But Delpy said he also knew from the start that he was venturing into fraught territory with his creation; in his attempt to bring attention to a serious flaw in Windows' security, he was bringing it to the attention of the internet's most dangerous actors, too.

"Mimikatz wasn't at all designed for attackers. But it's helped them," Delpy acknowledged, with the understatement that sometimes results from a limited English vocabulary. "When you create something like this for good, you know it can be used by the bad side too."

∎

Microsoft had underestimated the severity of its security flaw. But Delpy had underestimated the danger of the tool he'd created to exploit it—even after he knew it was being used by foreign spies. He assumed that Mimikatz's tricks must have already been known to most state-sponsored hackers; surely he couldn't have been the only one to spot Microsoft's mistake in leaving passwords so vulnerable.

So in early 2012, when Delpy was invited to speak about his Windows security work at the Moscow conference Positive Hack Days, he accepted. The result, almost immediately after his arrival in Moscow, was his unnerving run-in with a strange Russian man in his hotel room.

That clumsy hands-on hacking apparently failed. Or so Delpy believes, because after that incident, the Russians tried a more straightforward approach. Two days later, after Delpy gave his conference talk to a crowd of hackers in the old Soviet chocolate factory where the conference was being held, another man in a dark suit approached him. He demanded Delpy put his conference slides and a copy of Mimikatz on a USB drive.

Trying to avoid a dramatic confrontation, Delpy complied. Then, before he'd even left Russia, he publicly posted Mimikatz's source code on the software repository GitHub, both fearing for his own physical safety if he kept the tool's code secret and figuring that if hackers were going to use his creation, defenders should fully understand it too.

, Mimikatz became a nearly universal tool in
from benevolent penetration testers to cyber-
ated cyberspies. It showed up in all manner
, from the break-ins of the notorious Carbanak
Fancy Bear's espionage operation inside the German
Bundestag. "It's the AK-47 of cybersecurity," as CrowdStrike CTO
Dmitri Alperovitch at one point described it.

Delpy, for reasons that are tough to explain outside the strange
world of hacker culture, didn't distance himself from his creation,
even as it appeared in more and more crime scenes. Instead, he
continued to advance it. If alerting Microsoft to Windows' original passwords-in-memory problem had been worthwhile, why not
demonstrate other vulnerabilities he'd turned up, too?

So he piled new features into Mimikatz, from generating fraudulent "tickets" used by Microsoft's Kerberos system that let computers prove their identities to each other over a network, to stealing
passwords from the auto-populating features in Chrome and Edge
browsers. He even threw in a tool that could allow anyone to cheat
at the game *Minesweeper,* pulling out the location of every mine in
the game from the computer's memory. "It's my toolbox, where I put
all of my ideas," Delpy told me.

Before adding a potentially dangerous new hacking tool to that
toolbox, Delpy said he would alert Microsoft, or whoever else might
be able to fix the flaw he was exploiting. Sometimes they did, eventually, respond with new protections. In Windows 8.1, for instance,
Microsoft finally turned off WDigest by default, blocking Delpy's
original avenue for Mimikatz's infections.

But often the fix is incomplete. Jake Williams, no stranger to
offensive hacking operations in his penetration testing business, told
me that he frequently gains a foothold in a target network, only to
find that systems administrators left WDigest on, letting Mimikatz
rampage through their systems. Or in other cases, he can simply find
a way to turn WDigest back on himself. "My total time on target to
evade that fix is about thirty seconds," Williams said.

All of that might make Delpy seem like a naive or even reckless
enabler. But Nick Weaver, a Berkeley computer science researcher
whom I asked about Mimikatz, argued it's not so simple. Yes, Mimi-

katz is "insanely powerful," he said. But perhaps it's just a repl___
tion of vulnerabilities that sophisticated hackers would have lea___
to exploit sooner or later, regardless—perhaps with less attention. ___
think we must be honest: If it wasn't Mimikatz, there would be some
other tool," said Weaver. "These are fundamental problems present
in how people administer large groups of computers."

Sandworm, however, did not write its own Mimikatz. It simply
took Delpy's. Like any ravenous, omnivorous predator, it was as
happy to scavenge low-hanging fruit as to hunt big game. Oleksii
Yasinsky first detected Ukraine's tormentors using Mimikatz in the
2015 penetration of StarLightMedia. It had appeared again in the logs
of the long, patient operation leading up to the Ukrenergo blackout
in late 2016.

With the leak of EternalBlue and its integration into WannaCry,
however, Sandworm's programmers saw an opportunity to elevate
Delpy's tool from a simple, manual shim into something far more
elegant and automated. The NSA's code presented one half of a
powerful, incendiary chemical reaction. Mimikatz offered the other.

24

NOTPETYA

Early on the morning of June 27, 2017, Colonel Maksym Shapoval was driving his Mercedes-Benz in the quiet Solomyansky district of western Kiev. When he stopped at an intersection next to the leafy campus of the State University for Telecommunications, a lump of explosives tucked under the Ukrainian military officer's car equivalent to about two pounds of TNT exploded. He was killed instantly in a ball of fire. Parts of his vehicle flew dozens of feet in every direction. Two pedestrians walking nearby were hit with shrapnel in the legs and neck. They would be the first collateral victims of the day, but not the last.

■

On the edge of the trendy Podil neighborhood to the east of Kiev's center, coffee shops and parks abruptly evaporate, replaced by a grim industrial landscape. Under a highway overpass, across some trash-strewn railroad tracks, and through a concrete gate stands the four-story headquarters of Linkos Group, a small, family-run Ukrainian software business.

Up three flights of stairs in that building is a server room where a rack of pizza-box-sized computers is connected by a tangle of wires and marked with handwritten, numbered labels. On a normal day, these servers push out routine updates—bug fixes, security patches, new features—to a piece of accounting software called M.E.Doc, which is more or less Ukraine's equivalent of TurboTax or Quicken. It's used by nearly anyone who files taxes or does business in the country.

But starting in the spring of 2017, those machines had served another purpose. Unbeknownst to anyone at Linkos Group, Sandworm's hackers had hijacked the company's update servers to allow them a hidden backdoor into the thousands of PCs around the country and the world that had M.E.Doc installed. Then, on that same morning of June 27, the saboteurs used that backdoor to release their payload: the most devastating cyberweapon in the history of the internet.

■

Oleksii Yasinsky had expected a calm Tuesday at the office. Earlier that morning, he'd read with dismay the headlines about the brazen assassination of a Ukrainian colonel in the middle of Kiev, but then he'd commuted to work as usual and come into an abnormally quiet office. It was the day before Ukraine's Constitution Day, a national holiday, and most of his co-workers were either planning their vacations or already taking them. Not Yasinsky. His job description at ISSP no longer lent itself to downtime. Since the first blows of Russia's cyberwar had hit StarLightMedia in 2015, in fact, he'd allowed himself a grand total of one week off.

Yasinsky remained unperturbed when he received a call that morning from ISSP's director telling him that Oschadbank, the second-largest bank in Ukraine, was under attack. The company had told ISSP that it was facing a ransomware infection, hardly an uncommon crisis for companies around the world targeted by cybercriminals. But when Yasinsky walked into Oschadbank's IT department at its central Kiev office half an hour later, he quickly suspected this was something worse. "The staff were lost, confused, in a state of shock," Yasinsky says. Around 90 percent of the bank's thousands of computers were permanently locked. Some showed the "repairing file system on C:" message. Others displayed an "oops, your files are encrypted" ransom screen demanding $300 in bitcoins.

After an examination of the bank's surviving logs, Yasinsky could see that the ransomware attack was an automated worm. It looked vaguely like WannaCry, but different: It wasn't merely scanning the internet at random and infecting any vulnerable computers it could find, but instead had somehow obtained an administrator's credentials, giving it the run of the bank's network. It had then rampaged through Oschadbank's systems like a prison inmate who'd stolen the warden's keys.

As he analyzed the bank's breach back in ISSP's office, Yasinsky started receiving calls and messages from people around Ukraine, telling him of similar instances in other companies and government agencies. One told him that another victim had experimented with paying the worm's ransom. As Yasinsky already guessed, the payment had no effect. This was no ordinary ransomware. "There was no silver bullet for this, no antidote," he said. And unlike WannaCry, there was no kill switch.

A thousand miles to the south, ISSP's CEO, Roman Sologub, was attempting to take a Constitution Day vacation on the southern coast of Turkey, preparing to head to the beach with his family. His phone, too, began to explode with calls from ISSP clients who were either watching the mysterious worm tear across their networks or reading news of the attack and frantically seeking advice.

Sologub retreated to his hotel, where he'd spend the rest of the day fielding more than fifty calls from customers reporting, one after another after another, that their networks had been infected. ISSP's security operations center, which monitored the networks of clients in real time, warned Sologub that the new worm was saturating victims' systems with terrifying speed: It took forty-five seconds to bring down the network of a large Ukrainian bank. A portion of one major Ukrainian transit hub, where ISSP had installed its equipment as a demonstration, was fully infected in sixteen seconds. Ukrenergo, the energy company whose network ISSP had been helping to rebuild after the 2016 blackout cyberattack, had also been struck yet again. "Do you remember we were about to implement new security controls?" Sologub recalled a frustrated Ukrenergo IT director asking him on the phone. "Well, too late."

By noon, ISSP's co-founder, a serial entrepreneur named Oleh Derevianko, had sidelined his vacation too. Derevianko had been driving north to meet his family at his village house for the holiday when the calls began. Soon he had pulled off the highway and was working from a roadside restaurant. By the early afternoon, he was warning every executive who called to unplug their networks without hesitation, even if it meant shutting down their entire company. In many cases, they'd already waited too long. "By the time you reached them," Derevianko said, "the infrastructure was already lost."

■

The unfolding digital debacle soon had a name: NotPetya. Security firms around the globe immediately began examining the new worm, primed by the previous month's WannaCry outbreak. Researchers at Kaspersky noted that the new malware's code somewhat resembled a piece of criminal ransomware called Petya that had been circulating since early 2016. Like that older ransomware, when this specimen infected a new machine, it immediately set about encrypting the computer's so-called master file table—the part of a computer's operating system that keeps track of the location of data in storage. It also encrypted every file on the machine individually; the effect was like a vandal who first puts a library's card catalog through a shredder, then moves on to methodically pulp its books, stack by stack.

But the new ransomware was distinguished from that earlier criminal code by crucial modifications—hence its name. Within twenty-four hours, a French security researcher named Matthieu Suiche would discover that in fact the code didn't actually allow decryption after a ransom was paid. Instead, its extortion messages seemed like a familiar ruse, covering its true intention of simple, permanent data destruction.

NotPetya was also distinguished from its Petya namesake by another feature: It was honed for maximum virulence. The worm used both Mimikatz and EternalBlue in tandem. For the researchers pulling its code apart, exactly how the code was gaining its initial foothold on computer networks was, at first, a mystery. But once it had that first infection, they could see that Mimikatz acted as its primary tool of expansion. Sucking passwords out of computers' memories, it instantly hopscotched from machine to machine, using common Windows management tools that give administrators free rein to access other computers on the network if they possess the right credentials—the inmates-running-the-prison case Yasinsky discovered at Oschadbank.

But the NSA's EternalBlue code leaked by the Shadow Brokers—along with another tool called EternalRomance for older versions of Windows—provided an extra, explosive catalyst. If any computer on a network hadn't received Microsoft's EternalBlue patch, NotPetya would jump to that vulnerable computer and continue to branch out from that new infection with its Mimikatz trick. The two tools paired to multiply their reach, making NotPetya more contagious than the sum of its parts. "You can infect computers that aren't patched, and then you can grab the passwords from those computers to infect other computers that *are* patched," said Mimikatz's creator, Delpy. "When you mix these two technologies, it's very powerful."

The result was scorched-earth file corruption that spread automatically, rapidly, and indiscriminately. "To date, it was simply the fastest-propagating piece of malware we've ever seen," Craig Williams, a researcher at Cisco's security division Talos, told me. "By the second you saw it, your data center was already gone."

NotPetya was, in fact, more pestilential than likely even its creators intended. Within hours, it would spread beyond Ukraine and out to countless machines around the world. It crippled multinational companies including Maersk; the pharmaceutical giant Merck; FedEx's European subsidiary, TNT Express; the French construction company Saint-Gobain; Cadbury's and Nabisco's food-industry parent company, Mondelēz; and the U.K. manufacturer Reckitt Benckiser, whose products include Durex condoms and Lysol disinfectant. In each of those cases, it would cause hundreds of millions of dollars in damages. It even spread to Russia—the cybersecurity community's immediate prime suspect for NotPetya's origin—striking victims like the state oil company Rosneft, the steelmaker Evraz, the medical technology firm Invitro, and Sberbank.

But at a national scale, no country would feel NotPetya's effects quite like Ukraine. Even as the worm's tentacles were spreading out from its initial victims into networks across the globe, the mass of infections at its core was busy eating Ukraine's digital infrastructure alive.

25

NATIONAL DISASTER

That same Tuesday morning, Serhiy Honcharov began his long, strange commute, just as he did every day. In the far-north Ukrainian town of Slavutych, the bespectacled, taciturn engineer boarded a train that headed east, crossing the Dnieper River and then dipping briefly over the Belarusian border. The train passed through forty miles of landscape that had seen no human influence in more than three decades. Trees and grass grew as tall and wild as they had in a prehistoric era. From his train window, he saw deer and flocks of birds, all of which seemed to prefer the radioactive remnants of humans' civilization to humanity's presence. Finally the train crossed the Pripyat River and arrived at a station that served only one destination: the cleanup site for the Chernobyl nuclear reactor.

At the station, Honcharov put on his blue uniform and boarded a bus that took him to the building where he worked in the sprawling Chernobyl complex, with a footprint larger than a dozen football fields. On one end of the grounds stood a gleaming structure that staff called the Arch, a massive hangar-like building taller than the Statue of Liberty and wider than the Roman Colosseum, designed to contain the supremely toxic ruins of the Chernobyl nuclear reactors. Inside, there remained nearly two hundred tons of uranium fuel, barely touched since the initial, tragic 1986 cleanup effort. The monumental mission of the Chernobyl facility's staff was to pull that fuel out of the Chernobyl reactors with cranes and safely bury it on a site nearby in the Exclusion Zone, a process of such scale and delicacy that it's projected to take until 2064.

Honcharov arrived at a building on the opposite end of the complex, where he served as the Chernobyl facility's IT director. He had been in his office for only two hours when he started to receive calls that something was going terribly wrong: Across the site's dozen-plus buildings, staff were seeing their screens go dark, then show NotPetya's ransom messages after they rebooted. Honcharov hurried into the room full of systems administrators next to his office, who were shocked by the speed of the malware tearing across their network.

Within seven minutes, they'd made the decision to turn off all the thousand-plus Windows machines at the entire Chernobyl site. The critical functions of the equipment dealing with radioactive waste were disconnected from the infected network and wouldn't be affected. But all the computers for the site's administration and communication with the outside world were about to go dark.

A man's voice read a message over the emergency loudspeaker system that reached every building in the complex. Thirty-one years after Chernobyl's world-shaking nuclear disaster, the site reverberated with a warning for a very different sort of meltdown. "To all staff members, immediately turn off computers and unplug network cables. Await further instructions."

■

Around the same time, back in the capital, an IT administrator for Ukraine's Ministry of Health named Pavlo Bondarenko was watching NotPetya's wave begin to crest across social media, seeing the same ransom screens appear again and again on Facebook and Telegram. Bondarenko, a twenty-two-year-old, six-foot-seven tech consultant with a mane of curly blond hair and a build that resembled a pro wrestler more than a government employee, watched the growing signs from his desk in the ministry's office. He sensed that Kiev's government agencies would be next.

Bondarenko called the health minister, Ulana Suprun, and made an unthinkable proposal: Unplug the ministry's entire network, responsible for everything from payroll for workers to cataloging stores of medicines to the national database of organ donors and recipients. "Save the data," as he described the approach he pitched to Suprun. "Don't think about the consequences."

Suprun agreed. Bondarenko and his colleagues started frantically disconnecting the ministry's computers and turning off its network links. Within hours, practically every other federal agency in Ukraine had either followed suit or else watched NotPetya tear through its systems, paralyzing everything in its path. "The government was dead," summarizes the Ukrainian minister of infrastructure Volodymyr Omelyan. Soon, NotPetya had hit Ukraine's national railways, taking down its ticketing system just as in the late 2016 attacks. It tore through Kiev's Boryspil airport, blacking out the scheduling screens across its terminals.

By 1:00 p.m., NotPetya had begun to topple another major pillar of Ukrainian society: the post office. The first ransom screens began to appear in the service's iconic white stone headquarters on Kiev's Maidan. Within an hour, Oleksandr Ryabets, the national postal service's director of IT, was pacing the halls, speaking on a conference call with the service's CEO, Igor Smelyansky, who had been at a meeting in Lviv, in the west of the country. They'd spoken for just a few minutes when Smelyansky gave Ryabets the order to shut down the agency's entire national network.

In Ukrainian society, the postal service's IT systems are responsible for more than mere mail. They also handle money transfers, newspaper subscriptions, and, perhaps most critically, pension payments that support 4.5 million retirees, along with the payroll of the postal service's own 74,000 employees and the dispatch system for 2,500 postal trucks.

Ryabets, a balding, central-casting career civil servant with a permanently weary expression, paused for a moment to process his boss's unthinkable directive to turn off those vital digital services, which in many cases would mean handling their gargantuan complexity with pen and paper. Then he and his staff spent the next hour on their phones, spreading the shutdown order out to twenty-five regional headquarters responsible for 11,500 branch offices and a total of 23,000 PCs and servers. (In fact, they'd later find, the move to unplug had come too late: More than 70 percent of the postal service's computers had already been infected, a mind-boggling disarray from which it would take months to recover.)

That afternoon, when the last of those offices had received the message and the shutdown was complete, Ryabets remembers feeling an eerie, death-like quiet descending over the building. "There was a kind of shocking emptiness," he said. "It was like you're dancing at a disco party when suddenly the music turns off, and everything is silent."

■

Around 6:00 p.m., ISSP's chairman Oleh Derevianko finally left the roadside restaurant where he'd unexpectedly spent the day fielding calls from shell-shocked clients. Before getting back on the road, he stopped to refuel his car. That's when he discovered that the gas station's credit card payment system had been taken out by NotPetya too. With no cash in his pockets, he carefully eyed his gas gauge, wondering if he had enough fuel to reach his village.

Across the country, Ukrainians were asking themselves similar questions: whether they had enough money for groceries and gas to last through the blitz, whether they would receive their paychecks and pensions, whether their prescriptions would be filled.

One of them was Pavlo Bondarenko, the twenty-two-year-old Health Ministry and IT administrator. Bondarenko left his office around 7:00 and headed out into the still-light summer evening. But when he swiped his contactless credit card at the turnstiles of the Arsenalna subway station nearby, he found that it was unresponsive. Yet another NotPetya casualty.

He had no cash to buy a token. So he headed out into the neighborhood to use a nearby ATM, only to find that it was dead. So was the next one he tried. And the one after that. On his fourth try, he found one working cash machine, with a long line and a tiny withdrawal limit.

Bondarenko took out enough cash to buy a metro ride home, then emerged in the Obolon neighborhood, where he lived in the north of the city. On his way to the apartment he shared with his mother, he stopped in a grocery store to buy enough milk, meat, and bread to last a couple of days. At the checkout line, he found that there, too, the point-of-sale systems were down, and cashiers were taking only cash. He didn't have enough bills left. So he went back out into the street and repeated his desperate hunt for cash, trying another five ATMs before he was able to find one that worked.

Later, after he'd finally gotten home with his groceries, Bondarenko sat down in front of his computer to pay his Kyivenergo electricity bill. He found, in one final, comic frustration, that the site was broken; the electric utility's payment system had been pulled off-line.

"It felt like a bad end-of-the-world movie. You're disoriented. You can't understand what to do next. You feel like you've lost an arm and can't function properly," Bondarenko said. "Life went very fast from 'What's new on Facebook?' to 'Do I have enough money to buy food for tomorrow?'"

■

Even then, NotPetya's rampage through Ukraine wasn't over. At 10:00 p.m., Mikhail Radutskiy, the president of a group of Kiev hospitals known as Boris Clinic, was brushing his teeth in the bathroom of his house in the western suburbs of Kiev when he got his NotPetya call. He drove into the city to find that his hospitals had been hit hard: Virtually all their Windows machines were now encrypted, though medical equipment running Linux and IBM operating systems had been spared.

All upcoming appointments had to be canceled. The GPS system for locating the hospitals' ambulances was dead. The IT administrators had a full backup of their systems from three days earlier. But every test that had been performed since then, from blood analyses to MRIs to CAT scans, would have to be redone.

Radutskiy didn't go home that night. By morning, angry patients with canceled appointments were collecting in the clinics' lobbies, hallways, even the waiting room outside his office. "It was a mess," Radutskiy told me simply. "It was chaos."

In sum, by the end of June 27, NotPetya had struck at least four hospitals in Kiev alone, along with six power companies, two airports, more than twenty-two Ukrainian banks, ATMs, and card payment systems, and practically the entire federal government. According to ISSP, at least three hundred companies were hit, and one senior Ukrainian government official would later estimate that a total of 10 percent of all computers in the country were wiped; the country's internet was literally decimated. "It was a massive bombing of all our systems," Minister of Infrastructure Omelyan said.

That night, the outside world was still debating whether NotPetya was criminal ransomware or a weapon of state-sponsored cyberwar. But ISSP's Oleksii Yasinsky and Oleh Derevianko had already started referring to it as a new kind of phenomenon: a "massive, coordinated cyber invasion."

Meanwhile, amid that digital epidemic, one single infection would become particularly fateful for the shipping giant Maersk. In an office in Odessa, a port city on Ukraine's Black Sea coast, a finance executive for Maersk's Ukraine operation had asked IT administrators to install the accounting software M.E.Doc on a single computer. That gave NotPetya the only foothold it needed.

26

BREAKDOWN

The shipping terminal in Elizabeth, New Jersey—one of the seventy-six that make up the port-operations division of Maersk known as APM Terminals—sprawls out into Newark Bay on a man-made peninsula covering a full square mile. Tens of thousands of stacked, perfectly modular shipping containers cover its vast asphalt landscape, and two-hundred-foot-high blue cranes loom over the bay. From the top floors of lower Manhattan's skyscrapers, five miles away, they look like brachiosaurs gathered at a Jurassic-era watering hole.

On a good day, about three thousand trucks arrive at the terminal, each assigned to pick up or drop off tens of thousands of pounds of everything from diapers to avocados to tractor parts. The trucks start that process, much like airline passengers, by checking in at the terminal's gate, where scanners automatically read their container's bar codes and a Maersk gate clerk talks to the truck driver via a speaker system. The driver receives a printed pass that tells him where to park so that a massive yard crane can haul his container from the truck's chassis to a stack in the cargo yard, where it's loaded onto a container ship and floated across an ocean—or that entire process in reverse order.

On the morning of June 27, Pablo Fernández was expecting dozens of trucks' worth of cargo to be shipped out from Elizabeth to a port in the Middle East. Fernández is a so-called freight forwarder—a middleman whom cargo owners pay to make sure their property arrives safely at a destination halfway around the world.*

At around 9:00 a.m. New Jersey time, Fernández's phone started buzzing with a succession of screaming calls from angry cargo owners. All of them had just heard from truck drivers that their vehicles were stuck outside Maersk's Elizabeth terminal. "People were jumping up and down," Fernández says. "They couldn't get their containers in and out of the gate."

That gate, a choke point to Maersk's entire New Jersey terminal operation, was dead, along with the rest of Maersk's entire NotPetya-ravaged network. The gate clerks had gone silent.

Soon, hundreds of eighteen-wheelers were backed up in a line that stretched for miles outside the terminal. One employee at another company's nearby terminal at the same New Jersey port watched the trucks collect, bumper to bumper, farther than he could see. He'd seen gate systems go down for stretches of fifteen minutes or half an hour before. But after a few hours, still with no word from Maersk, the Port Authority put out an alert that the company's Elizabeth terminal would be closed for the rest of the day. "That's when we started to realize," the nearby terminal's staffer remembers, "this was an attack." Police began to approach drivers in their cabs, telling them to turn their massive loads around and clear out.

Fernández and countless other frantic Maersk customers faced a set of bleak options: They could try to get their precious cargo onto other ships at premium, last-minute rates, often traveling the equivalent of standby. Or, if their cargo was part of a tight supply chain, like components for a factory, Maersk's outage could mean shelling out for exorbitant air freight delivery or risk stalling manufacturing processes, where a single day of downtime costs hundreds of thousands of dollars. Many of the containers, known as reefers, were electrified and full of perishable goods that required refrigeration. They'd have to be plugged in somewhere or their contents would rot.

Fernández had to scramble to find a New Jersey warehouse where

* Fernández is not his real name. Like Henrik Jensen, this source asked that I refer to him using a pseudonym.

he could stash his customers' cargo while he waited for word from Maersk. During the entire first day, he says, he received only one official email, which read like "gibberish," from a frazzled Maersk staffer's Gmail account, offering no real explanation of the mounting crisis. The company's central booking website, Maerskline.com, was down, and no one at the company was picking up the phone. Some of the containers he'd sent on Maersk's ships that day would remain lost in cargo yards and ports around the world for the next three months. "Maersk was like a black hole," Fernández remembers with a sigh. "It was just a clusterfuck."

In fact, it was a clusterfuck of clusterfucks. The same scene was playing out at seventeen of Maersk's seventy-six terminals, from Los Angeles to Algeciras, Spain, to Rotterdam in the Netherlands, to Mumbai. Gates were down. Cranes were frozen. Tens of thousands of trucks would be turned away from comatose terminals across the globe.

No new bookings could be made, essentially cutting off Maersk's core source of shipping revenue. The computers on Maersk's ships weren't infected. But the terminals' software, designed to receive the electronic data interchange files from those ships, which tell terminal operators the exact contents of their massive cargo holds, had been entirely wiped away. That left Maersk's ports with no guide to perform the colossal Jenga game of loading and unloading their towering piles of containers.

For days to come, one of the world's most complex and interconnected distributed machines, underpinning the circulatory system of the global economy itself, would remain broken. "It was clear this problem was of a magnitude never seen before in global transport," one Maersk customer remembers. "In the history of shipping IT, no one has ever gone through such a monumental crisis."

■

Several days after Henrik Jensen had watched all the screens around him go dark in Maersk's headquarters, he was at home in his Copenhagen apartment, enjoying a brunch of poached eggs, toast, and marmalade. Since he'd walked out of the office the Tuesday before, Jensen hadn't heard a word from any of his superiors. Then his phone rang.

When he answered, he found himself on a conference call with three Maersk staffers. He was needed, they said, at Maersk's office in Maidenhead, England, a town west of London where the conglomerate's IT overlords, Maersk Group Infrastructure Services, were based. They told him to drop everything and go there. Immediately.

Two hours later, Jensen was on a plane to London, then in a car to an eight-story glass-and-brick building in central Maidenhead. When he arrived, he found that the fourth and fifth floors of the building had been converted into a 24/7 emergency operations center. Its singular purpose: to rebuild Maersk's global network in the wake of its NotPetya meltdown.

Some Maersk staffers, Jensen learned, had been in the recovery center since Tuesday, when NotPetya first struck. Some had been sleeping in the office, under their desks or in corners of conference rooms. Others seemed to be arriving every minute from other parts of the world, luggage in hand. Maersk had booked practically every hotel room within tens of miles, every bed-and-breakfast, every spare room above a pub. Staffers were subsisting on snacks that someone had piled up in the office kitchen after a trip to a nearby Sainsbury's grocery store.

The Maidenhead recovery center was being managed by the consultancy Deloitte. Maersk had essentially handed the U.K. firm a blank check to make its NotPetya problem go away, and at any given time as many as two hundred Deloitte staffers were stationed in the Maidenhead office, alongside up to four hundred Maersk personnel. All computer equipment used by Maersk from before NotPetya's outbreak had been confiscated, for fear that it might infect new systems, and signs were posted threatening disciplinary action against anyone who used it. Instead, staffers had gone into every available electronics store in Maidenhead and bought up piles of new laptops and prepaid Wi-Fi hot spots. Jensen, like hundreds of other Maersk IT staffers, was given one of those fresh laptops and told to do his job. "It was very much just 'Find your corner, get to work, do whatever needs to be done,'" he said.

Early in the operation, the IT staffers rebuilding Maersk's network came to a sickening realization. They had located backups of almost all of Maersk's individual servers, dating from between three and seven days prior to NotPetya's onset. But no one could find a backup for one crucial layer of the company's network: its domain controllers, the servers that function as a detailed map of Maersk's systems and set the basic rules that determine which users are allowed access to which machines.

Maersk's 150 or so domain controllers were programmed to sync their data with one another so that, in theory, any of them could function as a backup for all the others. But that decentralized backup strategy hadn't accounted for one scenario: where every domain controller is wiped simultaneously. "If we can't recover our domain controllers," a Maersk IT staffer remembered thinking, "we can't recover anything."

After a frantic search that entailed calling hundreds of IT admins in data centers around the world, Maersk's desperate administrators finally found one lone surviving domain controller in a remote office—in Ghana. At some point before NotPetya struck, a blackout had knocked the Ghanaian machine off-line, and the computer remained disconnected from the network. It thus contained the singular known copy of the company's domain controller data left untouched by the malware—all thanks to a power outage. "There were a lot of joyous whoops in the office when we found it," a Maersk administrator remembers.

When the tense engineers in Maidenhead set up a connection to the Ghana office, however, they found its bandwidth was so thin that it would take days to transmit the several-hundred-gigabyte domain controller backup to the U.K. Their next idea: put a Ghanaian staffer on the next plane to London. But none of the West African office's employees had a British visa.

So the Maidenhead operation arranged for a kind of relay race: One staffer from the Ghana office flew to Nigeria to meet another Maersk employee in the airport to hand off the very precious hard drive. That staffer then boarded the six-and-a-half-hour flight to Heathrow, carrying the keystone of Maersk's entire recovery process.

With that rescue operation completed, the Maidenhead office

could begin bringing Maersk's core services back online. After the first days, Maersk's port operations had regained the ability to read the ships' inventory files, so operators were no longer blind to the contents of the hulking 18,000-container vessels arriving in their harbors. But several days would pass after the initial outage before Maersk started taking orders through Maerskline.com for new shipments, and it would be more than a week before terminals around the world started functioning with any degree of normalcy.

In the meantime, Maersk staffers worked with whatever tools were still available to them. They taped paper documents to shipping containers at APM ports and took orders via personal Gmail accounts, WhatsApp, and Excel spreadsheets. "I can tell you it's a fairly bizarre experience to find yourself booking five hundred shipping containers via WhatsApp, but that's what we did," one Maersk customer said.

About two weeks after the attack, Maersk's network had finally reached a point where the company could begin reissuing personal computers to the majority of staff. Back at the Copenhagen headquarters, a cafeteria in the basement of the building was turned into a reinstallation assembly line. Computers were lined up twenty at a time on dining tables as help desk staff walked down the rows, inserting USB drives they'd copied by the dozens, clicking through prompts for hours.

A few days after his return from Maidenhead, Henrik Jensen found his laptop in an alphabetized pile of hundreds, its hard drive wiped, a clean copy of Windows installed. Everything that he and every other Maersk employee had stored locally on their machines, from notes to contacts to family photos, was gone.

THE COST

Five months after Maersk had recovered from its NotPetya attack, the company's chair, Jim Hagemann Snabe, sat onstage at the World Economic Forum meeting in Davos, Switzerland, and lauded the "heroic effort" that went into Maersk's IT rescue operation. From June 27, when he was first awakened by a 4:00 a.m. phone call in California, ahead of a planned appearance at a Stanford conference, he said, it took just ten days for the company to rebuild its entire network of four thousand servers and forty-five thousand PCs. (Full recovery had taken far longer: Some staffers at the Maidenhead operation continued to work day and night for close to two months to rebuild Maersk's software setup.) "We overcame the problem with human resilience," Snabe told the crowd.

Since then, Snabe went on, Maersk has worked not only to improve its cybersecurity but also to make it a "competitive advantage." Indeed, in the wake of NotPetya, IT staffers told me that practically every security feature they've asked for has been almost immediately approved. Multifactor authentication has been rolled out across the company, along with a long-delayed upgrade to Windows 10.

Snabe, however, didn't say much about the company's security posture pre-NotPetya. Maersk security staffers told me that some of the corporation's servers were, until the attack, still running Windows 2000—an operating system so old Microsoft no longer supported it. In 2016, one group of IT executives had pushed for a preemptive security redesign of Maersk's entire global network. They called attention to Maersk's less-than-perfect software patching, outdated operating systems, and above all insufficient network segmentation. That last vulnerability in particular, they warned, could allow malware with access to one part of the network to spread wildly beyond its initial foothold, exactly as NotPetya would the next year.

The security revamp was green-lighted and budgeted. But its success was never made a so-called key performance indicator for Maersk's most senior IT overseers, so implementing it wouldn't contribute to their bonuses. They never carried the security makeover forward.

Few firms have paid more dearly for dragging their feet on security. In his Davos talk, Snabe claimed that the company suffered only a 20 percent reduction in total shipping volume during its NotPetya outage, thanks to its quick efforts and manual workarounds. But aside from the company's lost business and downtime, as well as the cost of rebuilding an entire network, Maersk reimbursed many of its customers for the expense of rerouting or storing their marooned cargo. One Maersk customer described receiving a seven-figure check from the company to cover the cost of sending his cargo via last-minute chartered jet. "They paid me a cool million with no more than a two-minute discussion," he said.

All told, Snabe estimated in his Davos comments, NotPetya cost Maersk between $250 million and $300 million. Most of the staffers I spoke with privately suspected the company's accountants had lowballed the figure.

Regardless, those numbers only start to describe the magnitude of NotPetya's damage. Logistics companies whose livelihoods depend on Maersk-owned terminals weren't all treated as well during the outage as Maersk's customers, for instance. Jeffrey Bader, president of a Port Newark–based trucking group, the Association of Bi-State Motor Carriers, estimates that the unreimbursed cost for trucking companies and truckers alone was in the tens of millions. "It was a nightmare," Bader said. "We lost a lot of money, and we're angry."

The wider cost of Maersk's disruption to the global supply chain as a whole—which depends on just-in-time delivery of products and manufacturing components—is far harder to measure. And, of course, Maersk was only one victim. Only when you start to multiply Maersk's story—imagining the same paralysis, the same serial crises, the same grueling recovery—playing out across dozens of other NotPetya victims and countless other industries does the true scale of Russia's cyberwar crime begin to come into focus.

Merck, the $200 billion, New Jersey–based pharmaceutical giant, was hit early on the morning of NotPetya's judgment day. It lost fifteen thousand Windows computers in ninety seconds, according to one of the company's IT staffers, before administrators managed to shut down its entire network. Merck maintained a backup data center for exactly this sort of crisis, but the staffer told me it was a "hot site," connected to Merck's network to enable faster recovery, rather than a "cold site," which would have been disconnected for greater security. That meant that it, too, was wiped out in NotPetya's tsunami. "We didn't have a great plan for what we'd do if both sites get infected at the same time, and that's exactly what happened," the IT staffer told me. "Something that would just take down *all* of our Windows systems—we hadn't imagined something of that scale."

Just as NotPetya shut down Maersk's port terminals worldwide, it immediately rippled out to Merck's physical processes, too, paralyzing its drug research and shutting down a significant swath of its pharmaceutical manufacturing. "Without computers these days you can't do anything," one Merck scientist lamented to *The Washington Post*. In its financial report to shareholders a few months later, the company would reveal that it had been forced to borrow a quarter-billion dollars' worth of its own vaccine for cancer-causing human papillomavirus from the federal Centers for Disease Control and Prevention. Two congressmen would write in a letter to the Department of Health and Human Services that the effects of NotPetya on Merck "raise questions about how the nation is prepared to address a significant disruption to critical medical supplies."

Eight months after the attack, Merck told shareholders it had totaled its losses due to the malware to a staggering $870 million. FedEx, whose European subsidiary, TNT Express, was crippled in the attack and required months to recover some data, took a $400 million blow. The French construction giant Saint-Gobain lost around the same amount. Reckitt Benckiser, the British manufacturer, lost

$129 million, and Mondelēz, the food producer, took a $188 million hit. Untold numbers of victims without public shareholders counted their losses in secret.

In total, the result was more than $10 billion in damages, according to a White House assessment confirmed to me by the former homeland security adviser Tom Bossert, who at the time of the attack was President Trump's most senior cybersecurity-focused official. Bossert emphasized, in fact, that this eleven-figure number represents a floor for their estimate, not a ceiling; it might well have been much higher. "While there was no loss of life, it was the equivalent of using a nuclear bomb to achieve a small tactical victory," Bossert said. "That's a degree of recklessness we can't tolerate on the world stage."

To get a sense of what that $10 billion in damages means on the spectrum of cyberattacks, consider that when a nightmarish but more typical ransomware attack paralyzed the city government of Atlanta in March 2018, it cost an estimated $17 million. In other words, less than a fifth of a percent of NotPetya's price. Even WannaCry, at the time an unprecedented internet catastrophe, was believed to have cost around $4 billion by most estimates. Nothing since has come close.

"This was a very significant wake-up call," as Maersk's chairman, Snabe, had said at his Davos panel. Then he'd added, with a Scandinavian touch of understatement, "You could say, a very expensive one."

■

But not all of NotPetya's costs could be measured in dollars. Another of its collateral victims was a little-known company called Nuance, focused on speech-recognition software. Nuance's code was used in the first version of the iPhone's Siri, for instance, and the voice command system in Ford cars. By 2017, however, much of Nuance's business came from a vast array of institutions that relied on its technology in matters of life and death: hospitals.

As it had for so many other massive multinationals, NotPetya sprang out from Nuance's Ukraine office to instantly paralyze the company's digital systems across its seventy locations, from India to Korea to its headquarters in Burlington, Massachusetts. And just as at Maersk, desperate IT administrators would struggle for weeks to recover thousands of PCs and servers encrypted by the worm. "It was trench warfare," one former Nuance staffer who participated in the rescue effort told me. "The office was in a state of triage. People were working 24/7. Every empty conference room had beds in it."

Ultimately, Nuance would report a loss of $92 million from Not-Petya, just a fraction of the damage to firms like Merck and FedEx. But Nuance's transcription service for electronic medical records, aided by the company's team of human transcriptionists, was used by hundreds of hospitals and thousands of clinics around the world. And that's where the real toll of its outage would be felt.

On the morning of the attack, Jacki Monson was sitting in a conference room in an office park in Roseville, California, a suburb of Sacramento. Monson served as the chief privacy and information security officer for Sutter Health, a network of more than twenty-four hospitals and clinics from Utah to Hawaii. Early that morning, she'd received a jarring message from Merck's chief information security officer about the company's crippling NotPetya infection, via a mailing list for the Health Care Industry Cybersecurity Task Force, a group created by the Obama administration to examine cybersecurity risks to medical organizations. By 9:00 a.m. Pacific time, Monson was on a tense conference call with health-care security executives around the world, all hoping to somehow avoid NotPetya's ballooning effects.

Half an hour into that meeting, Monson received another call from Sutter's head of health-care information management systems. Sutter hospitals still didn't seem to be infected with NotPetya, Monson was relieved to hear. Instead, they were facing a less obvious problem: For the last hour, Nuance's systems had been down and, with them, the ability of every doctor at every Sutter hospital to dictate changes into patients' medical records.

Monson quickly began to see the seriousness of that bottleneck. All across Sutter's hospitals, doctors were reading changes into Nuance's transcription service—in some cases, hours of audio at a time—and now none of those changes would show up in patients' files. People scheduled to go into surgery that morning might not have the final approvals they needed to be cleared for their operations. Others, like transplant recipients whose doctors constantly monitor and adjust their drugs, might miss crucial changes in treatment.

Sutter's emergency response team soon began racing to sort through thousands of patients' records at dozens of hospitals, trying to identify which ones might face serious consequences from their Nuance choke point. Meanwhile, Monson and her IT colleagues were desperately searching for an alternative system that would allow their hospitals' doctors to keep making changes to health records at their normal pace. Though Nuance's human-aided dictation services were off-line, its fully automated software, installed on Sutter's own systems, was still working. But that software was error-prone and struggled with accents. The hospitals' own transcriptionists were overwhelmed. It would take Sutter two weeks to switch to one of Nuance's competitors. And within just twenty-four hours, Sutter was facing a backlog of 1.4 million changes to patients' records, every one of which might have a real impact on a human being's health.

On the other side of the country, another hospital network was grappling with NotPetya more directly. Heritage Valley Health System, a small two-hospital network in Pennsylvania, had itself been infected by the worm. According to one of the IT staffers at those hospitals who spoke to me, its administrators had been logged in to a Nuance server at the time of the company's infection, allowing the worm to spread directly into the hospitals' own systems. Before 8:00 a.m. eastern time, it had corrupted two thousand computers and hundreds of servers.

According to that Heritage Valley staffer, equipment like X-ray machines and CT scanners weren't running Windows, so they weren't infected. But the shutdown of every Windows machine nonetheless crippled the hospitals' operations. "The MRI didn't get touched. But the computer that has the software to get the MRI image *off* the machine, that got hit," he told me. "Tests are no good if you can't see the damn things."

Both Heritage Valley hospitals continued to serve existing patients, but new patients were turned away for around three days, the staffer said. The Associated Press reported that some of the hospitals' surgeries had to be delayed. One woman, fifty-six-year-old Brenda Pisarsky, told the AP that her gallbladder surgery was interrupted by a hospital-wide loudspeaker announcement calling staffers to a "command center" to deal with the NotPetya crisis.

"Europe or somewhere in that vicinity hacked into Beaver Medical Hospital and Swickley Hospital and shutdown all their computer system! It happened right after I got into the operating room!!!" Pisarsky wrote on Facebook. "Thank God no computer was used for my type of surgery. Others weren't so lucky and had to be cancelled."

∎

Heritage Valley's case was an outlier. The vast majority of hospitals that suffered from NotPetya, like Sutter Health, felt its effects through Nuance's malware outbreak, not their own. One call to deal with Nuance's swelling transcription backlog had more than two hundred participants, Jacki Monson remembered.

In Sutter's case, Monson claimed, the hospital network ultimately tracked down every urgent case and made sure doctors and IT staff updated medical records in time to prevent harm. "Fortunately, because of how proactive we were, we didn't have any patient safety issues," she said.

But not every hospital staffer was so sure. One IT systems analyst at a major American hospital—she declined to tell me which one—had a more troubling story to tell. After NotPetya's outbreaks, she had initially focused on how to prevent her own institution from getting infected. It was only one afternoon a week later that a furious co-worker on the edge of panic had alerted her to two children's diagnostic reports that were missing from their medical records due to the Nuance outage. Both kids were scheduled for treatments whose safety depended on their records being up-to-date. One had been transferred to another hospital for surgery the next morning.

The IT staffer felt the blood drain from her face. Did her hospital even have a copy of the dictated record changes? Would they have to delay a potentially lifesaving procedure? With only hours to spare, she located the hospital's own raw archive of the dictations, listened to close to forty audio files, located the crucial one, and sent it out for transcription by a backup service, barely squeezing in the request in time for the child's surgery to proceed the next day.

Over the next week, the IT staffer found two more cases where pediatric patients' medical records were missing dictated reports, each time with only a day or two to spare before a major treatment was scheduled. In one case, a doctor had to manually retype his dictation after reexamining an ultrasound scan of a child's heart.

In all four cases, the IT staffer told me, the hospital managed to deal with its glitches in time to prevent any delay or incorrect treatments. But even a year and a half later, she told me that those cases, where children's care was put in jeopardy by a cyberattack, continued to haunt her. The hospital's Nuance outage and its effects had dragged on for more than four months. Yes, the four cases she'd seen had happy endings, she told herself. But what about the hundreds of other hospitals affected by NotPetya, and their many thousands of cases? After her own close calls, could she really believe that not one among those thousands of patients had been harmed? "I can't say how many patients were affected or what health problems might have been caused as a result of the Nuance outage," she told me. "But there's a huge potential for it, just by the number of reports impacted, how long they were impacted, the critical nature of the care being provided."

If delays did occur in even a tiny fraction of those cases, the damage to human lives could have been real, argues Joshua Corman, an Atlantic Council security researcher who also served as a member of the Health Care Industry Cybersecurity Task Force. He points to a *New England Journal of Medicine* study that showed that even a traffic delay of less than five minutes in an ambulance caused patients to die 4 percent more often in hospitals over the following thirty days.

"Think of every hospital in the U.S. that uses Nuance. Think about how many days it was down, multiplied by the number of lab results, transfers, discharges, and how many of those are time sensitive," Corman said. "In some cases, time matters. Pain level is affected. Quality of life is affected. Mortality is affected."

28

AFTERMATH

One week after NotPetya's outbreak, Ukrainian police dressed in full SWAT camo gear and armed with assault rifles poured out of vans and into the modest headquarters of Linkos Group, running up the stairs like SEAL Team Six invading the bin Laden compound.

They pointed rifles at perplexed employees and lined them up in the hallway, as the company's founder, Olesya Linnyk, would later describe it to me. On the second floor, next to her office, the armored cops even smashed open the door to one room with a metal baton, in spite of Linnyk's offer of a key to unlock it. "It was an absurd situation," Linnyk said after a deep breath of exasperation.

The militarized police squad finally found what it was looking for: the rack of M.E.Doc servers that had played the role of patient zero in the NotPetya pandemic. They confiscated the offending machines and put their hard drives in black plastic bags.

■

Anton Cherepanov, working at his desk in ESET's Houston room, had spotted NotPetya's connection to Linkos Group's accounting software in the very first hours of the worm's spread. Around ten o'clock on the chaotic morning of the attack, ESET's Ukrainian staff had sent him photos of the malware's ransom message, and he'd quickly dug through the fresh collection of malware pulled from ESET's antivirus software to find a sample. Taking apart NotPetya's lightly obfuscated code, he saw that the worm was being triggered by a file on victims' machines called ezvit.exe—a component of the M.E.Doc accounting application.

Cherepanov hadn't dwelled on that connection. He'd been too busy trying to push out an update to ESET's antivirus software to protect customers against the snowballing infections and then frantically searching in vain for a technique to unscramble NotPetya's encryption or even for a WannaCry-like kill switch in its code.

It was only in the days that followed NotPetya's initial mayhem that Cherepanov returned to the connection to M.E.Doc and began to untangle a long thread of forensic links—a thread complex enough that, more than a year later, I would have to ask him to walk me through it several times in a conference room of ESET's Bratislava headquarters.

Cherepanov had recognized the ezvit.exe file because he'd seen it in an earlier malware outbreak. The same program had been the carrier for a different infection he'd discovered in May 2017. Five days after WannaCry, he'd found that a piece of ransomware known as XData seemed to be spreading via that ezvit executable file, using Mimikatz but not EternalBlue. At the time, he thought that victims were perhaps being tricked into installing a malware-tainted version of M.E.Doc, the sort of spoofing that hackers often use to infect victims with ransomware and other criminal code.

He'd warned M.E.Doc's developers at Linkos Group in an email, received a brief acknowledgment, helped ESET to add protection against the new malware, and written a blog post about his findings. But in the days following the frenzy around WannaCry, few had taken notice of his warnings about an attack that had affected only a tiny fraction of WannaCry's number of victims.

Now, a month later, he had seen M.E.Doc used to spread Not-Petya, a vastly larger outbreak that dwarfed his earlier findings and even WannaCry. Cherepanov had downloaded all of M.E.Doc's 2017 updates from Linkos Group's website when he first detected its use to spread malware in May. In the wake of NotPetya, he quickly downloaded M.E.Doc's latest updates from May and June, just before the website was shut down by Linkos Group, and spent the rest of the week scrutinizing them. Looking at the code, he came to the realization that the hackers hadn't merely distributed a tainted version of M.E.Doc's software to infect victims, like a murderer serving tea laced with arsenic. They'd piggybacked on the software's actual, legitimate update mechanism, akin to corrupting the entire tea supply of India. That remarkable supply chain hijacking meant they must have penetrated deep into Linkos Group's servers. "M.E.Doc *was itself* the backdoor," Cherepanov thought.

For the rest of the week, he pored over that corrupted update code and ESET's malware records, working for more than twelve hours a day to understand exactly how the hackers had turned this innocuous piece of tax software into the vehicle that had carried NotPetya out into the world. It was now clear the same hackers had hijacked M.E.Doc's updates to spread a ransomware worm at least twice, first XData in May, and then the vastly more virulent NotPetya in June.

But then Cherepanov started to make other connections back from NotPetya based on a different fingerprint—a clue that would allow him to piece together a much longer timeline.

He'd been closely following the group he called TeleBots, that others called Sandworm. as it had rampaged through Ukrainian networks with data-destroying, FSociety-themed attacks in December of the previous year—the ones that had led up to the second blackout attack. Cherepanov had since seen the group carry out more intrusions in February and March 2017. In each of those cases, in addition to that Telegram backdoor, he'd also seen the hackers install another backdoor access tool written in a programming language known as Visual Basic Scripting Edition, or VBS.

Therein lay the fingerprint that caught Cherepanov's attention. As he investigated the M.E.Doc hijacking mechanism, one major Ukrainan financial institution—he declined to tell me which one—shared with him another, remarkable clue: Before it had been infected with NotPetya, that same VBS backdoor and another, similar VBS script had also been installed on its network via the corrupted M.E.Doc software. One of those two VBS tools seemed to be a kind of secondary foothold—designed to persist even if the M.E.Doc one were discovered and deleted. The second appeared to be a method for testing the M.E.Doc backdoor's controls before it was used to deliver its final NotPetya payload.

Those VBS tools, Cherepanov realized, matched the attacks he'd seen for more than six months, tying NotPetya all the way back to the wave of data-destroying breaches starting in December 2016. He now saw the glowing links that chained together the entire series of incidents: It all came back to Sandworm.

Looking further in Sandworm's history, he realized that Not-Petya was, even more, a direct descendant of the KillDisk attacks that stretched all the way back to 2015. The techniques for wanton data destruction had evolved over nearly three years in the attackers' minds. In fact, looking into its code, he could see that a list of dozens of file extensions targeted for deletion in the December 2016 attacks almost exactly matched a list targeted for encryption in NotPetya. "From the attacker's perspective, I could see the problem. KillDisk doesn't spread itself," he explained. "They were testing this tactic: how to find more victims, looking for the best infection vectors."

As he dug back through his archive of M.E.Doc updates, Cherepanov could see that they'd found that perfect carrier in Linkos Group's accounting software. In fact, he discovered that Sandworm had first tested pushing out backdoor code through M.E.Doc two months before NotPetya, in April. The hackers had enjoyed an extraordinary level of access to the networks of every M.E.Doc customer for months, long before they'd pulled the trigger on their ultimate payload. After years of experimentation, they'd found the perfect keys into the heart of the Ukrainian internet, ideal for espionage and sabotage alike. They'd tested it, bided their time, then used it to unleash a world-shaking worm. "It was so unique," Cherepanov marveled. "So dedicated, so patient."

When he finally comprehended the full picture, it was 3:00 a.m. on a Sunday, and Cherepanov was still at his desk in his home office in an apartment east of Bratislava's city center. Only the glow of his computer screens lit the room. His wife had gone to sleep hours earlier. He finished his work and got into bed, but adrenaline and the visions of Sandworm's years-long destructive campaign continued to run through his brain. He lay there awake until dawn.

■

Largely overlooked in the chaos of NotPetya's pandemic was a strange feature of the worm: NotPetya might not have had a kill switch or an antidote, but it did have a vaccine.

On that fateful Tuesday in late June, Amit Serper, a former Israeli government hacker with a job as a security researcher for the Boston-based firm Cybereason, was on vacation in Tel Aviv. He'd been visiting family in the suburbs of the city when he learned about NotPetya's spread from a television news report around 7:00 p.m. Israeli time—the same time zone as Ukraine. Serper had been planning to go out drinking with friends at 10:00 p.m. "I have three hours to kill," he thought. "Let's play."

Serper quickly obtained a copy of NotPetya and started pulling it apart on his MacBook and scanning its code. Within two hours, he'd stumbled onto something unexpected: an "exit process" function call. A function call is an instruction in code—in this case, one that stops a component of a program from running. Serper started working backward from that peculiarity to determine what part of the malware it might turn off and what might trigger it. Soon he came to a realization that left his mind almost numb with excitement: The feature he'd found hidden in the code could stop NotPetya's destructive encryption altogether.

Just before he headed into the city for drinks, Serper identified the exact "if/then" statement in the code that triggered that shutdown: If a file called "perfc" with no file extension was present in the main Windows directory, then NotPetya essentially quit, saving the machine's data from destruction. Perhaps the file was a vestigial feature of the ransom algorithm NotPetya was based on, designed to prevent the malware from encrypting data twice and rendering it unrecoverable? Regardless, if an administrator installed a file with that specific "perfc" name in that specific directory, a computer would be spared from NotPetya, like the Passover story of the angel of death sparing the firstborn sons of those who smeared lambs' blood on their doors.

Barely able to wrap his head around the notion he'd found a possible solution to a global crisis, Serper tweeted out his finding. Not-Petya had a "kill-switch," he wrote excitedly. Perhaps it wasn't too late to save the world from this plague after all. For the next few hours, as Serper and his friends drank beer in a Tel Aviv bar, his phone was bombarded with so many messages from security researchers, network administrators, and reporters that it repeatedly crashed.

But all of that excitement was, to some degree, misplaced. In fact, Serper hadn't exactly found a kill switch like the one Marcus Hutchins had discovered in WannaCry. The "perfc" check wasn't a single switch that could stop NotPetya's progress across the world. And to have any effect, that file had to be present in computers *before* they were infected. That meant the task of educating victims and distributing the fix faced all the same old epidemiological problems of patching software.

No doubt some potential victims of NotPetya did end up installing Serper's vaccine and preemptively saving their data. But by that night, when the vaccine had caught the attention of the security community, been tested, confirmed, and shared, it was too late for all but a small fraction of the plague's victims to make use of it. NotPetya's $10 billion worth of damage was largely, irreversibly, underway. The angel of death had already made its rounds.

■

If nothing else, however, Serper's work got the attention of the Ukrainian government. Cybereason contacted the Ukrainian authorities to offer its help. And following the strange, overdramatic raid those authorities had just carried out at Linkos Group's headquarters, the cops in Kiev answered Cybereason's staff with a unique opportunity: to aid in the analysis of Linkos Group's hacked, confiscated servers.

The day after Ukrainian police stormed into the Linkos server room, two of Serper's colleagues in Kiev were given access to the seized servers' hard drives, still in their black plastic bags. They quickly copied all of the data from the machines, and Serper remotely connected to the laptops of his colleagues on the ground to analyze the Linkos logs from the company's Boston headquarters. From around noon until late that evening, he worked to link together the fingerprints of the hackers who had penetrated the company's M.E.Doc infrastructure to its core. Serper was so engrossed, in fact, that he continued working on his laptop even as he rode home from the Cybereason office in an Uber. Rather than waste time with a shower that night, he continued reverse engineering in the bath, perching his computer on a shelf over his tub.

Serper eventually assembled a rough story of Linkos Group's breach: It began with the hackers exploiting a vulnerability in the content-management system of the company's web server, the software it used for editing its website's appearance. From there, the hackers had set up a "web shell" on the server, a kind of simple administration panel that acted as a foothold inside the computer, letting them install their own software on it at will.

They'd somehow leveraged their control of that web server to gain access to the M.E.Doc update server on the same network, though Serper couldn't explain to me exactly how. They essentially turned that update server into a command-and-control beacon for their backdoor software updates, hiding the entire back-end setup of a traditional malware infection inside Linkos Group's own infrastructure, like a community of parasites that's taken up residence in a host's extremities and brain at the same time.

Even more striking was the mode of communication between that hacked update server and the backdoor copies of M.E.Doc that it controlled around the world. M.E.Doc was designed to connect with Linkos Group's servers via http, the same basic internet communications that web browsers use to talk to websites. As such, those http messages include a standard channel for "cookies," the bits of data that websites plant in users' browsers to track their activities.

Now the command-and-control software installed on the hacked M.E.Doc server had used that same covert cookie channel to send commands to the computers it had backdoored. It could send a range of instruction, including not only installing files like NotPetya but also stealing any file the hackers chose from a machine running the accounting software, using M.E.Doc's own communication system to avoid detection. "The way they used M.E.Doc's infrastructure against itself was very elegant," Serper said. "It was a job well done."

Serper was struck by just how mismatched these hackers were for the defenses they were up against. These agile, innovative intruders were strolling through holes in M.E.Doc's server software that was years old, poorly configured, and shoddily patched. "This was not a challenge," he told me, as if refraining from saying something less polite.

But perhaps most remarkable of all was the sheer longevity of M.E.Doc's security woes. On the company's hard drives, Serper also discovered another, older set of log files from November 2015, a record of the company's network activity years before it became the epicenter of NotPetya's meltdown. In those logs, Serper found *another* hidden web shell.

There was no way to tell if that earlier infection had ties to Not-Petya or to any particular group of hackers. But it showed that someone had secret access to the same network that had served as the epicenter of a global calamity for at least twenty months. The company that would serve as the trigger for Sandworm's climactic cyberweapon had been quietly penetrated even before the hackers' first Christmas blackout.

29

DISTANCE

When Olesya Linnyk talks about NotPetya, she assumes the tired patience of someone who has gotten used to reliving the worst moment of her career again and again. "Emotionally, it has been a total horror movie," Linnyk told me in a tone of measured disgust, sitting in a Linkos Group conference room. "Our slogan was 'financial reporting without problems.' Then we became the problem."

Over the previous seven years leading up to the company's ill-fated moment in the spotlight, Linnyk had spun off M.E.Doc as a new product independent from her father's accounting software firm and nurtured it from a seed of an idea into its own thriving business. She had hired nearly three hundred people, simultaneously raised four children, and considered her company almost as another. "It's like my fifth child, the oldest one, and my other kids often get less attention," she told me with a fleeting smile. "Seven years of reputation, destroyed."

I was ready to ask the unkind question: Why then, with so much at stake for her, her company, and the world, didn't Linkos better protect itself? Why leave such a powerful mechanism for global infection so unsecured?

Linnyk spared me by answering the question before I could ask it. She insisted that her company hadn't willfully neglected to protect itself and its customers against cyberattacks. They had simply never imagined that they might be a target. "We do quite basic and simple things. We help out accountants," she said. "We saw ourselves as quite distant from cybersecurity issues."

That understanding of "distance" struck me as a kind of concise summary of the broader attitude that made NotPetya's epic effects on the global internet possible. Linkos Group hadn't remotely imagined that it could be a carrier for a worldwide digital contagion. The Ukrainian police, in the aftermath of the disaster, had staged a showy raid on the headquarters of the worm's unwitting launch point, while the real perpetrators of the attack watched with impunity, likely thousands of miles away. The American intelligence community—and to a lesser extent the creator of Mimikatz—hadn't reckoned with the potential consequences of their tools falling into the enemy's hands. Even NotPetya's own creators seem not to have understood the extent of the worm's collateral damage beyond Ukraine, both to the West and to Russia itself.

But the largest of those blind spots, perhaps, can be found in the West's attitude to Ukraine and silence in the face of the cyberwar afflicting it. For a decade, the United States had treated Russian cyberattacks on its neighbors—Estonia, Georgia, and Ukraine, above all—as a "distant" problem. The Obama administration had watched since 2015 as Ukraine became a helpless victim and a nation-sized laboratory for Russia's cruelest hacking techniques. It allowed those hackers to cross one red line after another, including not one but two unprecedented blackout attacks. The second had been well timed to slip through the diplomatic cracks, coming as the administration already had one foot out the door, ending its tenure without a single public rebuke of those sabotage campaigns.

The Trump administration, of course, had made those concessions to Putin far more explicit. Trump's nihilistic denials had made Russia's hacking of American election targets a subject for debate—in the face of mounting, incontrovertible evidence—leaving no space for even a discussion of the vastly more aggressive hacking of critical institutions in Ukraine. At the same time, Trump had overtly praised Putin, repeatedly calling him a "strong leader" in public comments and even complimenting his response to the Obama administration's sanctions.

Meanwhile, his administration's broader isolationism telegraphed to the world that Ukraine would be entirely on its own in the face of Russian attacks—physical or digital. "Why should U.S. taxpayers be interested in Ukraine?" Trump's secretary of state, Rex Tillerson, callously asked a group of diplomats at a gathering in Italy, three months before NotPetya's release.

NotPetya provided a tidy answer to Tillerson's question. Americans ignored Ukraine's escalating cyberwar in the face of repeated warnings that the attacks there would soon spread to the rest of the world. Then, very suddenly, exactly that scenario played out, at an immense cost.

The result of all these combined myopias was the closest thing the earth has yet seen to the long-predicted, infrastructure-crippling cyberwar doomsday. To an extent never seen before or—as of this writing—since, a single surprise cyberattack took a chunk out of the foundation of civilization, from pharmaceuticals to shipping to food. Distributed across the world, and in a far more concentrated sense for Ukraine itself, NotPetya was the "electronic Pearl Harbor" that John Hamre had first warned of in 1997.

Even Thomas Rid, a professor of strategic and military studies at Johns Hopkins who has written skeptically about the potential for cyberwar, criticizing overblown metaphors of "cyberweapons" and an impending "cyber 9/11," has said that NotPetya finally represented an event that warranted that sort of hyperbole. "If anything comes close to 'cyber 9/11,'" Rid told me, "this was it."

■

Reckoning with the extent of NotPetya's damage, its victims often described it to me in the terms of an uncontrollable pathogen or natural disaster. But of course, there was nothing natural about it. The worm was man-made, imbued with its creators' malicious intentions. The question remained: What *were* those hackers' intentions?

Nearly a year after the attack, I visited the new, upgraded headquarters of ISSP, which had ditched its old, dismal neighborhood and moved into a trendy complex of start-ups that included a satellite office of Uber. In a conference room inside, I met with Oleksii

Yasinsky, whose appearance had shifted in the opposite direction of his surroundings: Instead of ironed business casual, he now wore torn jeans, a white T-shirt, and several days' stubble, the uniform of the overworked cybersecurity expert.

Yasinsky and his boss, ISSP's co-founder Oleh Derevianko, quickly launched into their explanation of NotPetya's purpose with all the usual theories about Ukraine's cyberwar: intimidation, experimentation, collateral damage. But they added another striking claim: that NotPetya was intended not merely for destruction but also as a cleanup effort. After all, they pointed out, the hackers who launched NotPetya first had months of unfettered access to victims' networks via their hijacked M.E.Doc infrastructure. On top of the panic and disruption it caused, NotPetya might have also wiped away evidence of espionage or even reconnaissance for future sabotage.

In fact, when Yasinsky had looked at the networks of Ukrainian NotPetya victims in the days and weeks after they were struck by the worm, he'd found something that no one else had described to me: The "perfc" file that Amit Serper had identified as NotPetya's vaccine appeared on computers that hadn't actually been affected by the worm, close to 10 percent of machines in some cases. The victim companies' administrators told him that they hadn't installed the vaccine. But those computers had, nonetheless, been spared from encryption.

Yasinsky believed that the "vaccine" had, in fact, served a different purpose in the hands of the hackers: It was designed to preserve their access. Even after a victim rebuilt his network, he might not rebuild those vaccinated, unscathed computers. And those machines might have some other, clever infection that neither the victims nor ISSP had yet identified. "Ukraine was used as a backdoor into the whole world," Yasinsky told me. And some part of that backdoor, he warned, might remain open.

As I spoke to other cybersecurity analysts about NotPetya, the notion that non-Ukrainian companies hit by the worm were unintended collateral damage came to seem like an oversimplification, too. Serper, ESET, and Cisco's Talos security division had all noted that the M.E.Doc backdoor had the ability to upload to the hackers a certain Ukrainian government-issued tax identification number known as an EDRPOU, pulling that number from every installation of M.E.Doc. That ID would allow the hackers to look up each legal entity that had registered with the Ukrainian government, creating an exact catalog of each potential victim before unleashing the worm into its system. If they'd wished to, they could have carefully avoided the vast majority of collateral damage, instead coordinating a campaign of precision-guided missile strikes.

Cisco's Craig Williams argued that meant Russia knew full well the extent of the pain the worm would inflict internationally. The fallout, he posited, was no accident. Instead, it was a kind of hyper-aggressive trade embargo, meant to explicitly punish anyone who would dare even to maintain an office inside the borders of Russia's enemy. "Anyone who thinks this was accidental is engaged in wishful thinking," Williams said. "This was a piece of malware designed to send a political message: If you do business in Ukraine, bad things are going to happen to you."

Other debates about NotPetya's intentions persist even today. Some cybersecurity researchers point to the vast damage it did to Russian companies as evidence that it couldn't have been a Russian government operation. Vesselin Bontchev, a security researcher at the Bulgarian Academy of Sciences, has highlighted errors in the coding of NotPetya's ransomware component that he argues must be the work of unsophisticated hackers, not Russian government agents, though he notes that the M.E.Doc backdoor does have all the hallmarks of a government intelligence operation. In fact, the mysteries over the thinking hidden beneath NotPetya's layers of misdirection may never be definitively solved, absent its creators themselves revealing their intentions.

But regardless of its targeting and purpose, the most enduring object lesson of NotPetya may simply be the strange, extradimensional landscape of the battlefield where it was launched. This is the confounding geography of cyberwarfare: In ways that still defy human intuition, phantoms inside M.E.Doc's server room in a gritty corner of Kiev spread chaos into the gilded conference rooms of the capital's federal agencies, into ports dotting the globe, into the stately headquarters of Maersk on the Copenhagen harbor, into operating rooms in U.S. hospitals, and across the global economy.

"Somehow the vulnerability of this Ukrainian accounting software affects the U.S. national security supply of vaccines and global shipping?" Joshua Corman, the cybersecurity fellow at the Atlantic Council, asked me, as if still puzzling out the shape of the wormhole that made that cause and effect possible. "The physics of cyberspace are wholly different from every other war domain."

In those physics, NotPetya reminds us, distance is no defense. Every barbarian is already at every gate. And the network of entanglements in that ether, which have unified and elevated the world for the past twenty-five years, can, over a few hours on a summer day, bring it to a crashing halt.

PART V

IDENTITY

Treachery within treachery
within treachery.

30

GRU

By late 2017, I had been tracking Sandworm for more than a year. I'd spent much of that time studying how its NotPetya apotheosis had played out across the globe. The group now had my full attention: Its members had distinguished themselves in my mind as the most dangerous hackers in the world. And it offended my sensibilities as a reporter that I still had practically no sense at all of who Sandworm *was*.

Yes, they seemed to be Russian and almost certainly controlled by the Russian government. But I wanted more. I wanted to learn about the individual people unleashing Sandworm's chaos from behind their keyboards and computer screens, their names, faces, and personal motives—or as close as I could get to any of those details about a group operating half a world away, with years of professional experience exploiting the internet's potential for anonymity.

Sandworm was becoming a kind of obsession for me, just as it had become for John Hultquist three years earlier. And I also shared something else with Hultquist, as well as with others like Oleksii Yasinsky and Rob Lee: I had joined the lonely club of Cassandras determined to bring attention to the group even as the rest of the world seemed determined to ignore it.

Along with its unprecedented devastation, Sandworm's NotPetya worm left in its wake six months of inexplicable silence. For the rest of the summer, the fall, and into the winter of 2017, no victim of NotPetya outside Ukraine would name Russia as the perpetrator of the attack. Nor did any government other than Ukraine's speak out to name the Kremlin. Russia seemed to have launched a cyberwar weapon that had crossed countless borders, violated practically every norm of state-sponsored hacking imaginable, and yet earned not a single reproach from the West.

Three days after NotPetya's outbreak, the NATO Cooperative Cyber Defence Centre of Excellence, established in Estonia in the wake of Russia's early, crude wave of cyberattacks there in 2007, had issued a milquetoast statement: It had called on the international community to take action and noted that NotPetya was very likely the work of some government, somewhere. "NotPetya was probably launched by a state actor or a non-state actor with support or approval from a state," the statement read. "Other options are unlikely."

But it had stopped short of naming Russia. And it had noted that any countermeasures would require definitive attribution of the attack to its source, which it argued was still a mystery. Even with firmer attribution, the statement had claimed naively or legalistically, NotPetya didn't actually inflict "consequences comparable to an armed attack," and thus didn't trigger Article 5 of NATO's collective defense provision—the one that required member states to treat a military attack against one of them as an act of war against them all.*

Other than brief public statements like those of Maersk's chairman, Snabe, at the World Economic Forum, the international victims of NotPetya shared the very minimum amount of information necessary to explain the ballooning damages they were legally required to report to shareholders. Even as red ink poured down their balance sheets, none of those major multinationals would name Russia as their abuser. It was as if the companies were politely backing away from the messy melee of geopolitical conflicts, or, perhaps more likely,

---

* In late 2018, this claim that NotPetya didn't rise to the level of an act of war would be formally disputed by an unexpected victim of the worm's damage: an insurance company. When food producer Mondelēz filed for a $100 million payout from Zurich Insurance Group for its NotPetya damages, the insurer rejected its claim, citing a fine-print provision that its insurance didn't cover any "hostile or warlike act" by a "government or sovereign power." Mondelēz sued, and as of this writing the case is ongoing.

trying to avoid fanning the flames of a story they feared would draw attention to their cybersecurity vulnerabilities.*

In fact, the evidence of Russia's responsibility was already clear enough for me. Anton Cherepanov at ESET had published his analysis of the meshed lines of forensic clues showing that Sandworm was very likely behind NotPetya. Reams of other public reporting showed that the same group was responsible for the escalating cyberwar in Ukraine, including its two blackouts, all signs pointing to the Kremlin's culpability.

The Western world's apathy as those earlier sabotage operations homed in on Ukraine had seemed rational, if cruelly self-interested. Now, somehow, the same countries were turning a blind eye to an attack that had materialized with epic effects on their own soil.

That seeming indifference, particularly on the part of the United States, was maddening. Was President Trump's unwillingness to acknowledge the Russian hacking that had aided his campaign now extending to *all* Russian hacking, no matter how destructive? Or was his administration simply incompetent or misinformed? "They've never even *named the actor,*" Rob Lee told me in late 2017, marveling at the government's continued nonresponse to Sandworm's provocations.

"NotPetya tested the red lines of the West, and the result of the test was that there are no red lines yet," Johns Hopkins's Thomas Rid said. "The lack of any proper response is almost an invitation to escalate more."

■

Finally, in January 2018, the first cracks in that wall of silence began to appear. Ellen Nakashima, the veteran intelligence agency reporter

* Learning the details of those attacks, such as those I included in the previous chapters of this book, would instead require months of anonymous, back-channel conversations with current and former staff at victim companies like Maersk, many of whom were terrified of having their careers ruined if superiors learned they were talking to a reporter about NotPetya's effects.

at *The Washington Post* who had first broken the news of the Democratic National Committee breach, published a brief story of just 424 words. It had the headline "Russian Military Was Behind 'NotPetya' Cyberattack in Ukraine, CIA Concludes." The story cited unnamed U.S. intelligence officials who had seen a CIA report from the previous November that asserted with "high confidence" that Russian military hackers had created NotPetya. Such a statement from an intelligence agency like the CIA would carry even more meaning than a similar finding from a private intelligence firm like CrowdStrike or FireEye. The CIA, like the NSA, has unique abilities to penetrate to the source of a cyberattack with human and digital spying techniques that would be illegal for practically anyone else.

Nakashima's report didn't merely suggest that the U.S. government strongly believed the Russian state was behind the attack. It also went on to name the exact organization NotPetya's programmers worked for: the Main Center for Special Technology, or GTsST, a part of Russia's military spy agency known as the Main Intelligence Directorate, or Glavnoye Razvedyvatel'noye Upravleniye, commonly referred to by its Russian acronym. The GRU.

Suddenly anonymous government sources were not only holding Russia accountable but pointing to an answer—albeit without any explanation—to the larger mystery of Sandworm's identity. That answer, that the GRU was responsible for NotPetya and, by inference, that the years-long campaign of escalating attacks on Ukraine fell under the auspices of the GRU, too, was simultaneously a major revelation and not entirely surprising. The GRU was, after all, the same agency whose Fancy Bear hackers had already been revealed as the chief meddlers in both the 2016 U.S. presidential election and the 2014 Ukrainian presidential election—the latter under the guise of the hacktivist group CyberBerkut. The notion that Sandworm, the ultimate crosser of cyberwar's red lines, was part of the same institution responsible for those other reckless, norm-breaking attempts to sabotage democracy seemed to fit.

I had, in fact, heard hints of Sandworm's connection to the GRU's Fancy Bear hackers before. A year earlier, I'd been sitting with John Hultquist on the lawn of a hotel on the eastern shore of the Caribbean island of St. Martin. We were eating lunch during a break from the Security Analyst Summit run by the Russian security firm Kaspersky. I started quizzing Hultquist about his favorite topic, the hacker group he'd helped to discover and name and who had only months earlier taken down a Ukrainian power grid for the second time.

"This is just rumint," he'd prefaced his answer, lowering his voice. ("Rumint" is a half-joking piece of intelligence community jargon: Just as "sigint" refers to intelligence collected from intercepted signals and "humint" is intelligence gathered from human sources, "rumint" means clues gleaned from the intelligence community grapevine—in other words, unsubstantiated gossip.)

Sandworm and Fancy Bear, Hultquist said he'd been told by well-placed sources, were one and the same. "I've even heard people use the names interchangeably," he'd said with a raised eyebrow. I'd responded, confused, that the two groups seemed to have distinct tool sets, missions, and even personalities—that Sandworm focused on sophisticated infrastructure disruption while Fancy Bear practiced noisy, more basic hacking operations like political leaks and smear campaigns.

Hultquist had shrugged, seeming as puzzled as I was. His rumint went that far, and no further.

Now the *Washington Post* story seemed to offer one way to interpret his tip: Sandworm and Fancy Bear were both hacker teams within the GRU. Maybe Hultquist's government contacts simply hadn't bothered to differentiate between them, painting both hyperaggressive GRU operations with the same broad brush.

In the months that followed the *Post*'s story, I at one point met with a pair of officials at the SBU, Ukraine's main intelligence agency, in a closed-curtained conference room in central Kiev. When I asked them about the attacks attributed to Sandworm, they made exactly the same confusing claim that I'd heard in Hultquist's rumint. "Different factors allow us to agree with our American colleagues that this is a group called Fancy Bear," an SBU analyst named Matviy Mykhailov told me, again lumping Sandworm in with what I had thought was a distinct hacker entity. "The GRU is probably behind the disruptive attacks on Ukrainian infrastructure."

An older, more cautious lawyer colleague sitting next to Mykhailov raised a finger. "Maybe," he added in English. (When I mentioned that strange conversation to the Russia-watcher Mark Galeotti at the Institute of International Relations, he said intelligence sources had told him that Sandworm was GRU in less uncertain terms. "A conversation with no lawyers and with alcohol tends to lead to more candid discussion," he said.)

The clues were jumbled and incomplete. But by the beginning of 2018, they were adding up to something remarkable: A single agency within the Russian government was responsible for at least three of the most brazen hacking milestones in history, all in just the past three years. The GRU, it now seemed, had masterminded the first-ever hacker-induced blackouts, the plot to interfere in a U.S. presidential election, and the most destructive cyberweapon ever released. A larger question now began to loom in my mind: Who are the GRU?

31

DEFECTORS

For most of the hundred years since the GRU's founding in the early days of the Soviet Union, the institution has been almost entirely shrouded in mystery. The agency didn't merely hide its goals, its tactics and tools, or its organizational structure. For decades, it hid the very fact of its existence.

The GRU was created by Lenin in 1918—and initially called the Registration Directorate, or RU—both to serve as the eyes and ears of the Red Army and to balance the power of the dreaded KGB, then known as the Cheka. The military spy agency's mission, unlike the KGB's, was assigned to foreign operations and didn't share in the surveillance and elimination of domestic enemies that gave the KGB its terrifying reputation. That foreign focus meant that the GRU never needed to instill fear in Soviet subjects, as the KGB did. It didn't advertise its insidious power with a grand headquarters on a central square in Moscow. Nor did it ever take the public blame for internal purges, repressions, and mass executions when the Communist Party needed a scapegoat for those atrocities, as when Khrushchev blamed the wanton political massacres known as the Great Terror on the KGB.

For most of its long, obscure history, that discipline of institutional secrecy had its intended effect: Even as the GRU wielded several times the budget and manpower of the KGB in its foreign spying and sabotage operations—and even as it outlived the KGB, which was officially dissolved after the Soviet Union's collapse—the GRU's name was for decades only rarely written or spoken in public. It operated quietly, little known to Soviet or Russian citizens and less known still in the foreign countries where it stealthily carried out its work.

Most of what the world does know about the history of the GRU and the people inside it comes from its rare defectors and moles. And the GRU has minimized those leaks by imposing legendarily severe consequences on anyone who dared betray it. Vladimir Rezun, a GRU captain who did successfully defect in 1978, wrote in his memoir how, on the first day of his training at the agency, he was shown a video of a turncoat colonel who was bound to a stretcher with wire and then pushed into a fire, cremated alive. On another occasion, he writes, he was told by a superior that a disloyal agent had been placed alive in a coffin and buried.

Neither of those horror stories has been independently confirmed. Instead, the West's first publicly recorded story of an ill-fated GRU source was that of Pyotr Popov, a young lieutenant colonel stationed in Vienna. In 1953, Popov dropped a note into the parked car of a U.S. diplomat offering to serve as an American spy inside the GRU. The twenty-nine-year-old had grown up the son of poor farmers in the northern region of the Volga River and had never forgiven Stalin's regime for its brutalization of the peasant class, which in the 1930s had devastated some regions of Russia just as thoroughly as it had Ukraine.

Over the next six years, as he worked to recruit Soviet agents in Vienna and then Berlin, Popov also met with the CIA and identified nearly the entire GRU command structure, including more than 650 GRU officers. Then, in 1959, after a botched operation escorting a Soviet spy flying out of Berlin, Popov was investigated by Russian authorities who promptly arrested him, briefly turned him into a double agent, and then shot him.

Popov's role as a top GRU leaker for Western intelligence was quickly replaced by a far more valuable source: Oleg Penkovsky. The GRU colonel, code-named HERO by the CIA, would become one of the highest-ranking and most prolific moles in the history of the Cold War. Like Popov, Penkovsky had deep resentment for the Soviet regime rooted in historical grievances: His father had been killed in a siege during Russia's civil war while serving in the tsarist White Russian army, and he felt that his own advancement in the Soviet military was stymied by that family history. He also hoped to make enough money with his secret betrayal to buy a car and a dacha outside Moscow, to escape the two-room apartment where he lived with three generations of his family, and to someday relocate his family to the West.

Starting in 1961, after contacting U.K. intelligence through a British businessman, he spent eighteen months feeding the British and American governments a steady flow of top secret reports and photographs. He'd pass the materials to officials in London—where he was assigned to carry out industrial espionage for the Soviets—or in meetings in a Moscow park with a British intelligence officer's wife, who hid film canisters inside boxes of candy in her baby carriage.

Those leaks are widely credited with changing the course of history. They included detailed information on the size of the Soviet nuclear arsenal, which the U.S. government had vastly overestimated in its perceived arms race. In 1961, most crucially, Penkovsky provided clues that later allowed the White House to deduce Khrushchev's tactics as the Soviet leader moved to place nuclear missiles in Cuba. By some accounts, it was that warning that allowed President John F. Kennedy to confront Khrushchev and begin negotiations to remove the weapons days before they were operational.

Almost immediately afterward, Penkovsky's treachery was identified by Russian intelligence. He was arrested, repeatedly interrogated, and then executed. Exactly how he was caught has never been revealed.

Penkovsky gave the West an unprecedented understanding of the inner workings of the Soviet military and Khrushchev's strategic thinking. But he also gave his Western handlers, less intentionally, a new sense of the callous, hyperaggressive mind-set of a top-ranking GRU officer.

Penkovsky made that stark impression in his very first meeting with the CIA and the British MI6 in a London hotel. After a break in the interview to eat sandwiches and drink dry German white wine, Penkovsky suggested, without prompting, that he was ready to lead a team that would hand-place small nuclear weapons equivalent to two thousand tons of TNT around the Moscow headquarters of the Soviet military, Communist Party, and KGB. At the Brits' or Americans' command, his team would then blow up all of those buildings, killing the entire senior staff of the U.S.S.R.'s government.

Penkovsky calmly explained that he could help locate similar targets in every major Soviet city, as well as the residential and commercial buildings surrounding them that could serve as hiding places for the atomic weapons. He made no mention of the many thousands of civilians who would die in the explosions and the subsequent radioactive fallout.

Penkovsky's Western interrogators were stunned. According to transcripts of the meeting, they ignored his proposal and continued asking him about Soviet capabilities. But in history's understanding of Soviet military intelligence, Penkovsky's suggestion might have been one of his career's most telling moments: a glimpse of how the GRU's officials perceived new innovations in mass destruction and their willingness to use them.

■

If Popov and Penkovsky served as the best sources of information on the GRU in the windowless back rooms of Western intelligence agencies, Vladimir Rezun would fill that same role for the Western public: the GRU's most prolific storyteller.

In 1978, Rezun defected from his position as a GRU captain, passing a note to the British embassy in Vienna and eventually making his way to London. As he later described it, he had been ordered to betray a friend at the agency and never forgave the Soviet system that had forced him to make that decision. In his new life, he became a remarkably prolific writer of tell-all accounts of his time in Soviet intelligence—though with most of their truly valuable secrets removed or obscured, and other details fabricated or exaggerated, some intelligence experts warn. His most revelatory books, written under the pen name Viktor Suvorov, include *Inside Soviet Military Intelligence* (which he dedicated to Oleg Penkovsky) and a memoir called *Inside the Aquarium,* a reference to the glass-encased, nine-story building on Moscow's Khodinka airfield that once served as GRU headquarters.

In those books, Rezun tells his own personal story of being plucked from his low-ranking position as a tank company commander and groomed for the GRU. He describes a weeklong entrance exam that consisted of thousands of questions for seventeen-hour days, sometimes without food or water, and his rise through the agency from a lowly "borzoi" tasked with supporting other officers to a "viking," an accomplished spy running his own informants. Rezun went on to detail the daily work of recruiting Western civilians as sources and searching out and cataloging "dead drops," secret locations where information could be hidden and picked up by other agents, sometimes in compartments stashed underground, underwater, or posing as tiny mundane objects like false rivets on a bridge's supports.

According to Rezun, practically any technology expo or conference was swarming with GRU agents, who saw the events as bonanzas for acquiring sources for industrial espionage. Space, too, was the GRU's domain: He writes that a third of all Soviet satellites were used by the GRU, and the "vast majority" of cosmonauts devoted roughly half their time to the GRU's spying tasks. Rezun's own innovation, as he tells it, was to come up with the idea of buying a series of hotels in Europe that were entirely controlled by the GRU, designed to attract Western officials taking alpine vacations and target them as potential sources.

But Rezun's account of the GRU isn't limited to mere espionage. He also spent a short stint in the special forces branch of the agency known as *spetsnaz*, devoted to sabotage, assassination, and terrorism. Each of the Soviet armed forces' fifty or so intelligence departments included such a subgroup, he says. "This company, which numbers 115 saboteurs and cut-throats, is capable of penetrating into the enemy's territory to murder and kidnap people, blow up bridges, electric power stations, dams, oil pipelines and so on," Rezun wrote.

He describes how those special forces parachuted behind enemy lines wearing oxhide "jump boots" with soles designed for deception: Depending on their mission, the interchangeable soles' patterns could be designed to mimic those of an adversary or another nation. In some cases, he wrote, they wore boots that left footprints with the heel in front and the toe behind, so that they appeared to be traveling in the opposite direction, each member of the group stepping in the others' prints to conceal their numbers.

Some of the more sensational details Rezun described of the *spetsnaz*'s practices seem to blur the line between fact and red-scare fiction. He describes how the soldiers would hone their hand-to-hand combat skills by fighting "puppets"—desperate inmates from Soviet prisons condemned to death. (While that description has been disputed, an Amnesty International report in 1996 noted that *spetsnaz* were indeed authorized to use prisoners in their training, many of whom were tortured or mistreated in the process.) He went further in another, questionably accurate book titled *Spetsnaz.* In that volume, he claims that in addition to plastic explosives, mines, and other typical saboteur tools the special forces carried chemical and biological weapons, as well as small nuclear weapons with a charge equal to about two kilotons of TNT, the same size of atomic bomb as Oleg Penkovsky had suggested be planted in the center of Moscow.

As dubious as Rezun's descriptions of those mass-destruction weapons may be, another GRU defector would repeat them in even more shocking terms a decade later. Stanislav Lunev, a GRU colonel who defected to the United States in 1992, would write his own tell-all memoir, titled *Through the Eyes of the Enemy.* In that slim volume, Lunev, who said he was disaffected with the corruption of the Russian government after the collapse of the U.S.S.R., didn't merely double down on Rezun's claims of the GRU's massive sabotage plots. He also claimed that Russia and the GRU had only advanced them in the post-Soviet era.

Lunev's book stated that GRU agents had, in fact, *already* planted suitcase-sized nuclear weapons on American soil, ready to be set off in the event of war. More speculatively, he argued that Russian military agents were also prepared to poison the water supplies of American cities with chemical and biological weapons. "One likely target would be the Potomac River, targeting the residents of Washington, DC," he wrote. "Small amounts of the weapons would cause minor epidemics. Large amounts could have unimaginable deadly impact."

After congressional hearings on that suitcase scare, Lunev's nuke claims would be partially discredited when the FBI told Congressman Curt Weldon in 2001 that Lunev had exaggerated the threat. But other Soviet defectors confirmed that the U.S.S.R. had indeed manufactured small, tactical nuclear weapons roughly in line with Lunev's descriptions and that Russia had continued to plan for the release of biological weapons in the United States in the event of a full-scale war.

Lunev's broader claims of wide-scale sabotage preparations, like many of Rezun's, may never be confirmed or proven false; the GRU was, after all, designed from its earliest inception to elude that sort of certainty about its practices. But in Lunev's book, he does provide a passage that seems to offer one of the clearest possible views inside the minds of the GRU saboteurs who would carry out similar attacks on every level of their enemies' civilian society, via the internet, two decades later. "It should not be shocking that *Spetznatz* would infiltrate America," he wrote.

> It is simply good military practice. War is war. It sounds simple, but many Americans seem to believe that there should be a gentlemen's code, that war should be fought by soldiers in remote battlefields. Americans believe that war should be sterile, because it has never hit their home soil since the Civil War of 130 years ago, and even then, only in the south-eastern part of the country. Russia has been rampaged for centuries by every would-be world conqueror. Millions of Russians have died on their homeland during wars. This is a feeling Americans do not know. The only way you get an enemy to submit is by bringing the war to its people.

■

There exists no Rezun or Lunev for today's GRU. The last high-ranking GRU defector known to the public is Sergei Skripal, a former paratrooper who reached the rank of colonel before secretly beginning to work for Britain's MI6 in 1996. He met with his U.K. handlers secretly in Italy, Malta, Portugal, and Turkey and at one point wrote notes in invisible ink in the margins of a novel his wife passed to agents in Spain. Skripal knew few operational details but would outline the GRU's structure for British intelligence and name hundreds of GRU agents. By most accounts, he remained a Russian patriot; he simply betrayed his colleagues for the money.

In 2004, Skripal was arrested by the FSB, the successor to the KGB focused on domestic affairs. He spent six years in prison before being released as part of an international spy swap. Reporting by the BBC would later suggest that he quietly continued to act as a source to Western intelligence agencies for years to come.

Then, in early March 2018, Skripal and his thirty-three-year-old daughter, Yulia, were found on a bench in Salisbury, the town eighty miles southwest of London where he had moved since his defection. The father and daughter were both semiconscious, convulsing, frothing at the mouth, and struggling to breathe.

In the months that followed, a pair of GRU agents were revealed to have traveled to Salisbury and poisoned the Skripals with a deadly nerve agent known as Novichok, designed to cause paralysis and suffocation. The highly potent poison had been sprayed on the front door of Skripal's house, and traces of the toxin also appeared at two restaurants he and his daughter had visited.

Both Yulia and Sergei Skripal were admitted to a nearby hospital and spent months in recovery, narrowly escaping death.* But the message had been sent, to Skripal and to any other would-be memoirist of Russia's modern military intelligence agency: This is what happens to those who spill secrets.

When the Skripal poisoning hit the news, I was in the last stages of reading a small mountain of biographies and autobiographies of past GRU defectors, working my way through the agency's history toward its present. But Skripal's case made it clear: If I was going to learn more about the same institution today, it wouldn't be by reading tell-all books. It would be by piecing together hints and glimpses of the truth, to find my own path in the dark.

---

* Tragically, two British citizens were hospitalized months later with the same symptoms as the Skripals, seemingly after picking up a bottle of the Novichok nerve agent discarded by Skripal's would-be assassins. One of them, forty-four-year-old Dawn Sturgess, died nine days later.

32

INFORMATSIONNOYE PROTIVOBORSTVO

For all its defectors' menacing talk of sabotaging infrastructure far behind enemy lines, tactical nukes, and chemical weapons, the GRU seems to have arrived late to the notion that the internet might be the vehicle for a new breed of unconventional weaponry. In my conversations with the rare sources I could find who had actually spoken to recent Russian intelligence insiders, no one could point to much evidence that the GRU had been involved in Russia's earliest, primitive experiments in cyberwar or even basic cyberespionage, from Moonlight Maze to the blitz of the Estonian web.

It was, after all, the KGB, not the GRU, who had hired the West German freelance hackers who invented state-sponsored hacking in the 1980s, as told in Cliff Stoll's *Cuckoo's Egg*. Andrei Soldatov, one of the few Russian journalists and authors who has spent years investigating Russian intelligence agencies, told me that in the 1990s era of Russian cyberspying, Kremlin hacking and cybersecurity were dominated by an agency called FAPSI—the Federal Agency of Government Communications and Information—that acted as Russia's equivalent of the NSA.

In 2003, FAPSI was cannibalized by its intelligence siblings, with most of its key roles falling to the FSB, one of several agencies created from the remains of the KGB. The result, as Soldatov described it, was that the FSB took over most of the Kremlin's state-sponsored hacking for the rest of that decade. "When FAPSI merged with the FSB, they were put in charge," he told me when I interviewed him in a hotel bar before his talk at PutinCon, a New York conference devoted to hosting the Russian president's most outspoken critics. "On all levels, they defined the rules." That hierarchy meant that the GRU had taken a backseat to the FSB throughout Russia's inchoate cyberwars in Estonia and Georgia, relegated to traditional intelligence in direct support of the military rather than the exciting new realm of digital offensive operations.*

But the 2008 war in Georgia was a turning point for the GRU: It was, in the eyes of the Kremlin, considered evidence of the agency's unforgivable incompetence. While Russia had dominated the Georgian conflict, and the GRU's *spetsnaz* forces had by all accounts performed well in it, the agency's faulty intelligence had also led to embarrassments like bombing already-abandoned Georgian airstrips. The GRU's spies had missed that the Georgians possessed anti-aircraft missiles that threatened Russian air force operations. Attempts to intercept Georgian communications had failed. Moscow came to see the GRU as too obsessed with its *spetsnaz*-style run-and-gun raids and not focused enough on subtler espionage and influence operations.

The result, in the vicious environment of Russian interagency backstabbing, was that the GRU was stripped of its responsibilities and humiliated. Russia's then president, Dmitry Medvedev, handed many of its intelligence duties to the FSB and the foreign intelligence service known as the SVR. A thousand GRU officers were cut or reassigned, along with almost the entire *spetsnaz*, who were moved to another branch of military control.

The Kremlin considered a bureaucratic demotion that would have altogether deprived the agency of direct contact with President Medvedev and the source of all real power, Putin. (The GRU was even threatened with removal of its *G,* making it simply *an* intelligence directorate rather than the "main" one. Instead, it would strangely be renamed the Main Directorate, or GU, though most in the West

---

* One clue does hint at the GRU's involvement in the Georgian cyberattacks: The website StopGeorgia.ru, which seemed designed to recruit and equip hacktivists to participate in those attacks, was hosted by a company called SteadyHost, which was headquartered next door to a known GRU research institute in Moscow.

continue to call it by its better-known three-letter name.) Even the emblem for the agency, a menacing black bat with its wings looming over a globe, was replaced with a far less fearsome image of a flower. "This, to me, was also meant to be a kind of insult," Soldatov said.

But the GRU, unlike the FAPSI before it, wasn't destroyed. Instead, it was in the resulting period of reform and mutation that the contemporary GRU was born.

Much of the interagency conflict that shaped that resurrection remains entirely hidden from outside observers. "It's like watching bulldogs fighting under a rug," said Keir Giles, a Russia-watcher for the British think tank Chatham House and a former consultant at the U.K. Defence Academy. "You just wait and see which one comes out on top."

The GRU's makeover benefited from two personnel changes over the next years: First came the firing of the agency's director, Valentin Korabelnikov, who had "seemed more comfortable accompanying Spetsnaz assassination teams in Chechnya than playing palace politics in Moscow," as Mark Galeotti wrote in *Foreign Policy*. Korabelnikov was eventually replaced in 2011 by Igor Sergun, who had both a closer relationship to Putin and far more talent at navigating the Kremlin's treacherous maze. Then came a new minister of defense in 2012, Sergey Shoygu, who supported the GRU's reemerging role as the tip of the spear of the Russian armed forces.

Beneath its cover of secrecy, meanwhile, the GRU began the process of reinventing itself as the most aggressive hacking agency in the Russian government—or perhaps the world. "They were in the doldrums, trying not to be demoted," said Galeotti, who has spent thirty years talking to Russian intelligence insiders, initially as a staffer at the U.K. Foreign Office, and has written more in the public record about the modern GRU than perhaps any other analyst. "From 2008 to 2014, the GRU was trying to re-demonstrate its role and value to the Kremlin. One way was getting more serious about cyber."

As it sought to reshape itself, according to Galeotti, the recent Georgian cyberwar gave the agency a rough model. "That's when the GRU said 'aha,'" Galeotti said. "Something as simple as knocking down and defacing websites can make a difference in war." (In

2010, Stuxnet would demonstrate a vastly more powerful model of cyberwarfare, but one that seemed to remain beyond the GRU's technological capabilities for years to come.)

No one I asked could tell me the internal details of the GRU's metamorphosis. But the timing of those changes struck me as more than a coincidence: The years aligned roughly with the timeline of the Sandworm attacks that John Hultquist's team at iSight Partners had discovered, from the hackers' first known breaches in 2009 to its emergence as a uniquely dangerous, critical-infrastructure-focused operation in 2014.

By the time Russia invaded Ukraine that same year, the GRU's revival was evident. The takeover of Crimea had been based on a plan derived largely from GRU intelligence. It was the GRU that led the invasion of "little green men" that armed and incited pro-Russian separatists in eastern Ukraine.* And unbeknownst to the world, the agency was already secretly laying the groundwork for a kind of cyberwar the internet had never before seen.

The new incarnation of Russia's hundred-year-old military intelligence agency had "shown the rest of the world how Russia expects to fight its future wars: with a mix of stealth, deniability, subversion, and surgical violence," Galeotti wrote in July of that year. "The GRU is back in the global spook game and with a new playbook that will be a challenge for the West for years to come."

■

None of this history, though, answered my underlying question: What was Sandworm thinking? What motivates cyberwar without limits, without discrimination between soldier and civilian?

One more recent document seemed to offer a keyhole view into

---

* In the spring of 2018, the investigative news outlet *Bellingcat* and the Russian news site *The Insider* would also name two GRU officers as responsible for the downing of Malaysian Airlines flight MH17, which resulted in 298 civilian deaths. In the following months, the same investigators would also name three GRU agents as the assassins responsible for the attempted murder of Sergei Skripal.

the thinking of the Russian military and its understanding of that distinction. In 2013, the Russian-language journal *Voenno-Promyshlennyi Kur'er,* or *Military-Industrial Courier,* had published a two-thousand-word article with an absurdly dry title: "The Value of Science in Prediction." It was based on a speech given by the chief of the General Staff of the Russian military, General Valery Gerasimov. The article was little noticed in the West, but Mark Galeotti published a translation in his blog a year later.

"In the 21st century we have seen a tendency toward blurring the lines between the states of war and peace," the article began. "Wars are no longer declared and, having begun, proceed according to an unfamiliar template."

> New information technologies have enabled significant reductions in the spatial, temporal, and informational gaps between forces and control organs. Frontal engagements of large formations of forces at the strategic and operational level are gradually becoming a thing of the past. Long-distance, contactless actions against the enemy are becoming the main means of achieving combat and operational goals. The defeat of the enemy's objectives is conducted throughout the entire depth of his territory.

A graphic published with the article succinctly listed the "new forms and methods" of war as bullet points. They included:

- "Reduction of the military-economic potential of the state by the destruction of critically important facilities of its military and civilian infrastructure in a short time."
- "Warfare simultaneously in all physical environments and the information space."
- "The use of asymmetric and indirect operations."

As the prime example of this new form of war, Gerasimov had pointed to the Arab Spring revolutions across North Africa, arguing they showed how external political factors could weaken or destroy a regime. That part of his analysis reflected the dubious conspiracy theory—no doubt commonly held within the Kremlin—that the uprisings in Tunisia, Egypt, and Libya had all somehow been secretly fomented by Western governments.

But as Galeotti wrote in his commentary on the Gerasimov article, the Arab Spring comparisons seemed to be only a pretense to talk about how Russia itself could weaken or destroy its own enemies. And the way to do that, Gerasimov argued, was with nontraditional, asymmetric, covert attacks on the pillars of their social stability, often by means of what he called *informatsionnoye protivoborstvo,* or "informational confrontation."

When Galeotti published his take on Gerasimov's speech in July 2014, titling his post "The 'Gerasimov Doctrine' and Russian Non-linear War," he saw in the speech a prescient explanation of the strategy Russia had already used in the earliest months of its Ukrainian invasion. Even before any signs of a cyberwar had come to light, Russia was secreting troops across the border out of uniform, flooding the Ukrainian media with disinformation, and exploiting internal instabilities.

But when the GRU's meddling in the U.S. presidential election emerged two years later, it suddenly seemed to suggest an even more far-reaching and insidious example of the ideas Gerasimov described, now put into practice. As the frenzy around Russia's election-related hacking grew in late 2016 and 2017, the Gerasimov Doctrine began to be referred to in mainstream Western media as the key to understanding all Russian warfare. The notion was repeated widely enough that Galeotti himself felt the need to step back from it, pointing out that Gerasimov had hardly been the first to suggest waging hybrid wars that extended past the traditional military front—the Georgian war offered a clear example five years earlier—and that his "Gerasimov Doctrine" wasn't even a formal or comprehensive doctrine so much as a momentary peek into the evolution of Russian military thinking.

But in early 2018, after Sandworm had been connected directly to the Russian military, I couldn't help but see how Gerasimov's ideas explained Sandworm's actions, too. The "informational confrontation" Gerasimov suggested wasn't necessarily limited to disinformation or propaganda. In fact, both Galeotti and Giles emphasized to me that there is no distinction in common Russian vocabulary between "information war" and a concept of "cyberwar" that suggests disruptive or physical consequences of hacking. Both fall under the same term, *informatsionnaya voyna*. "Whether it's to change someone's mind or achieve a physical effect, it's the same thing," Giles said.

The "long-distance, contactless actions" against enemy targets "throughout the entire depth of his territory" that Gerasimov described matched Sandworm's modus operandi perfectly, from blackouts to NotPetya. Sandworm was not some aberrant or rogue element in the Russian armed forces. It was a direct expression of the strategy of its most senior leaders.

■

If the vague outline of the GRU and Russian military thinking was tough to discern at the official level, it was far harder still to get inside the mind of its rank and file. When I asked Galeotti and Soldatov about the psychological profile of the average GRU hacker, they both started with a simple answer: They're following orders.

The FSB, as Galeotti explained, had notoriously mixed its staff's hackers with recruited cybercriminals, often forcing them to cooperate to avoid prison. When the GRU began building its own hacking operations in 2008, Galeotti says it instead went through the far slower but more reliable process of recruiting its hackers at the age of eighteen or nineteen and then training them, as it would any soldier.

On the most prosaic level, that meant GRU hackers were more likely to wear a uniform and to work in actual GRU buildings, compared with other Russian agencies' hackers. But that soldier mentality also meant GRU hackers had fewer qualms about carrying out high-risk or even highly destructive campaigns, Galeotti said. The agency maintains a macho, military culture that rewards risk taking, even to the point of shortsightedness. "They're more likely to be promoted because they gave something a try, even if it didn't work, than because they're a pair of safe hands," Galeotti told me. "If you prove you're aggressive and effective, bosses will smile on that."

Despite many *spetsnaz* having been moved out from under GRU control years earlier, it still served as the home of special-ops killers and saboteurs, Galeotti reminded me, and that spirit infected the entire agency. "The defense attaché and the commando who goes behind enemy lines to blow up bridges and assassinate people are in the same organization," he told me. "Sometimes they're the same person. At the very least, they feel an association."

Much of the rank-and-file GRU mentality, as the Russia-watchers I spoke to described it, seemed also to line up with Gerasimov's cynicism, the same conspiracy theorizing that led him to believe the West had incited the Arab Spring. Ukraine's sovereignty, many Russian soldiers held, was entirely a creation of the West, its recent revolutions just more U.S.-triggered coups. Attacking the pseudo-nation of Ukraine was not only an expedient task to please their superiors but a patriotic duty in an ongoing, undeclared second cold war with Europe and the United States.

That stereotypical portraiture of a GRU hacker, however, was far from universal, Soldatov warned me. Some, contrary to Galeotti's description, are in fact outside contractors and freelancers from the private sector, conscripted for their services with little choice in the matter.

For those secondary players in the GRU's orbit, their personal motivation is different. Refuse to lend your services as a researcher, as a developer, or even as an operational hacker, and you could face the destruction of your business, your career, or worse. "People disguise fear with many things: with patriotism, with cynicism," Soldatov told me. "But when you talk to people, you see that fear plays a big part. You scratch them, and under the surface you see fear."

33

THE PENALTY

One afternoon in February 2018, the Trump White House released an extremely short, straightforward statement:

> In June 2017, the Russian military launched the most destructive and costly cyber-attack in history.
>
> The attack, dubbed "NotPetya," quickly spread worldwide, causing billions of dollars in damage across Europe, Asia, and the Americas. It was part of the Kremlin's ongoing effort to destabilize Ukraine and demonstrates ever more clearly Russia's involvement in the ongoing conflict. This was also a reckless and indiscriminate cyber-attack that will be met with international consequences.

With those four sentences displayed on a page of the White House website, the U.S. government had finally, publicly acknowledged Russia's cyberwar in Ukraine. That acknowledgment had come nearly three and a half years after the siege had begun and almost eight months after it exploded out to the rest of the world.

The announcement seemed belated even on the timescale of that day: The British intelligence agency GCHQ had published its own statement pinning NotPetya on Russia earlier that morning, pre-empting the White House. But after the U.S. statement in the late afternoon, intelligence agencies from Canada, Australia, and New Zealand would all follow with their own confirmations. By that night, all of the so-called Five Eyes—the loosely allied agencies of those five English-speaking countries—had assembled a rare, joint set of confirmations tying NotPetya to Russia and condemning the attack, intended to leave no room for doubt of their findings.

The Kremlin, of course, denied them anyway. "We strongly reject such accusations, we consider them to be groundless, they are part of the similarly groundless campaign based on hatred against Russia," Putin's spokesperson Dmitry Peskov told reporters in Moscow.

The White House would never publicly back up its statement with evidence. But it had promised consequences, and a month later those consequences arrived: The U.S. Treasury announced new sanctions against nineteen people and five organizations. Most of the named individuals, however, seemed to have nothing to do with NotPetya. The listed culprits were lumped together in a broad collection of Russian misbehavior, largely still focused on interference in the 2016 election. They included a dozen staffers at the Internet Research Agency, the St. Petersburg–based institution that had paid civilian workers to flood social media with divisive and pro-Trump content, as well as a consultant firm and a catering company linked to that business. But they also named the GRU and its director, Igor Korobov, along with three deputy chiefs of the agency. While those GRU officers had already been listed in Obama's earlier sanctions, the new list included one deputy chief who hadn't been sanctioned before, as well as the head of the GRU's training academy.

Like most sanctions, the punishment was purely financial. But it would have a personal impact on its targets nonetheless. For those named, living a life divorced from interaction with all American companies—and any other businesses that want to remain friendly with the United States—wouldn't be easy, the Center for Strategic and International Studies' Russia-watcher James Lewis told me at the time. "It makes you sort of an outcast on Wall Street," Lewis said. "You're going to take a vacation to Hungary and present them with a Russian credit card? What's a Russian credit card? You're cutting these people off from the American economy, and that has a global effect."

After all of its denials of Russian hacking, the Trump administration seemed to have realized, with glacial timing, that it could no longer ignore the Kremlin's escalating digital rampages. "Hard as it may be to believe, it looks like the White House attitude towards Russia is hardening," Lewis said.

In a phone call with reporters on the day the sanctions were announced, President Trump's homeland security adviser, Tom Bossert, made clear that it was in fact NotPetya that had most required redress—that it had violated a red line, spoken or unspoken, around how the United States expects fellow countries to behave on the internet. "The United States thinks any malware that propagates recklessly, without bounds, violates every standard and expectation of proportionality and discrimination. Truly responsible nations don't behave this way," Bossert said on the call. "We have an additional expectation that tools like NotPetya not be used in a reckless fashion, causing $10 billion or more in damage across the globe, not only in Europe but in the United States."

With that day's sanctions, Bossert said, the U.S. government meant to leave no doubt about the contours of that red line. "We've made clear the rule," Bossert added. "We've started to make clear the penalty associated with that rule."

■

The rebuke to Russia from the White House struck an optimistic note for anyone who hoped to prevent the full-scale cyberwars of the future: Finally, the worst cyberattack in history had earned *some* sort of response, rather than the sheer impunity that had seemed to shield Sandworm's actions for years.

But it was shaded by another, simultaneous note of menace: In an announcement made on the same day as the sanctions, the FBI and the DHS also confirmed that Russian hackers had, starting in 2016, targeted a wide range of American critical infrastructure targets, including water and energy utilities, some of which were nuclear power plants. And unlike in previous warnings about that targeting, like Sandworm's initial breaches of U.S. utilities in 2014, these hackers had dug in deep.

In a handful of cases—thankfully not in nuclear facilities—the intruders had penetrated beyond the utilities' traditional IT networks and into their industrial control systems. They hadn't crossed the line of causing actual disruptions to physical equipment. But they had gained enough access to that equipment's controls that they could have started to manipulate it at will. Months later, Secretary of Homeland Security Kirstjen Nielsen would explain that the operation seemed like reconnaissance—what she described as an attempt to "prep the battlefield."

By all accounts, these hackers were distinct from Sandworm. As far as security researchers could tell, the new group used none of Sandworm's unique tools, techniques, or infrastructure. The security firm Symantec had first detailed their attacks in a report six months earlier and attributed the intrusions to a group it called Dragonfly 2.0, without naming any nation where the hackers might be based. But Symantec did note that never before had anyone found evidence of such deep penetrations into utilities' networks—except in Ukraine's two blackouts.

"There's a difference between being a step away from conducting sabotage and actually . . . being able to flip the switch on power generation," Eric Chien, a Symantec security analyst, had told me at the time. "We're now talking about on-the-ground technical evidence this could happen in the U.S., and there's nothing left standing in the way except the motivation of some actor out in the world."

Now, in March 2018, the U.S. government was confirming what everyone had suspected: that the actor with its fingers on that switch was Russia, the only nation whose hackers had dared to turn off the power to civilians before. Even as the world was waking up to Sandworm's threat, the group's experiments in societal sabotage seemed to be metastasizing out to other Russian hackers' operations—and to new victims.

BAD RABBIT, OLYMPIC DESTROYER

The attribution of NotPetya to the Russian military was the strongest confirmation yet of Sandworm's GRU identity. But just as that identity seemed to be coming into focus in the first months of 2018, two strange events clouded the picture, each of which seemed intuitively linked to the hacker group's trail of disruption. And yet they included mysterious aberrations from Sandworm's profile, breaking any clean mental model that I had tried to use to make sense of its actions.

The first had come as a kind of NotPetya aftershock. Early on the morning of October 24, 2017, ESET's Anton Cherepanov was sitting in the same seat in the same Houston room of ESET's headquarters when he once again began to receive screenshots of ransomware messages taken from the security company's eastern European customers. This time those messages had the unexplained words "BAD RABBIT" displayed above their demand that victims make a Bitcoin payment to decrypt their files. Once again, the malware was spreading quickly through Ukrainian networks. Soon it had hit Odessa's airport and the Kiev metro, again paralyzing the transit system's credit card payments.

Cherepanov would describe the feeling as a kind of déjà vu. Just as he had done with NotPetya four months earlier, Cherepanov dug up a fresh sample of the malware from ESET's antivirus collection and began to take its code apart. He quickly found that, as before, the malware used Mimikatz and a leaked NSA technique to branch out its infections from machine to machine. But surprisingly, it didn't include the EternalBlue code used in NotPetya. Instead, it used only the EternalRomance program from the NSA's leaked tool set, which targeted older versions of Windows, along with a custom-coded mechanism that cycled through a collection of common passwords as it attempted to spread via the same computer-to-computer communications feature of Windows that those NSA hacking tools exploited.

Stranger still were the statistics ESET began to pull from the computers around the world that ran its antivirus software. They showed that this time the worm had only encrypted a few hundred machines—a tiny fraction of the destructive results of NotPetya. And weirdest of all, the victims' numbers had flipped: The vast majority of infected computers weren't in Ukraine but in Russia. Fully 65 percent of the victims that ESET detected were Russian, compared with just a little over 12 percent in Ukraine.

As ESET and analysts at the Russian security firm Kaspersky analyzed the source of the Bad Rabbit malware (as they'd immediately named it), they found that it had spread via a so-called watering hole attack, the technique of hacking certain websites to infect those sites' visitors. The hackers had broken into a series of news sites in Russia, Ukraine, Bulgaria, and Turkey and planted code on their pages that asked visitors to install a fake Flash software update containing the ransomware. That technique seemed crude and sloppy compared with the powerful, Ukraine-focused backdoor that had carried NotPetya's payload.

But there was little doubt that Bad Rabbit had been released by the same hackers as NotPetya. It contained fully 67 percent of the same code, according to the security firm CrowdStrike. Kaspersky revealed within hours of Bad Rabbit's outbreak that there was stronger proof, still: NotPetya, it turned out, had also been distributed via a watering hole attack in at least one case. Kaspersky had found that the Ukrainian news site Bahmut.com.ua had been hacked and used to deliver NotPetya back on its June 27 trigger date. The company's analysts had then connected that website's breach to a series of attacks on thirty other sites, many of which were now spreading Bad Rabbit. NotPetya's masterminds, it seemed, had been laying the groundwork for their Bad Rabbit follow-up for months.

But why? Even in the fall of 2017, before Sandworm had been officially linked to the Russian military, all signs hinted that the group's hackers were working in the service of the Kremlin. What would motivate Russian government hackers to purposefully infect hundreds of Russian computers with malware?

As Cherepanov and his boss, Robert Lipovsky, puzzled over the incongruent clues, they noted one suspicious element of the Bad Rabbit attack: Exactly how the malware had reached Ukrainian infrastructure like subway and airport networks remained unexplained, but those infections appeared to be highly targeted. Meanwhile, the watering hole attack that had hit Russian computers struck them as far more random.

"It seemed like a smoke screen," Lipovsky told me. "They had targets they wanted to infect. Then they released their malware everywhere else as a distraction."

Lipovsky cautioned that he could only speculate—that Bad Rabbit still defied an intuitive explanation. But his theory implied that the attack had, perhaps, two distinct goals: It had scored one more blow, in passing, against Ukraine's infrastructure. And at the same time, it had created a new layer of confusion for investigators. "It blurs things," Lipovsky told me. "It makes it impossible to attribute the attack based on the targeted country."

Was the GRU really so callous as to randomly destroy the computers of Russia's own citizens, simply as a feint? In fact, its next operation would reveal that it was willing to go far further still in the interests of sowing uncertainty.

■

Just before 8:00 p.m. on February 9, 2018, high in the northeastern mountains of South Korea, Sang-jin Oh was sitting behind the press section of the Pyeongchang Olympic Stadium, a few hundred feet away from the vast, circular stage on which the 2018 Winter Olympics' opening ceremony was about to start.

Anticipation buzzed through the 35,000-person crowd. But few felt it more intensely than Oh. For more than three years, the forty-seven-year-old civil servant had held the position of director of technology for the Pyeongchang Olympics organizing committee. He'd overseen the setup of an IT back end for the games that comprised more than 10,000 PCs, nearly 25,000 mobile devices, 6,300 Wi-Fi routers, and 300 servers in two Seoul-based data centers, with more than 100 additional servers in partner companies' facilities.

A few minutes earlier, he'd gotten word from one of those partner companies that it was having some sort of technical issue. The firm's glitches, in fact, had been a long-term headache. Oh's response had been annoyance: Even now, with the entire world's spotlight on the event they were managing, the company was still working out its bugs?

The data centers in Seoul, however, weren't reporting any such problems, and Oh's team believed the issues at the partner's data center were manageable. He didn't yet know that they were already preventing some attendees from printing tickets that would let them enter the stadium. He'd settled into his seat, ready to watch a highlight of his career unfold.

Ten seconds before 8:00 p.m., numbers began to form, one by one, in projected light around the stage, as a choir of children's voices counted down in Korean to the start of the event:

"Sip!"

"Gu!"

"Pal!"

"Chil!"

In the middle of that countdown, Oh's Samsung Galaxy Note 8 phone abruptly lit up. He looked down to see a message from a subordinate on KakaoTalk, a popular Korean messaging app. The message shared perhaps the worst possible news that Oh could have received at that exact moment: Something was shutting down every domain controller in the Seoul data centers.

As the opening ceremony got underway, thousands of fireworks exploded around the stadium on cue, and dozens of massive puppets and Korean dancers entered the stage. Oh saw none of it. He was texting furiously with his staff as they watched their entire IT setup go dark. He quickly realized that what the partner company had reported wasn't a mere glitch. It was the first sign of an unfolding attack. He needed to get to his technology operations center.

As Oh made his way out of the press section toward the exits, reporters around him had already begun complaining that the Wi-Fi seemed to have suddenly stopped working. Thousands of internet-linked TVs showing the ceremony at the stadium and twelve other Olympic facilities had gone black. Every RFID-based security gate leading into every Olympic building was down. The Olympics' official app was broken, too, reaching out for data from back-end servers that suddenly had none to offer. That meant some unknown number of audience members had been unable to load their tickets to their phones, locking them out of the performance.

The feeling, for Oh, was both infuriating and surreal. The Pyeongchang organizing committee had prepared for this: Their cyber-security advisory group had met twenty times since 2015. They'd conducted drills as early as June of the previous year, simulating disasters like cyberattacks, fires, and earthquakes. But Oh could still hardly believe one of those nightmare scenarios was now playing out in reality. "It's actually happened," Oh thought to himself, as if to shake himself out of the sense that it was all a bad dream.

Once Oh made his way through the crowd, he ran to one of the stadium's exits, out into the freezing air of the Pyeongchang winter night and across the parking lot, now joined by two other IT staffers. They jumped into a Hyundai SUV and began the forty-minute drive east, down through the mountains to the coastal city of Gangneung, where the Olympics' technology operation center was located.

From the car, Oh immediately made calls to tell staffers at the stadium to start distributing Wi-Fi hot spots to reporters and to tell security to check badges manually, because all RFID systems were down. But he knew that in just over two hours the opening ceremony would end, and all of the tens of thousands of athletes, visiting dignitaries, and spectators at the event would find that they had no Wi-Fi connections and no access to the Olympic app full of schedules, hotel information, and maps. The result would be a humiliating confusion. And if they couldn't recover the servers by the next morning, the entire IT back end of the organizing committee—responsible for everything from meals to hotel reservations to event ticketing—would remain off-line. A kind of technological fiasco that had never before struck the Olympics would take place in one of the world's most wired countries.

By 9:00 p.m., halfway into the ceremony, Oh had arrived at the technology operations center in Gangneung, a large open room, one wall covered in screens, with desks and computers for 150 staffers. When he walked in, many of those staffers were standing, clumped together, anxiously discussing how to respond to the attack that had also locked them out of many of their own basic services like email and messaging.

All nine of the Olympic staff's domain controllers, the same backbone servers whose erasure had nearly crippled Maersk, had somehow been paralyzed. The staff decided to respond with a temporary workaround, setting all surviving servers that powered critical services, such as Wi-Fi and the Olympic app, to simply bypass those dead domain controllers. They managed to bring those systems back online just minutes before the end of the ceremony.

Over the next two hours, as they attempted to rebuild the domain controllers to re-create a more long-term, secure network, the staffers would find that the servers were mysteriously crippled again and again. Some malicious presence in their network remained, disrupting the servers faster than they could be rebuilt.

A few minutes before midnight, Oh and his administrators reluctantly decided to cut off all their systems from the internet in an attempt to isolate them from the saboteurs, who must still have maintained a presence inside. That meant taking down every service—even the Olympics' public website—while they worked to root out whatever malware infection was tearing apart their network from within.

For the rest of the night, Oh and his staff would work desperately to rebuild the Olympics' IT infrastructure. It wasn't until just after 5:00 a.m. that a Korean security company working with the organizing committee, AhnLab, managed to create an antivirus signature that could help Oh's staff vaccinate the network's thousands of PCs and servers against the mysterious malware that had been at the root of the attack, a file named simply winlogon.exe. At 6:30 a.m., the

Olympics' administrators reset 120 staffers' passwords to lock out whatever means of access the hackers might have stolen. Just before 8:00 that morning Korean time, almost exactly twelve hours after the cyberattack on the Olympics had begun, Oh and his sleepless staffers finished reconstructing their servers from backups and restarting every service.

Amazingly, their emergency triage response worked. The day's snowboarding, ski jumping, and curling events went forward with little more than a few Wi-Fi hiccups. Thousands of athletes and millions of spectators remained blissfully unaware that the Olympics' IT staff had just spent the prior night fighting off a cyberattack that threatened the entire event.

Even so, Oh still smoldered when he thought back to the night of the opening ceremony. "For me, the Olympics are about peace. It still makes me furious that without any clear purpose, someone hacked this event," he told me months later. "If we hadn't solved it, it would have been a huge black mark on these games of peace. I can only hope that the international community can figure out a way that this will never happen again."

35

FALSE FLAGS

Within hours, rumors began to trickle out into the cybersecurity community that the website, Wi-Fi, and app glitches during the Olympics' opening ceremony had been caused by foul play. The Pyeongchang organizing committee soon confirmed that it had indeed been the target of a cyberattack. But it refused to comment on the attack's source. Instead, the incident became a hacker whodunit on a global stage—with a vexing number of potential culprits.

The usual suspect for any cyberattack in South Korea is, of course, North Korea. The two countries had never officially called an end to the civil war that followed their split in 1945, and hackers working on behalf of the hermit kingdom had long used their southern neighbors as the same sort of online punching bag that Russia had made out of Ukraine. For a decade, North Korean hackers had hit South Korean targets with everything from crude waves of junk web traffic to data-wiping malware—broadsides as relentless as Sandworm's cyberwar tactics, if not as sophisticated. In the run-up to the Olympics, analysts at the cybersecurity firm McAfee had warned that Korean-speaking hackers had targeted the Pyeongchang Olympic organizers with phishing emails and what appeared to be espionage malware, hinting in a phone call with me that North Korea was likely behind the spying scheme.

But as the Olympics began, the North had seemed as if it were experimenting with a friendlier approach. The North Korean dictator, Kim Jong Un, had sent his sister as a diplomatic emissary to the games and had invited South Korea's president, Moon Jae-in, to visit the North Korean capital of Pyongyang. The two countries had even taken the surprising step of combining their Olympic women's hockey teams in a show of friendship. Why would North Korea launch a disruptive cyberattack in the midst of that charm offensive?

Then there was Russia. The Kremlin had its own motive for an attack on Pyeongchang: Its Fancy Bear hackers had, in fact, been hacking and leaking data from Olympics-related targets for years in retaliation for the anti-doping investigations that had punished Russian athletes for their coordinated performance-enhancing drug use. Ahead of the 2018 winter games, the International Olympic Committee had taken the final measure of officially banning Russia altogether. Russian athletes could compete but not wear Russian flags or national colors, and any medals would be credited to them individually, not to their home country.

It was exactly the sort of slight that might inspire the Kremlin to unleash a piece of disruptive malware against the opening ceremony. If the Russian government couldn't enjoy the Olympics, then no one would.

If Russia was trying to send a message with the attack on the Olympics' servers, however, it was hardly a clear one. Days *before* the opening ceremony, it had preemptively denied any Olympics-targeted hacking. "We know that Western media are planning pseudo-investigations on the theme of 'Russian fingerprints' in hacking attacks on information resources related to the hosting of the Winter Olympic Games in the Republic of Korea," Russia's Foreign Ministry had told Reuters. "Of course, no evidence will be presented to the world."

In fact, there would be plenty of evidence vaguely hinting at Russia's responsibility. But analyzing the attack's forensic fingerprints would turn out to be even more confusing than untangling its geopolitical motive.

Three days after the opening ceremony, Cisco's Talos security division revealed that it had obtained and dissected the Olympics-targeted malware, which it named Olympic Destroyer. Someone from the Olympics organizing committee or perhaps the Korean security firm AhnLab had uploaded the code for analysis on VirusTotal, where Cisco's reverse engineers found it. The description of Olympic Destroyer's anatomy that Cisco published broadly resembled both NotPetya and Bad Rabbit: It had a Mimikatz-like password-stealing tool, again combining those stolen passwords with legitimate Windows features to spread among computers on a network, and then a wiping component that deleted a boot configuration file from the machine before shutting the computer down so that it couldn't be rebooted.

But unlike Bad Rabbit, there seemed to be no clear code matches between NotPetya and Olympic Destroyer. Although it contained similar features, they had apparently been re-created from scratch or copied from elsewhere. Analysts at the security firm CrowdStrike would find other apparent Russian fingerprints: the version of the programming language C++ the Olympic malware used matched Sandworm's XData ransomware, for instance, as well as its mechanism for handling the credentials it stole from victim machines. But as malware analysts dug deeper, the clues became stranger. The data-wiping portion of Olympic Destroyer shared characteristics with a sample of data-wiping code that had been used not by Russia but by the North Korean hacker group known as Lazarus. When Cisco researchers put the logical structures of the wipers side by side, they seemed to roughly match. And both destroyed files with the same distinctive trick of deleting just their first one thousand bytes. Was North Korea behind the attack after all?

But there were still more contradictory signposts. The security firm Intezer noted that a chunk of the Mimikatz-like code in Olympic Destroyer matched exactly with tools used by a hacker group known as APT3. The company also traced a component Olympic Destroyer used to generate encryption keys back to a third group, APT10. They pointed out that the encryption component had never been used before by any other hacking teams, as far as the company's analysts could tell. Both APT3 and APT10 had been named by multiple cybersecurity companies as likely linked to the Chinese government.

Russia? North Korea? China? The deeper forensic analysts looked, the further they seemed to be from a definitive conclusion.

The security world had seen plenty of false flags before: The state-sponsored hackers behind every major attack for years had pretended to be something else, their masks ranging from those of cybercriminals to hacktivists to another country's agents. But this was different. No one had ever seen quite so many deceptions folded into the same piece of software. Wading into the Olympic Destroyer code was like walking into a maze of mirrors, with a different false flag at every dead end.

■

In the midst of that fog of confusion and misdirection, a leak to *The Washington Post*'s Ellen Nakashima cut through with an unequivocal statement. Her headline: "Russian Spies Hacked the Olympics and Tried to Make It Look Like North Korea Did It, U.S. Officials Say." Again, the *Post* cited anonymous U.S. intelligence sources—two of them—who claimed that the GRU's Main Center for Special Technology was behind the attack, the same hackers responsible for NotPetya. Olympic Destroyer, it seemed to follow, was the work of Sandworm, or at least its colleagues at the same agency.

The *Post*'s story rang true. Despite all its ruses, Olympic Destroyer had struck me as exactly the sort of reckless sabotage that Sandworm and the GRU had been engaged in for years. But Nakashima's report cited no evidence—at least nothing that the public could verify. With the Kremlin's proactive denial of any Olympics hacking, the result was a kind of standoff between two governments' contradictory claims. Though one of those governments was vastly more credible than the other, the debate was hardly settled for the cybersecurity community's skeptics. How could they be certain that anonymous "U.S. officials" had solved the mystery and not simply fallen for one of Olympic Destroyer's layered lies?

Soon another set of clues emerged from an unlikely source: Kaspersky Labs. After the Shadow Brokers' theft from the NSA had been linked to Kaspersky's software, the cloud of suspicions around the Moscow-based security firm had only grown thicker. But in March 2018, it waded into the Olympic Destroyer morass and emerged with evidence that actually bolstered the case against Russia.

Kaspersky had obtained its copy of the Olympic Destroyer malware not from the Olympics organizing committee, but from a ski resort hotel that had also been struck in the attack. It seemed, in fact, that the hackers had attempted to hack a wide range of Olympics-related targets beyond the Olympics themselves, but Kaspersky could confirm only that two ski resorts had been breached (along with a ski equipment automation firm and Atos, an IT services provider in France). The hotel that shared the malware sample with Kaspersky had been seriously infected, to the degree that its automated ski gates and ski lifts were temporarily paralyzed.

When Kaspersky's Korea-based staff sent the malware sample back to Moscow for analysis, its Global Research & Analysis Team had begun dusting it for fingerprints. But rather than focus on the malware's code, as other companies like Cisco and Intezer had immediately done, they'd looked at its "header," one part of the file's metadata that includes clues about what sorts of programming tools were used to write it. Comparing that header with others in Kaspersky's vast database of malware samples, they found it perfectly matched the same sample of North Korean data-wiping malware that Cisco's Talos had already pointed to as sharing traits with Olympic Destroyer.

But in this case, one senior Kaspersky researcher named Igor Soumenkov decided to look a step further. Soumenkov, a hacker prodigy who'd been recruited to Kaspersky's research team as a teenager years earlier, had a uniquely deep knowledge of file headers and decided to double-check his colleagues' findings. By the end of a late night at the company's Moscow office, he had determined that the header metadata didn't actually match other clues in the Olympic Destroyer code itself; the malware hadn't been written with the programming tools that the header implied. The metadata had been forged.

This was something different from all the other signs of misdirection that researchers had fixated on. The other red herrings in Olympic Destroyer had been so vexing in part because there was no way to tell which clues were real and which were deceptions. But now, deep in the folds of false flags wrapped around the Olympic malware, Soumenkov had found one flag that was *provably* false.

It was now perfectly clear that someone had tried to make the malware look North Korean and only failed due to a slipup in one instance and through Soumenkov's fastidious triple-checking. "It's a completely verifiable false flag. We can say with 100 percent confidence this is false, so it's *not* the Lazarus Group," Soumenkov would later say in a presentation at the Kaspersky Security Analyst Summit, using the name for the hackers widely believed to be North Korean. Still, whether out of skeptical rigor or some secret influence of the Kremlin, Kaspersky's researchers refused to state publicly who they believed was behind the malware.

If Olympic Destroyer was the work of the GRU, its timing seemed more than coincidental. Just as the Russian military was about to be publicly called out and punished for the biggest cyberattack in history, a piece of malware had conveniently appeared that seemed designed to call into question the fundamental ability of security researchers to determine the source of any cyberattack. "Even as it accomplished its mission, it also sent a message to the security community: You shouldn't be so quick to attribute things," Cisco's Craig Williams told me. *"You can be misled."* It was as if the GRU, feeling the proximity of investigators on its tail, had dropped a smoke bomb and made its escape.

All signs, more than ever, pointed to Russia, not North Korea, as the perpetrators of the Olympic hacking. But as the mystery unfolded, I was reminded of the jump boots Vladimir Rezun had described the *spetsnaz* wearing, with soles designed to impersonate enemy tracks. The false flags were serving their purpose: Once they appeared, every piece of evidence was tainted with doubt, even when the truth was displayed plainly in front of your eyes.

36

74455

On a warm fall day in September 2018, I stepped out of John Hultquist's car and onto the driveway of his two-story house in an idyllic suburb of Washington, D.C., complete with a well-furnished backyard and a very affectionate goldendoodle named Penny.

Hultquist, wearing a green T-shirt and shorts, invited me in. We were meeting at his home because he'd been out of the FireEye headquarters on paternity leave for the last month, following the birth of his second child. That time away from the office, of course, had not diminished his obsession with Sandworm. When we sat down at his kitchen table, he first told me that he was ten thousand words into writing a Tom Clancy–style novel—purely fictional, of course—about a cybersecurity researcher who finds himself tracing the trail of destruction of a team of über-hackers. His working title, for the moment: "Johnny Saves the Internet."

But Hultquist had continued to work on his nonfictional hacker hunting, too. He'd asked me to come down from New York because he and his team of researchers had made new connections he wanted to map out for me in person—significant ones and, he'd warned me, very, very complicated. I turned on the voice recorder on my phone.

"I think . . . 7-4-4-5-5," Hultquist suddenly said without preamble. "I think that's your man."

I paused, dumbstruck. "What does that mean?" I asked slowly, puzzling over what sort of code this series of numbers might represent.

"I think 7-4-4-5-5 is Sandworm," he said matter-of-factly.

"What is 7-4-4-5-5?" I asked, still entirely confused and wondering if Hultquist was enjoying this game.

"That's the unit," Hultquist spelled out patiently, as if speaking to one of his children. "I think Unit 74455 is your boys."

It took me a moment longer still to understand what Hultquist was telling me: an answer, in some sense, to the mystery that had dogged me for more than a year, and Hultquist far longer. He meant that Sandworm was Unit 74455 of the GRU.

Before Hultquist had even explained the evidence behind his claim, hearing this number alone felt like an epiphany. Those five digits themselves didn't immediately tell me anything about Sandworm that I didn't already know. But they held the promise of representing the secret name Sandworm calls itself. That unit number might also hold the key to understanding the hidden human beings behind that code name, sitting on the other end of the internet.

When I asked Hultquist to explain how he'd come to that connection, he opened his laptop and pulled up a report from FireEye dated June 2018, which he said the company had distributed to some of its intelligence clients but hadn't shared publicly. It was titled "Targeting of US and French Elections Connected to Olympics Incident and Others." I could see at a glance it contained pages and pages of charts and graphed links among technical data points. For the next two hours, Hultquist would walk me through a series of connections that would thoroughly redefine how I thought of Sandworm, its place within the GRU, and its mission.

"Basically you can get from NotPetya to the Olympics to hacking election infrastructure," Hultquist summarized as we got started. "You've got yourself quite a web here, my friend."

■

When Hultquist's researcher Michael Matonis found the loose thread that would unravel that web in February 2018, it wasn't by searching for clues in the code of the Olympic Destroyer payload. Instead, in the days immediately following the news of the Olympic cyberattack,

Matonis had looked at a far more mundane element of the operation: the fake, malware-laced Word document that had served as the first step in the nearly disastrous Olympic sabotage.

When Matonis pulled the infected document from VirusTotal, he saw that the bait had been sent to staff at the International Olympic Committee more than two months before the Olympics began, in late November 2017. The Word file spoofed a list of VIP delegates to the games but hid inside it a malicious macro script, the same simple program-in-a-document trick Hultquist's team had first seen Sandworm using in 2014 and that it had continued to deploy as late as its first blackout attack.

Just as Drew Robinson had done when he was working in iSight's office on another investigation for Hultquist's team, three years earlier, Matonis began combing FireEye's historical collection of malware and VirusTotal, looking for matches to that code sample. On a first scan, he found none. But Matonis did notice that a few dozen malware-infected documents from the archives corresponded to his file's rough characteristics: They similarly carried embedded Word macros and, like the Olympic-targeted file, had been built to launch a certain common set of hacking tools called PowerShell Empire.

The malicious Word macro traps, however, looked very different from one another. Each one had layers of obfuscation—just like that first piece of Sandworm malware Robinson had unpacked in iSight's office—and that encoded layer of noise seemed altogether distinct for each sample.

But as Matonis compared the malware specimens, scouring their noise for clues, he struck upon a connection. Matonis refused to tell me the pattern he'd pulled out of that randomness; like a good gambler, he wanted to keep the hackers' "tell" secret so he could use it again in the future. But the result, in the most abstract sense, was that while the files looked different, the *way* they looked different looked uniform. In fact, like teenage punks who all pinned just the right obscure band's buttons to their jackets and styled their hair in the same shapes, their attempt to look unique had made them part of a distinctly recognizable group.

Matonis soon put together that the source of that signal in the noise was a common tool used to create each one of the booby-trapped documents. It was an open-source program, easily found online, called Malicious Macro Generator. Matonis speculated that the hackers had chosen the program to blend in with other malware authors. But beyond their shared tools, the malware group was also tied together by the author names Matonis pulled from the files' metadata: Almost all had been written by someone named either "AV," "BD," or "john." When he looked at the command-and-control servers that the malware connected back to—the strings that would control the puppetry of any successful infections—all but a few of the IP addresses of those machines overlapped, too.

The fingerprints were hardly exact. But over several weeks, he had assembled a loose mesh of clues that added up to a solid net, tying the fake Word documents together.

When he had established those connections, it was the actual, visible content of those Word files, not their hidden malware, that got Matonis's blood pumping. Two documents from the collection, which stretched back to the spring of 2017, seemed to target Ukrainian LGBT activist groups, using infected files that pretended to be a gay rights organization's strategy document and a map of a Kiev Pride parade. Others targeted Ukrainian companies and government agencies with a tainted copy of draft legislation.

In Matonis's mind, all other suspects for the Olympic attack fell away. Only one country would have been targeting Ukraine in the same hacking campaign, nearly a year earlier, and it wasn't China or North Korea.

Strangely, other infected documents in the collection Matonis had unearthed seemed to target victims in the Russian business and real estate world. Had a team of Russian hackers been tasked with spying on some Russian oligarch on behalf of their intelligence taskmasters? Were they engaged in profit-focused cybercrime as a side gig? Regardless, Matonis felt that he was on his way to finally, definitively cutting through the Olympic cyberattack's false flags to reveal its true origin: the Kremlin.

■

After Matonis had made those first, thrilling connections from Olympic Destroyer to a very familiar set of Russian hacking victims, he wanted to see how far those new links would take him. He told Hultquist that he wouldn't be coming into the FireEye office for the foreseeable future. Instead, he locked himself in his basement-level apartment in the D.C. neighborhood of Capitol Hill. For the next three weeks, he barely left that four-hundred-square-foot box, instead working on his laptop from a folding chair, with his back to the only window in his home that produced sunlight, poring over every data point that might reveal the next cluster of the hackers' targets.

A pre-internet-era detective might start a rudimentary search for a person by consulting phone books. Matonis started digging into the online equivalent, the directory of the web's global network known as the domain name system, or DNS. DNS servers translate human-readable domains like "facebook.com" into the machine-readable IP addresses that actually describe the location of a networked computer that runs that site or service, like 69.63.176.13. Matonis began painstakingly checking every IP address his hackers had used as a command-and-control server in the campaign of malicious Word documents he'd just uncovered, translating those domains into any IP addresses that had ever hosted them. At the same time, he'd use a reverse-lookup tool to flip the search, finding every domain that had been hosted on any single IP address to assemble a branching graph.

Once he'd created these treelike maps for dozens of the IP addresses and domain names connected to the Olympic attack, one branch of that exploration led to a domain that lit up like neon in Matonis's mind. Three links down his daisy chain of IP addresses and domains, there it was: account-loginserv.com.

A photographic memory is a helpful trick for an intelligence analyst. As soon as Matonis saw the account-loginserv.com domain, he instantly knew that he had seen it nearly a year earlier in an FBI "flash," a short alert sent out to U.S. cybersecurity practitioners and potential victims. This one had offered a new detail into the hackers who in 2016 had breached the Arizona and Illinois state boards of elections: The same intruders had also spoofed emails from a voting technology company, VR Systems, in an attempt to trick more election-related victims into giving up their passwords.*

Matonis drew up a jumbled map of the connections on a piece of paper that he slapped on his refrigerator with an Elvis magnet and marveled at what he'd found. Based on the FBI flash—and Matonis told me he confirmed the connection with another human source he declined to reveal—the fake VR Systems emails were part of a phishing campaign that had also used a spoofed login page at the account-loginserv.com domain he'd found in his Olympic Destroyer map. At the end of his long chain of IP addresses and domains, Matonis had found a fingerprint that linked the Olympic attackers back to a hacking operation that directly targeted the 2016 U.S. election.

Matonis had, since his teenage years, been a motorcycle fan. When he was just barely old enough to ride one legally, he had scraped together enough money to buy a 1975 Honda CB750. Then one day a friend let him try riding his 2001 Harley-Davidson with an 1100 EVO engine. In three seconds, he was flying along a country road in upstate New York at sixty-five miles an hour, simultaneously fearing for his life and laughing uncontrollably.

When Matonis had finally drawn his forensic web, outsmarting the most deceptive malware in history, he says he felt that same feeling, a rush that he could only compare to taking off in that Harley-Davidson in first gear. He sat alone in his D.C. apartment, staring at his screen and laughing.

---

* The whistle-blower Reality Winner, working at a contractor firm, had leaked documents to the news site *The Intercept* revealing that the same hackers had breached VR Systems, too.

THE TOWER

When Matonis reported his findings to his boss, John Hultquist, they agreed there was no longer any doubt: The hackers behind Olympic Destroyer were Russian. But was this the work of their favorite rampaging team of cyberwarriors, Sandworm?

Matonis had made some solid, but not quite definitive, connections between the new nexus of operations he'd uncovered and Sandworm's older activity: The Olympic hackers had placed their command-and-control servers in data centers run by specific companies like Fortunix Networks and Global Layer, most likely chosen because those firms accepted Bitcoin payments that made any follow-the-money forensics far more difficult. And in a handful of cases, he could see that those hosting companies overlapped: Fortunix had been used for some of the original BlackEnergy attacks, and then again by the Olympic hackers. Other attacks in the Olympics cluster seemed to have been hosted with Global Layer, just like the command-and-control servers Sandworm had used to control its hijacked M.E.Doc servers.

Soon, Matonis made an even more remarkable connection: One of the same set of command-and-control servers Sandworm had used in its smaller-scale destructive attacks ahead of NotPetya was also tied to the hacking-and-leaking operation targeting the campaign of the French presidential candidate Emmanuel Macron.* The same group

---

* The clues that led Matonis to make that connection, tying Sandworm to a French

of back-end servers Sandworm was using for its pre-NotPetya experiments had doubled as the infrastructure for another election-targeted hack-and-leak operation. NotPetya was connected to French election interference, just as Olympic Destroyer was linked to U.S.-focused election meddling. The lines of FireEye's vast web of analysis violated any clean boundary I might have imagined between political information warfare and destructive cyberwar.

The first time I'd spoken to Matonis about Sandworm in early 2018, he had described it to me as the hammer in the Russian hacker tool kit. "You call on them when you want to fuck shit up," he'd told me over breakfast at a conference. But his notion of Sandworm's mission was changing—as would mine. Any simple concept of Sandworm as the arm of the GRU focused purely on sabotage now seemed incomplete. The GRU's hacker teams, it was becoming clearer, worked hand in hand.

■

By June, FireEye had assembled Matonis's findings into the intricate report for its clients that Hultquist would later show me in his kitchen. In the meantime, Matonis had made one more connection: The same campaign of infected Word documents that targeted Ukrainian activists, Russian real estate businesses, and the Olympics had also targeted the Organisation for the Prohibition of Chemical Weapons, a Spiez, Switzerland–based chemical weapons research group that was investigating the poisoning of the GRU defector Sergei Skripal and his daughter. The arrows pointing to Russian involvement were clearer than ever.

One month after FireEye privately published those findings, the U.S. government provided another, final piece of the puzzle Matonis and Hultquist were assembling. On July 14, the U.S. Department of Justice released an indictment targeting twelve GRU hackers for their role in interfering in the 2016 U.S. election. Those criminal charges would demonstrate the penetrating level of detail that can be revealed

---

election-focused hacking operation, represent another long and intricate path through the web of his investigation. For a complete breakdown, see the appendix.

about even faraway, state-sponsored hackers when the full investigative powers of American intelligence agencies are brought to bear.

The indictment, filed by Special Counsel Robert Mueller as part of the independent investigation created to suss out Russia's full role in the 2016 election, went so far as to name exactly which GRU staffers had played which role in the hacking operation: A GRU agent named Aleksey Viktorovich Lukashev, for instance, was charged with sending the phishing emails that targeted the Democratic Party and the Clinton campaign staff. Sergey Aleksandrovich Morgachev had allegedly supervised the team that built and ran the malware used to spy on the DNC staff for months. Another GRU officer, Ivan Sergeyevich Yermakov, was accused of stealing the emails from the DNC server that were later leaked to disastrous effect. The document even named the specific GRU unit most of the hackers worked for—26165—and the address of its building in Moscow: 20 Komsomolsky Prospekt.

Like most indictments of foreign governments' hackers, the alleged perps would almost certainly never face those charges in court. Instead, they were designed to send a message—to name and shame the individual hackers involved—and to impose draconian restrictions on their lives. They'd never again be able to set foot in a country that had an extradition treaty with the United States without facing arrest.

When I first read the indictment, as revelatory as it might have been about Russia's election-focused hacking—the initiative led by the team known as Fancy Bear—I saw it as irrelevant to the search for Sandworm's more destructive hackers. But Hultquist, with the secrets of Matonis's findings fresh in his brain, read it differently. He instead homed in on the accusations against one GRU hacker among the twelve in particular: Anatoliy Sergeyevich Kovalev.

Kovalev was singled out in the document for having hacked into at least one of the state boards of elections in 2016, allegedly stealing data for about 500,000 voters, including names, addresses, dates of birth, driver's license numbers, and partial Social Security numbers. The indictment went on to blame Kovalev for the breach of a company whose software was used to verify voter registration information.

These breaches, Hultquist could see, were part of the web Matonis had drawn: In the infrastructure that had enabled those attacks on the boards of elections, Matonis had found forensic clues that linked strongly to the attack against the Olympics and, more circumstantially, to NotPetya and Sandworm. This election-hacking indictment revealed culprits who were connected to that far wider network of chaos.

Kovalev, the indictment against him detailed, wasn't part of the same Unit 26165 as most of the hackers it charged. He and two other GRU staffers—Aleksandr Vladimirovich Osadchuk and Aleksey Aleksandrovich Potemkin—were instead part of Unit 74455, based in a different location just outside Moscow: 22 Kirova Street in the neighboring city of Khimki, a building identified in the indictment as "the Tower."

Unit 74455 had provided back-end servers for Unit 26165's intrusions into the Democratic National Committee and the Clinton campaign, the indictment stated. But more surprisingly, the indictment accused 74455 of "assisting in" the operation to leak the emails stolen in those operations. Unit 74455, the charges stated, had helped to set up DCLeaks.com and even Guccifer 2.0, the fake Romanian hacker persona that had claimed credit for the intrusions and given the Democrats' stolen emails to WikiLeaks.

A new theory crystallized in Hultquist's mind. Unit 26165 was Fancy Bear. Unit 74455 was Sandworm. The operations of those two teams were tightly intertwined, different sides of the same GRU coin. And the addresses where they worked were now on full public display.

■

The FBI had provided photographs of eleven of the twelve indicted hackers on its website, and after meeting with Hultquist, I stared at the pictures of the three members of Unit 74455. Aleksandr Osadchuk, the colonel who led the unit, was a fifty-six-year-old man with brown eyes and the broad, blocky features of a *Dick Tracy* character. In his photograph, he wore a navy-blue-colored Russian military uniform weighed down with medals and pins.

On the website of a Ukrainian seller of antiques and collectibles, one of those pins seemed to be offered for sale—the FBI's photograph was too low-resolution to know for sure—a round chunk of golden metal engraved with the image of a white diamond at its center. A lightning bolt and a sword slashed across the circle, crossing behind the gem. At the bottom of the image was a sash with the numbers "74455" written across it. On the other side of it was an engraving that translated to "in service of the fatherland."

I was more intrigued by the two other faces: Anatoliy Kovalev and Aleksey Potemkin were both far younger men. Potemkin, the older of the two at thirty-five, wore a blue shirt and tie, along with a green cap that hid what looked like closely buzzed hair. His light blue eyes stared into the camera with a steely, almost contemptuous gaze.

Kovalev, accused of the hands-on hacking of at least one U.S. state's board of elections website, was listed as only twenty-seven years old. His photograph, cut off at the neck, showed no sign of his uniform, and despite his close-cropped hair he had the sort of open, intelligent face I could imagine seeing on any hacker in a cybersecurity company or graduate school across the world. In 2017, Kovalev had been listed on the website of the cybersecurity conference Positive Hack Days as an attendee. He'd noted his affiliation as Moscow State Technical University. My Russian translator called the school; she found that no one there had ever heard of him.

I now had three names, three faces, and an address. They were the barest of clues. But they were also, I began to realize in the days that followed my meeting with Hultquist, the closest thing to solid leads I was going to get. With those names and the address of the Tower burned in my mind, I booked a flight for Russia.

38

RUSSIA

In late November 2018, I arrived in St. Petersburg, deep into one of the city's subzero, seventeen-hour winter nights. The next morning I walked into the A2 Green Concert club near the city's center, a massive music venue with its internal brick walls lit in glowing green and purple and thrumming with bass. In two of those rooms, hackers on stages presented technical research on everything from industrial control system hijacking methods to ATM hardware reverse engineering. In the rest of the building, young, darkly dressed people milled around the venue's hallways and bars. At one table, Russia's state-owned bank Sberbank was recruiting security engineers. At another, hackers crowded around with their laptops, trying to win a contest to breach an email server in the shortest possible time. This was ZeroNights—one of the two largest hacker conferences in Russia and what I hoped might be my best chance to learn about how Russia's hacker community interacted with the GRU.

For the next two days at the conference, I'd ask any Russian hacker with whom I could start a conversation about a topic that was perhaps the event's worst possible icebreaker: their country's intelligence services. Most of them grew visibly distant as soon as I brought it up, told me they had nothing to say on the topic, and found an excuse to walk away. The few who did talk said they didn't know the three members of the GRU's 74455 I was looking for or any other GRU agents. What they told me instead seemed to lead me even further from the truth, or in circles: *The Russian government doesn't have sophisticated hackers; it can't pay enough to afford them. No one at an event like this works with Russian intelligence agencies. No Russian hacker with any skill is both smart enough to be a talented hacker and dumb enough to be a patriotic GRU agent. I don't want to talk to anyone who believes the story that Russia hacked the U.S. election. The Ukrainian power grid? You don't even have to hack it. You just wait a while and it will fall apart on its own.*

Finally, one security researcher sat down with me and openly admitted that he and others he knew did sell hacking tools to the Russian government—if indirectly. In his case, he offered a subscription service for zero-day vulnerabilities and the tools to exploit them. The targets of his hacking wares, he said, were industrial control system software.

Among his buyers were penetration testers seeking to suss out their clients' vulnerabilities, U.S. government agencies, and, he believed, Russian companies that served as fronts for Kremlin intelligence staff, though he politely declined to pinpoint any customers by name. He told me he didn't know anyone who had been coerced into working with the FSB or GRU, but had no doubt that he and his hacker associates had—wittingly or not—done deals with them. "They don't need to pressure you, that was only in years past," he said calmly, as we sat on the venue's balcony, the smell of stale cigarettes wafting out of the smoking room next to us. "Money solves a lot of problems."

Did he believe GRU agents or their front companies were at Zero-Nights now, recruiting or buying tools? He didn't know, but he had certainly seen them at other Russian conferences, he told me. "They don't walk around wearing badges," he said. "They could be anyone here."

■

I left St. Petersburg after the conference, more confused by my conversations than enlightened, and boarded the Sapsan bullet train to Moscow. That evening I emerged from Leningradsky station into the core of Russia's capital just as a light snow was beginning to fall. But even as I was approaching the geographic heart of the GRU, I found myself still banging my head against its wall of secrecy.

I felt that impenetrability tangibly the next day when I paid a visit to the global headquarters of Kaspersky Labs, arriving at its sleek glass building along a highway in Moscow's northwest, with orchids and a Salvador Dalí sculpture of an elephant decorating its white-paneled lobby. In a conference room on the fourth floor, I met with Igor Soumenkov, the brilliant security researcher who had found the first, most telling clue exculpating North Korea for the Olympic Destroyer attack.

For the next hour, I interviewed him about that impressive finding, and the thin, kind-faced thirty-two-year-old laid out the case for North Korea's innocence in perfect English, with all the confidence and clarity of a university professor. At the conference room's whiteboard, he drew charts of how software compilers function, to explain the mismatch in the malware's header that showed its failed attempt at a false flag. Kaspersky had, by then, also made most of the same connections out from Olympic Destroyer that FireEye's Michael Matonis had found, linking the Olympic hackers to attacks targeting Ukraine, Russian businesses, and the Swiss chemical weapons laboratory. (Soumenkov didn't mention those hackers' link to the attacks on the U.S. state boards of elections, which tied them to Unit 74455 of the GRU. Because Matonis and Hultquist had shared that key data point with me in confidence, I didn't mention it to Soumenkov, either.)

Near the end of my hour-long briefing with Soumenkov, I summarized what he seemed to have laid out for me: The Olympic attack clearly wasn't the work of North Korea. "It didn't look like them at all," Soumenkov agreed.

And it certainly wasn't Chinese, despite the more transparent false code hidden in Olympic Destroyer that fooled some researchers early. "Chinese code is very recognizable, and this looks different," Soumenkov agreed again.

Finally, I asked the glaring question: If not China, and not North Korea, then who? It seemed that the conclusion of the process of elimination was practically sitting there in the conference room with us and yet couldn't be spoken aloud.

"Ah, for that question, I brought a nice game," Soumenkov said, affecting a kind of chipper tone. He pulled out a small black cloth bag and took out of it a set of dice. On each side of the small black cubes were written words like "Anonymous," "Cybercriminals," "Hacktivists," "USA," "China," "Russia," "Ukraine," "Cyber-terrorists," "Iran." I'd seen these so-called attribution dice before: a prop designed to illustrate the nihilistic notion that no cyberattack could ever be traced to its source and anyone who tried was simply guessing.

As he held the dice, Soumenkov's cheeks had taken on a mild red flush. Perhaps the room was stuffy, although I hadn't felt it. Or perhaps Soumenkov was feeling the embarrassment of concealing an answer that his own innate intellectual honesty had helped uncover. Or perhaps he was feeling the fear that Andrei Soldatov had described to me among Russia's cybersecurity community, hiding just a scratch's depth beneath the skin.

Soumenkov tossed the dice on the table. "Attribution is a tricky game," he said. "Who is behind this, it's not our story, and it will never be."

■

On my last morning in Russia, I walked out of my hotel and along the bank of the Moscow River toward 20 Komsomolsky Prospekt, the home of GRU Unit 26165, the primary actor in Russia's interference operation targeting the 2016 U.S. election. As I approached the now-notorious address named in the U.S. indictment against those hackers, I passed an ornate Orthodox church and then came to a series of long, faded yellow buildings that filled an entire block. The center third of each building had a series of Greek columns in its facade, as if to signal its innocuous identity as an academic institution—officially, the Institute of Military Instructors.

But seeing the building in person made clear it contained something far more carefully guarded than a school. Its front door had been boarded up neatly with red wooden panels, and its side entrance was absurdly well protected: Guards screened visitors through a metal gate, surrounded by three fortified mounds of sandbags, each fronted by a curved steel plate with a slot for a rifle. Each of the three miniature bunkers was painted green and covered in camouflage netting, and thus looked ludicrously conspicuous on the central Moscow sidewalk. I watched as two older men in black coats and then a younger man in a green winter uniform entered the gate. Then I hurried away before the guards could notice my staring.

Perhaps Sandworm was inside that gate. But Hultquist's theory, the only one that had even attempted to trace a line all the way from the very first BlackEnergy attacks in Ukraine to an actual unit number and address, had pointed elsewhere. I wanted to see that building, too. As snow began to fall again, I boarded the metro and took it northward to nearly the end of the line. After close to an hour, I emerged and took a taxi across the Moscow River to the suburban city of Khimki. The cabdriver dropped me off at 22 Kirova Street: the Tower, home of GRU Unit 74455.

The neighborhood of Khimki that abuts the Moscow River is made up of 1960s- and 1970s-era Soviet brick apartments. On that afternoon, their quiet courtyards were blanketed in snow, an idyllic picture of communist nostalgia. But on the banks of the river, the Tower loomed over them, more than twenty-five stories of glass and steel.

I walked past an auto body shop, a community gym, and the tower's fortified gate, marked as the Glavnoye Upravleniye Obustroystva Voysk—translating roughly to the "General Directorate for the Arrangement of Troops"—which was surrounded by surveillance cameras. Then I descended a metal staircase to a path by the river, which had broadened north of the city and frozen, becoming a perfect flat ribbon of white snow.

With the river to my back, the Tower stood directly above me, blocked off by a high iron fence on a steep hill. I couldn't make out a single human figure through its windows without using a pair of binoculars, which I wasn't brave enough to try.

It struck me that this was as close as I was likely ever going to get to the hackers I'd now been following for two years. After traveling close to five thousand miles, I was no nearer to understanding or unmasking Sandworm than I had been in John Hultquist's kitchen in northern Virginia.

I had felt the need to seek out the place where Sandworm lived. But now it seemed as though I'd been tricked by the same peculiarity of cyberwar's geography that had made the Ukrainian police's raid on the M.E.Doc server room so absurd. Just as NotPetya had defied human intuition about the physical origin of a weapon's launch—just as distance hadn't protected its victims—proximity hadn't brought me meaningfully closer to its perpetrators.

A security guard appeared on the edge of the parking lot above me, looking out from within the Tower's fence—whether watching me or taking a smoke break, I couldn't tell. It was time for me to leave. I walked north along the Moscow River, away from the Tower, and through the hush of the neighborhood's snow-padded parks and pathways to the nearby train station. On the train back to the city center, I glimpsed the glass building one last time from the other side of the frozen river before it was swallowed up in the Moscow skyline.

THE ELEPHANT AND
THE INSURGENT

When Hultquist told me that Unit 74455 of the GRU was Sandworm, I wanted to believe him. Those five digits, as impenetrable as they might have been, seemed to offer a kind of solution to Sandworm's mystery. But even before I flew to Russia with the Tower hanging in my imagination, I couldn't ignore the nagging skepticism telling me that the full story wasn't so simple.

Rob Lee, with his official pedigree as an NSA hacker-hunter, had warned me months earlier that the international researchers tracking Sandworm—from FireEye to Kaspersky to ESET—were all only seeing pieces of the picture. For the most part, he pointed out, they were analyzing clues in the malware left behind in the wake of the hackers' attacks, not other evidence such as the intrusion data pulled from victims' logs.

The problem with that malware analysis approach, Lee explained, was that highly sophisticated hacking operations aren't typically carried out by a single team working alone. Instead, like in any well-developed industry, the hackers inside any competent intelligence agency specialize. One team might be assigned only to build tools. Another might focus on gaining initial access to target networks. A third might be assigned to take over that foothold, monitoring implanted spyware or carrying out the next stage of the intrusion, like penetrating from the IT network to the computers that connect to industrial control systems.

The problem with the story of Sandworm as I knew it, Lee pointed out, was that the group had mostly been tracked via clues in the software it used. Even its name had come from the *Dune* references in the code of its BlackEnergy infections. The cybersecurity research community had started from those initial fingerprints, finding other software hints that connected to those intrusions and grouping those operations as the work of Sandworm. But what if those operations shared only the same software developers, and different operations teams had deployed that code in their attacks? "You're tracking the malware. The people who develop it are not always the same people who use it," Lee warned me in a phone call. The result might be misconceptions along the lines of tying together a series of murders as the work of a single gang, when in fact they had simply all been carried out with weapons from the same gun shop.

It seemed true, I had to admit, that there were at least two distinct threads within Sandworm's cyberwar fronts: one that seemed intent on destroying data, from KillDisk to NotPetya, and one that seemed to be honing attacks with physical effects, culminating in Crash Override, a.k.a. Industroyer. What if they were different groups, linked only by a shared software development team?

At Dragos, Lee had sought to clarify the distinction by creating a new name for what he considered Sandworm's development team, calling it "Electrum" in a reference to its blackout malware. In fact, he argued, that team of developers might even be not part of the same agency but a private contractor. "Shit, what we're tracking as Electrum could be the Booz Allen of Russia," Lee had mused. "They could be GRU, but they could also be a shared resource."

The security firm CrowdStrike, which had initially led the analysis of Fancy Bear's attacks on U.S. election targets, suggested to me that it had a different but similarly thorny theory: Sandworm—or Voodoo Bear, as CrowdStrike named the group—might be the heavyweight crew called in late in an operation when Russian intelligence was looking to inflict maximum damage. CrowdStrike's vice president of intelligence, Adam Meyers, hinted to me—but declined to show evidence to back up—that he had seen the group's fingerprints appear alongside multiple other Russian hacking groups, including one that CrowdStrike believed wasn't even a GRU operation but FSB.

Meyers's working theory was that Voodoo Bear/Sandworm might be a shared resource of a different kind from what Lee had described: That other group might be assigned to gain access, and Sandworm would take over when it was time to drop the payload. "Voodoo Bear could be a specialized sabotage group that's a collaborative effort between GRU and FSB," Meyers said. "It could be kind of like a team effort that comes in to do disruptive or destructive attacks."

FireEye had, in the fall of 2018, shared with me an entirely different theory. Hearing Michael Matonis's analysis of overlapping command-and-control servers between the Olympic attacks, NotPetya, and election-hacking operations, I couldn't help but consider whether this represented yet *another* distinct way to track Sandworm that might confuse the picture further still. Matonis was, after all, tracking the infrastructure links between different attacks and connecting them with Sandworm's operations and malware. But if Lee was right, those three elements—the software, the servers, and the hands on the keyboard—might all be the work of different teams.

The larger research community surrounding Sandworm had begun to remind me of the story about the blind men surrounding an elephant. One man grabs the elephant's tail and decides it's a rope. Another touches its leg and declares it's a pillar. A third feels its ear and swears the elephant must be a kind of large fan.

The detectives tracking Sandworm were running their hands over those same bits of anatomy and coming to equally disparate conclusions. Some, like Hultquist and Matonis, were taking the logical leap necessary to assemble their tactile experiences into an idea of a single, complex animal. Others, like Lee, were carefully describing only what they could directly observe—a trunk here, a tail there, each of which might be an independent organism. After all the years of effort and forensic breakthroughs, stretching back to Sandworm's first traces, the full shape of that animal remained a frustrating mystery.

■

Just days after my visit with John Hultquist, however, the U.K. government's National Cyber Security Centre released a remarkable document. It served as a final confirmation of the GRU's connection to Sandworm, establishing a layer of ground truth beneath the fog of cyberwar.

As I'd come to expect from government statements on state-sponsored hacking, it provided only conclusions, not the clues that led to them. But it served as a kind of omnibus reproach to the Russian government for almost all of the cyberattacks I'd associated with Sandworm over the previous two years. And it settled any last, lingering questions of which intelligence agency might be ultimately responsible.

"Our message is clear: together with our allies, we will expose and respond to the GRU's attempts to undermine international stability," read the statement from the U.K. foreign secretary, Jeremy Hunt. "The GRU's actions are reckless and indiscriminate: they try to undermine and interfere in elections in other countries; they are even prepared to damage Russian companies and Russian citizens. This pattern of behaviour demonstrates their desire to operate without regard to international law or established norms and to do so with a feeling of impunity and without consequences."

The statement was followed by two lists. One enumerated the aliases that the cybersecurity community had used for groups whose association with the GRU the British government could now confirm. Those names included practically every way of referring to all the known Russian players in the story of this book: "Fancy Bear," "Black Energy Actors," "Cyber Berkut," "Voodoo Bear," and finally "Sandworm."

The document went on to list a series of operations it tied to those actors: NotPetya. Bad Rabbit. The attacks on the Democratic National Committee. The intrusions of the World Anti-Doping Agency. The attempted breach of the Organisation for the Prohibition of Chemical Weapons that Matonis had tied to Olympic Destroyer. For each of those operations, the National Cyber Security Centre stated (with its emphasis) that it had "*high confidence* that the GRU was *almost certainly* responsible."

There was no longer room for doubt about this underlying fact: Whatever the shape of Sandworm, almost every attack that anyone had ever attributed to it had now been named as the work of the GRU.

That clarion signal came, in fact, just as the clear boundaries describing Sandworm as an entity were beginning to break down. My sense of the distinction between Sandworm and Fancy Bear was dissolving.* I had believed Sandworm to be a single cyberwar unit focused on physical disruption, but it now seemed to be something less defined. The line between development and operations teams was blurring, too. Its mission, as I understood it, no longer had the purity of a cyberattack sabotage campaign but was mixed up with election-focused influence operations.

All of that meant conceiving of the group Hultquist's team had discovered in 2014 as a distinct, named entity, with its own discrete set of operations, was losing its usefulness. That simple model no longer fit reality. The story of Sandworm, in that sense, was over.

The underlying mystery of its identity, however, had been solved. The answer was the one that had been coming into focus all along. It didn't matter which part of the elephant the blind men were touching. The animal was the GRU, working in the service of the Russian Federation and its president, Vladimir Putin.

■

Hultquist's unified theory of Sandworm, that it mapped cleanly onto Unit 74455 and its Khimki Tower, might have been correct—or perhaps not. No one outside an intelligence agency may ever be able to confirm or refute it.

But when Hultquist described his theory to me in his kitchen on

---

* Around the same time, another set of new clues was also blurring the line between Sandworm and Fancy Bear: ESET in October 2018 had revealed a tool kit it called GreyEnergy, which the company said Sandworm had used as a successor to Black-Energy to target industrial control system victims in Ukraine and Poland. Then, in February 2019, Kaspersky exposed a connection between that GreyEnergy malware and Fancy Bear, pointing out that a group within Fancy Bear seemed to be targeting the same victims at the same time as that GreyEnergy malware and using the same command-and-control servers.

that warm autumn afternoon in 2018, it had been, in some sense, too unwieldy for my brain to process. The same GRU hackers had turned off the lights in Ukraine, unleashed NotPetya, attacked the Olympics, hacked the U.S. state boards of elections, and even helped to set up the bizarre fake persona Guccifer 2.0? How could those absurdly disparate missions all fall under the remit of one hacking team within the GRU?

For Hultquist, however, linking Sandworm to 74455 held a certain counterintuitive, explanatory power. As he described it to me, that connection brought the purpose behind the group's entire history into focus. Now he could see that there wasn't some line between the influence operation of election meddling and disruptive attacks on infrastructure. *All of it* was an influence operation, he now believed.

"It's not about turning out the lights," Hultquist said, his eyes wide with epiphany. "It's about letting people *know* you can turn out the lights."

Russia's cyberwar in Ukraine hadn't, in fact, resulted in any concrete military wins, Hultquist pointed out. No territorial gains, enemy casualties, or other tactical victories. Its entire purpose was psychological: to reduce the will of the Ukrainian people to fight. "It's not about specific changes on the battlefield. It's about making people feel they're not safe anymore," Hultquist insisted. "There was no military, long-term objective. It was about a *psychological* objective, taking that war out of the eastern front and bringing it right to Kiev."

Just as election hacking is meant to rattle the foundations of citizens' trust that their democracy is functioning, infrastructure hacking is meant to shake their faith in the fundamental security of their society, Hultquist told me, echoing the unified sense of information warfare Gerasimov's paper had described five years earlier. "The foundation for government is the ability to protect their people," Hultquist continued, holding forth as if my questions had unlocked a torrent of ideas he'd been bottling for months. "If they can't do that—if they can't protect these soft targets—they look illegitimate."

The threat, Hultquist argued, was in essence the same one he'd battled in Iraq and Afghanistan: sudden, unpredictable destruction aimed more at shattering a sense of security than actually furthering military control. "The reason you carry out terrorism is rarely to kill *those* particular victims," Hultquist said. "It doesn't degrade the fighting capability of the adversary. That's never why someone tried to hit me with an IED. It's about scaring the shit out of people so they lose the will to fight, or change their mind about the legitimacy of their own security service, or overreact."

The theory of cyberwar Hultquist was describing sounded less like a new front for traditional wars than a new form of insurgency. And as he spoke, it occurred to me that this role—as an insurgent—might be the most accurate description of Russia's place in modern geopolitics. Putin has little hope of outgunning the West as the center of global power in a symmetric face-off. Russia's economy is smaller than Italy's or Canada's. And even with its outsized spending on war relative to that economy, its military budget is just over a tenth the size of America's.

Yet Russia sets off its IEDs—NotPetya, interference in the U.S. election, the attack on the Olympics—as cheap, asymmetrical tactics to destabilize a world order that's long ago turned against it. "This is Russia: embattled, short on resources, reaching out and touching people," Hultquist finally concluded.

He left unspoken the other corollary of this theory of cyberwar, the one that he knew all too well from his experience in Iraq and, most of all, Afghanistan. One of those wars stretched to almost a decade. The other began when Hultquist was still in college and continues as of this writing, eighteen years later. Counterinsurgencies are long. And for this digital one, there's no end in sight.

PART VI

LESSONS

*The concept of progress acts as a protective mechanism
to shield us from the terrors of the future.*

40

GENEVA

One afternoon in late January 2018, just over a year after J. Michael Daniel walked out of the White House as an executive branch official for the last time, I met him for coffee on the sixty-fourth floor of 1 World Trade Center, the building where I work for *Wired* magazine. The meeting was a kind of belated exit interview, a chance to look back at his record as Obama's top cybersecurity official, responsible for overseeing the administration's handling of every conflict on the internet over the nearly five years he held the post.

Daniel was proud of that record, which included carefully calibrated responses to everything from Iranian DDoS attacks on American banks to the North Korean attack on Sony to Russian attacks on the U.S. election. But I wanted to talk to him instead about the one series of events where the Obama administration had offered practically no response at all: the Ukrainian cyberwar and, in particular, the world's first-ever blackout attacks carried out by Sandworm just before Christmas 2015.

"I believe the White House and the Obama administration handled those incidents reasonably well given what we knew at the time and the evolving understanding," Daniel said judiciously, after he'd sat down on a couch overlooking a view of downtown Manhattan.

I followed up with an impolite question: With years of hindsight, and the knowledge that the same hackers would go on to unleash the most expensive, global malware pandemic in history, did he regret not acting against those hackers earlier, at the time of their

first unprecedented infrastructure attack? If not sanctions or indictments, why not at least answer those blackouts with a public statement calling out the power grid attacks as unacceptable behavior on
the international stage?

Daniel's first, clearest answer was that he very well might have
advocated those sorts of responses—if the attacks had targeted Americans or even NATO members. "There's a distinction between what
happens overseas and what happens to a U.S. company or on U.S.
soil," he said.

But then Daniel followed with a darker, more realpolitik justifica-
tion for America's inaction in the face of Ukraine's cyberwar: that the
United States might not *want* wartime cyberattacks against critical
infrastructure to be considered off-limits—that it wants the freedom
to carry out those attacks itself. "That's the fundamental tension,"
he continued. "We don't want to take any options for ourselves off
the table."

In the late 1990s war in Kosovo, Daniel pointed out, NATO planes
dropped bombs that exploded in the air over targets and released
showers of tiny carbon fibers designed to short out electrical equipment, shutting down five power plants that distributed electricity to
the Serbian armed forces. "We need to consistently advocate for not
disrupting infrastructure during peacetime," Daniel said. "You can
argue that in wartime the power grid is a legitimate target."

But none of that offered an entirely satisfying answer. Ukraine
might have been at war with Russia, but the power grid serving western Ukrainian civilians on the opposite side of the country from that
fighting couldn't remotely be called a military target. And Ukraine's
non-NATO status hadn't stopped the world from publicly condemning Russia's invasion of Crimea and Donbas, and even hitting Russia
with sanctions for that physical aggression, less than a year before it
gave the country an unspoken pass for its subsequent digital attacks.

As I pressed Daniel further, his responses became more ellipti-
cal: He wasn't present for all the discussions about Russian relations
at the time, he said. Other parts of the executive branch were factor-
ing the Ukraine cyberattacks into a bigger, tangled web of relationships that also included the bloody unraveling of Syria, where Russia
and the United States were at odds. The administration's policy on

Russia was still recalibrating after its earlier attempt at a friendly "reset" with the Kremlin, a détente shattered by the Crimean invasion. He didn't want to reveal private conversations with the president that he considered protected by executive privilege. He didn't want to "Monday-morning quarterback."

But the third time I asked him whether he regretted not doing more, Daniel overtly admitted that he did. "I wish that we could have been more up-front and done a bigger push about this issue, yes," he said.

Then he offered something unusual for a lifelong political official: a series of honest thoughts that, beyond his legalistic arguments, sounded like a deeply considered analysis of a past decision he was still not sure he'd made correctly. "This is an incredibly new area," Daniel said, now speaking in a different, unguarded tone. "We haven't made the shift to thinking about this nodal, light-speed network that doesn't play by the physics that the real world plays by and yet is intimately connected with the real world, and more connected every day.

"Our understanding is still growing. What's important is that we take these lessons and apply them going forward," he concluded. "Because it will be one of those issues that will come back up. It will happen again."

■

Four months later in May 2018, it was Tom Bossert's turn for an exit interview. Until April, Bossert had been Trump's homeland security adviser, and thus his most senior official focused on cybersecurity. Then came the latest reorganization of Trump's tumultuous cabinet, this time led by his sharp-elbowed new national security advisor, John Bolton. Bossert had resigned after a little more than a year on the job—on friendly terms, he was careful to assure me.

I found the newly unemployed Bossert in Manhattan's Union Square with his meetings over, a couple hours to spare before his train back to D.C., and in urgent need of a bagel. "You can't come to New York and not eat a bagel," he told me as I speed-walked down the street to keep up with him. Tall and handsome, Bossert projected a politician's importance and impatience, and I found myself instinctively acting as his personal assistant, consulting Yelp to find Bossert's bagel for him. He considered my suggestion and, in an executive decision, dismissed it as too far to walk, instead turning around and hurrying into an Au Bon Pain.

Bossert, even more than Daniel, was fiercely proud of his accomplishments in the White House. He was, after all, the one who finally cracked down on Sandworm with actual sanctions in response to NotPetya after years of inaction. "My premise coming in, which I maintained through my entire time there, was to be aggressive, active about attribution," he told me once he'd sat down at a window table with his bagel sandwich. "It isn't for the sake of knowledge alone. It's for the sake of punitive action when you've determined a culprit."

Sure, the sanctions on the GRU in response to NotPetya came eight months after the fact. But they sent the necessary message, and just in time, Bossert adds, to pressure European Union allies into voting to continue the wider sanctions on Russia that had been enacted in response to its 2014 invasion of Ukraine.

But Bossert insisted, with the logical precision of his legal training, that the decision to sanction NotPetya's perpetrators was based on a rule that remained distinct from the wider context of Russia's behavior in Ukraine. "There's an expectation of discrimination and proportionality," he said, laying out his argument like a judge giving a rapid-fire sentencing statement. "The theory behind my anger with that particular cyberattack is that its spreading damage was not only predictable; it was obvious that it would propagate without control outside of Ukraine."

That all sounded fine, I agreed. But what about all the attacks that the GRU launched against Ukraine *before* the one that spilled out to become the largest cyberattack in history? What about the arguments made by Rob Lee, Thomas Rid, and others that the use of unprecedented cyberattacks on Ukraine's civilian infrastructure for years, including two blackout attacks, should already have been enough to trigger a response? After all, the Industroyer/Crash Override malware that took down the Kiev power grid came to light in June 2017, well into Bossert's watch.

"They were annoyed that blackout attacks in Ukraine didn't meet with a U.S. response against Russia?" Bossert asked me with raised eyebrows. "Forget about the cyber component and wrap your head around any act of aggression. Suggest to yourself that there are regional acts of aggression going on in any number of places in the world. What's the U.S.'s responsibility and risk calculus in entering that fray?"

The Cassandras' warnings about Sandworm and their calls for early deterrence, Bossert argued, ignored the massive burden of that imagined policy, the sheer number of conflicts the United States would be signing up for if it were unilaterally imposed. "They're taking the world police responsibility of the U.S. to a ridiculous extreme," he said evenly, as if taming his outrage. "Imagine the resources we'd have to impose on the taxpayers of the U.S. to provide a blanket defense against all malicious cyberactivity."

But the administration's critics aren't asking for a policy that requires a response to "all malicious cyberactivity," I suggested. What about a simpler, narrower policy: a norm we set for the world, that even in wartime no one should use cyberattacks to turn out the lights on civilians?

Bossert paused. "I'd have to think about whether I mean that," he responded, slowing down. "I don't think I believe that. I don't subscribe to that policy.

"In the case of war, we reserve the right to do whatever is in our self-interest and within the law of armed conflict," he continued, echoing the point that Michael Daniel had expressed to me months before. "If you and I put ourselves in the Captain America chair and decide to go to war with someone, we might turn off their power and communications to give ourselves a strategic and tactical advantage. In fact, it's even condoned in the law of war to conduct all sorts of sabotage against the enemy."

But these blackouts weren't aimed at achieving tactical military gains, I pointed out. They were targeted well beyond the front lines and intended to intimidate civilians.

"Agreed, and I do not condone them," Bossert said. "But put yourself in Putin's perspective." Putin was willing to send little green men into Ukraine, to shoot down planes, to hack power grids, Bossert noted. All of that was justified, in Putin's view, by his original, dubious rationale for the invasion of Ukraine.

"If a similar hypothetical situation confronted the U.S., and if we similarly didn't care what the international opinion was, meaning we had reached the conclusion it was in our national self-defense interest, we might easily do the same," Bossert said. "*We* would shoot down airplanes if we were at war with someone. *We* would take down power. We would do all those things. The difference here becomes whether Putin was justified militarily being in the Ukraine. We all believe he wasn't."

Only after Bossert finished his lunch, shook my hand, and jumped in a cab to Penn Station did I manage to mentally unwrap the layers of policy he'd put forward: Putin's invasion of Ukraine broke the rules. So did the sloppy, reckless destruction NotPetya inflicted as part of that invasion, but on different grounds. But those rules drew red lines that still preserved the ability to carry out all manner of cyberattacks on civilian critical infrastructure.

If any nation were instead to aim its cyberattacks carefully and start a war for the right reasons, against the right country, those red lines would offer no impediment. In that future cyberwar, in other words, the ends would justify the means.

■

On November 9, 2017, Microsoft's president, Brad Smith, stood before a crowd at the United Nations building in Geneva and reminded them of a particular thread of their city's history. A century and a half earlier, a dozen countries had met in Geneva to hammer out an agreement that they would no longer kill one another's medical personnel on the battlefield. Over the next century, a growing group of nations would meet three more times, culminating in the signing of the Fourth Geneva Convention in that very spot, setting down the basic protections for noncombatants in wartime that the world largely abides by today.

"It was here in Geneva in 1949 that the world's governments came together and pledged that they would protect civilians even in times of war," Smith said. "And yet let's look at what is happening. We're seeing nations attack civilians even in times of peace."

Smith walked through the cybersecurity disasters that had racked the globe in just the prior months: first WannaCry, then NotPetya. Back-to-back acts of state-sponsored hacking had called into question the fundamental security of human infrastructure worldwide—from hospitals to manufacturing to shipping—just as the rifle-and-artillery horrors of the Battle of Solferino in 1859 had brought attention to the need to create what would ultimately become the Red Cross, and World War II had shown the need to protect civilians.

"We live in a world where the infrastructure of our lives is ultimately vulnerable to the weakest link," Smith told the crowd, notably skipping the fact that some of the weakest links in both of the cyberattacks he'd mentioned had been security flaws in Microsoft's own Windows operating system. "It's clear where the world is going. We're entering a world where every thermostat, every electrical heater, every air conditioner, every power plant, every medical device, every hospital, every traffic light, every automobile will be connected to the Internet. Think about what it will mean for the world when those devices are the subject of attack."

Then he made his pitch. "The world needs a new, digital Geneva Convention. It needs new rules of the road," Smith said, intoning the words slowly for emphasis. "What we need is an approach that governments will adopt that says they will not attack civilians in times of peace, they will not attack hospitals, they will not attack the electrical grid, they will not attack the political processes of other countries."

Smith's speech was, perhaps, the broadest, most public articulation of the ideal that I'd heard stated for years, most notably by Richard Clarke, a former national security counterterrorism adviser to three presidents whose 2010 book *Cyber War* had advocated a "Cyber War Limitation Treaty." Clarke's imagined treaty would ban "first-use" cyberattacks on critical infrastructure, and even forbid planting sabotage malware on targets like power grids, railroads, and financial institutions.

The cyberwar doves' position boiled down to Rob Lee's maxim: No one, anywhere, should be hacking anyone else's civilian critical infrastructure. For those who'd been in the trenches of the recent cyberattacks spilling out from Ukraine, it seemed obvious. The world needs new red lines beyond the ones I'd heard from officials like J. Michael Daniel and Tom Bossert. It needs straightforward new norms, enshrined in international law, limiting the use of a powerful and dangerous new class of weapon before it costs human lives or cripples entire societies.

But it wouldn't be so simple. "I think there's room for a set of agreed-upon rules in cyberspace," Bossert told me in a follow-up phone call after our meeting, when I'd brought up the Geneva Convention idea. "But it's hard to imagine all the caveats I'd have to place on that."

Countries frequently probe each other's infrastructure or even infect it with malware but stop short of pulling the sabotage trigger, Bossert pointed out. Would those probes violate the letter of the hypothetical new rules? "I just want to make sure whoever writes the rules understands what they're trying to sign up to," Bossert said. "If they interpret 'attack' to mean scanning and taking control but not actually turning the lights out, we might be going to war unnecessarily. I've lived in that gray zone too much."

But there was a more fundamental roadblock to a digital Geneva Convention, according to Joshua Corman, who was at the time of Smith's speech the director of the Cyber Statecraft Initiative at the Atlantic Council: Countries like the United States still think they benefit more from their own ability to wage cyberwar than they would from depriving their enemies of that power. "There's no appetite to go straight to the Geneva Convention. None," Corman told me. "The Microsoft thing is dead on arrival, because there's no way we're going to give up that freedom of movement."

American officials, Corman explained, still look at the NSA's superior capabilities and believe that cyberwar favors those with the best offense. What they don't consider is the degree to which the West has become dependent on the internet and automation—vastly more than adversaries like North Korea or even Russia. "As one of the most connected nations, we're more dependent and more exposed," Corman said. "And we stand to lose much more."

Instead of a full Geneva-style answer, though, Corman advocates a narrower set of rules: no cyberattacks on hospitals, for instance—

what he calls a "cyber no-fly zone" around medical targets. "Fine, just say hacking hospitals, deliberately or otherwise, constitutes a war crime," Corman said. "Cyber's gonna cyber, but you better be damn flawless in your execution. You fuck up and hit a hospital, you get the international war crime, you're going to The Hague."

Of course, any debate over those diplomatic measures remains academic. Russia, China, North Korea, and Iran have no intention of giving up their cyberweapons. The Trump administration, too, has seemed determined to move in the opposite direction from hacker pacifism. In 2017, Trump announced he would elevate the authority of the Pentagon's Cyber Command and then the next year quietly increased that cyberwar force's mandate to preemptively attack foreign targets if it believed they were planning to strike the United States. Three months later, Trump reversed an Obama administration directive that required a complex set of federal agencies to sign off on any offensive hacking operation.

All of that followed through on a campaign promise Trump had made in October 2016, before his election. "As a deterrent against attacks on our critical resources, the United States must possess, and has to, the unquestioned capacity to launch crippling cyber counter attacks," Trump told a crowd at a speech to military veterans in Virginia. "I mean crippling. *Crippling.*"

A digital Geneva Convention remains a nice dream. In the meantime, the American government looks more likely to follow the most reflexive, primitive response to a cyberwar arms race: escalation.

BLACK START

On a wet day in early November 2018, a power utility engineer named Stan McHann was walking along a road on the southeastern coast of Plum Island, a tiny three-by-one-mile strip of land off the tip of Long Island's North Fork. He looked to his left, out to the expanse of the Atlantic Ocean, and felt a rare moment of peace in what had been a supremely rough week.

McHann and his colleagues had been fighting off a team of devious hackers who had proven themselves fiercely determined to take down their grid—and keep it down. He'd been locked in combat with the intruders for days, scrambling between distribution substations, sometimes in the midst of sixty-knot winds and sideways rain, to bypass corrupted digital equipment and diagnose problems. Each time the hackers seemed to have been expelled, they'd find another way to inject a new round of mayhem, sending McHann back out into the storm.

Just before 9:00 that morning, all his substations finally seemed to be back online. Out of an abundance of paranoia, McHann had decided to check them anyway, walking out of the utility's dispatch center near the north of the island and down the coastal road. That's when he heard a very particular sound.

"It was a *bam bam bam bam bam bam bam*," as McHann later described it to me. Seven pops like the explosion of a small-caliber gun, ringing out in succession across the island's landscape. Each "bam," he knew immediately, was a circuit breaker slamming open.

A startled Con Edison engineer walking with him asked what the strange and terrible noise had been. McHann answered, "That's all your power going off."

This disaster situation was not, thankfully, what it sounds like. McHann and his fellow engineers weren't fighting off the first-ever cyberattack to trigger a blackout on American soil. Instead, they were in the midst of a disturbingly realistic simulation of that dreaded scenario, defending a custom-built and isolated grid from a "red team" of skilled Department of Defense contract hackers, designed to let his "blue team" feel the pain of a utility-targeted cyberattack without inflicting that pain on American civilian victims.

The Plum Island test grid had been constructed by the Defense Advanced Research Projects Agency, or DARPA, the experimental arm of the Pentagon designed to develop technologies to fight future wars. DARPA is famously credited with inventing the internet and in recent decades helping to develop other world-changing technologies like GPS and unmanned aerial vehicles. On Plum Island, the agency had set out to find the tools that would allow electric utilities to fight off highly sophisticated hackers. And to test them, it had dropped those utilities' engineers into a worst-case scenario: one where they were tasked not with merely keeping the power on but with turning it *back* on after digital adversaries had already blacked out a grid for days.

As the red team hackers dragged his utility back to that blackout state, McHann was discovering just how painful that recovery could be. "Your heart sinks and your stomach falls through the ground," he said, describing the feeling of starting over yet again. "Then you suck it up and get back to work."

■

A few days before McHann had heard those seven shots ring out across Plum Island, DARPA had kicked off its cyberattack war game with an elaborate setup: Two utilities had been assembled on the island with a remote dispatch center and sixteen transmission substations housed in shipping containers dotting the landscape. One utility started the exercise fully dark; in the game's panic-inducing scenario, hackers have turned off the power for long enough—weeks or even months—that all its generators are down and even backup batteries are entirely depleted.

The second utility started the week with one diesel generator connected only to a "critical asset," which the blue team was told it must keep powered at all times. That asset, a crumbling building near the south of Plum Island that was once used by the Pentagon as a laboratory for germ warfare, represented in the world of DARPA's simulation something like a hospital or a defense command center—an imaginary, nonnegotiable consumer of power that's required to save lives or win a war. To allow the participants to see from a distance whether the critical asset was powered or not, a series of inflatable dancing wind-sock figures had been plugged in just outside the building, giving it the look more of a used-car dealership than an imperiled hospital.

The participants, engineers drawn from utilities around the country and cybersecurity researchers who submitted proposals to DARPA, were told they must perform a so-called black start. That meant bootstrapping one blacked-out utility's grid from scratch by spinning up its diesel generator, then building out a path of electrical distribution from both utilities' generators to their substations, and finally syncing the island's two utilities to create a redundant power source for the critical asset.

On the first day of the exercise, the utility engineers quickly discovered just how comprehensively they'd have to rethink their approach to running a power grid after it had been fully hijacked by digital saboteurs. Some senior utility operators had begun by telling their teammates that they would restart the grid "by the numbers," McHann said. These engineers believed they could use their remote readings from networked, digital equipment to power up the grid just as they would after any natural disaster. "They were pretty sure it was going to be another hurricane-training scenario," he said drily.

Within twenty-four hours, according to McHann, those naive operators had learned that straightforward approach didn't work when every computer lied to you. The industrial control system software that the utility operators were accustomed to drew its readings of current and voltage from power equipment, displaying them on the dispatch centers' computers known as human-machine interfaces. But that software had now been fully penetrated by the hackers and offered only wildly inaccurate or even deceptive answers.

Worse, the operators soon discovered that not only those remote readings but even the panels on the equipment couldn't be trusted. "They knocked out routers, mucked with the data on screens, tripped breakers, routed power wrong," said McHann of the phantom hackers tormenting them. "You name it, it was coming at us."

The utility defenders tried to push the hackers out of their systems and rebuild them, only to find that the attackers would tenaciously dig their way back in again. "While we were cleaning things up, the adversary was countering our moves," one cybersecurity researcher, Stan Pietrowicz, told my *Wired* colleague Lily Hay Newman, who visited the island during the exercise, in the midst of one of its punishing rainstorms. On the third day, just as the defenders had almost restarted the entire grid, the attackers took down a key substation, throwing them back into chaos. "Even that small victory got taken away from us," Pietrowicz lamented.

Once the utility engineers conceded to their cybersecurity researcher teammates that their traditional computers were hopeless, they resorted to experimental tools designed to bypass the hacked network. Engineers eventually walked into each substation and connected sensors with clamps directly to power equipment. They connected those sensors with a "mesh" network built from portable computers—black boxes the size of a desktop PC—that talked to one another over encrypted channels protected from the rest of the utility's infections.

Communicating via that encrypted network and with voice commands by phone, the utility operators were finally able to make some progress toward stability. In the very last hours of the weeklong exercise, they finally, briefly synced the two utilities, though there was no guarantee the hackers wouldn't have taken it down again had the game continued.

Meanwhile, the red team had scored a different sort of victory: Twice, they had managed to take down the power to the "critical asset" the blue team had been ordered to protect. On both occasions, the inflatable sock-men had fallen limp on a concrete ramp outside the building, casualties of a conflict against an insidious, highly persistent enemy.

■

Hearing the experience of DARPA's guinea pigs, I was reminded of something Rob Lee had said to me a year and a half earlier, not long after the second Ukrainian blackout. We'd just met for the first time at the bare-bones Baltimore headquarters of his newly formed start-up, Dragos. Outside the window of his office, appropriately, loomed a series of pylons holding up transmission lines that carried power eighteen miles south to Washington, D.C.

"Taking down the American grid would be harder than Ukraine," Lee had told me at the time. "*Keeping* it down might be easier."

The DARPA exercise seemed to bear out that idea: American utility operators, more than Ukrainians, have learned to manage the generation and flow of power primarily through their computers and automated systems. Without those modern tools, they're blinded. Ukrainian operators, by contrast, are far more accustomed to those tools' failures, and thus ready to fall back on an analog option.

When Sandworm opened circuit breakers in utilities across western and central Ukraine, those utilities' staffers were ready within hours to drive out in trucks to manually flip the switches at those substations. When I asked Stan McHann why the blue team in the DARPA simulation hadn't simply disconnected devices like circuit breakers from automation and operated them manually, he told me that was, for some modern equipment, not even an option. "Some breakers have gotten so automated that they're software-controlled only," he said ruefully.

But even more than that lack of an analog fallback in American utilities, the DARPA exercise had illustrated a broader point Lee had made to me: that attacks on power grids or other industrial control systems could be far, far worse than what the world had seen thus far.

A future intrusion might target not a distribution or transmission station but an actual power plant. Or it could be designed not simply to turn off equipment but to destroy it, as Mike Assante's

Aurora experiment had demonstrated back in 2007. The massive, rotating generator killed in that proof-of-concept attack, after all, was safeguarded by the same protective relays that are found all over U.S. electrical systems, including transmission stations like the target of Sandworm's Kiev attack. With the right protective relay exploit, it's possible that someone could permanently disable power-generation equipment or the massive, often custom-made, multimillion-dollar transformers that serve as the backbone of the American electric transmission system.

Add in that destructive capability, and the dystopian scenarios start to expand well beyond the brief outages that Ukraine experienced, Lee told me. "Washington, D.C.? A nation-state could take it out for two months without much issue," he'd said calmly.

An isolated incident of physical destruction might not even be the limit to the damage hackers could inflict. When the cybersecurity community talks about state-sponsored hackers, they often refer to them as "advanced, persistent threats"—sophisticated intruders who don't simply infiltrate a system for the sake of one attack but stay there, silently keeping their hold on a target. If a victim is lucky enough to discover them and purge them from its systems—as the DARPA blue team had tried—it often finds that the hackers have left a backdoor for themselves in some obscure corner of its network and used it to silently take up residence again, like an infestation of hyperintelligent cockroaches.

In his nightmares, Lee had told me, American infrastructure is hacked with this kind of persistence: transportation networks, pipelines, or power grids taken down again and again by deep-rooted adversaries. "If they did that in multiple places, you could have up to a month of outages across an entire region," he'd said. "Tell me what *doesn't* change dramatically when key cities across half of the U.S. don't have power for a month."

■

A year and a half later, when I visited Dragos again, Rob Lee's critical infrastructure cybersecurity firm had moved across town into a sleek industrial space. In one corner of the new office was a small "pipe-

line" system of plumbing and pumps, along with a closet full of programmable logic controllers. In the other corner was a full in-house
industrial beer-brewing setup. All were intended to serve as targets
for Dragos's hacking demonstrations and training sessions—as well
as a virtually unlimited supply of in-house IPA and stout. The business of protecting customers from industrial control system attacks
seemed to be booming: Since my last meeting with Lee, his company
had exploded from twenty-two employees to eighty-four and raised
more than $48 million from investors.

I sat down with Lee at a conference table he's had custom-made
from a single oak trunk. He looked older and rounder than photographs from his air force days, with the bushy red beard of a Viking.
His transition from a military maverick to a confident, eccentric
CEO seemed to be complete. And he quickly made it clear that the
fuel of his and Dragos's prosperity was a very real escalation in critical
infrastructure hacking around the world.

"Nothing has gotten better," he summarized. "When I last saw you,
we were tracking three different groups targeting industrial sectors
specifically. We're tracking ten now."

Those ten infrastructure-hacking teams, Dragos's analysts believed,
work in the service of six distinct governments, though Lee declined
to list exactly which ones. "Russia, China, Iran, and North Korea are
not the only actors in this space," he hinted. "We're tracking one African state targeting industrial sectors. All of this goes completely outside of what people tend to think." And Lee estimated that despite
Dragos's extensive intelligence collection—now as the world's largest
cybersecurity incident response team focused on industrial control
systems—they'd found less than half the active hacking operations
infiltrating targets like grids, factories, pipelines, and water treatment
facilities around the world.

Late 2017, in fact, saw another landmark in that mostly invisible
conflict: Hackers of unknown origin hit the Saudi oil refinery Petro
Rabigh with a piece of malware called Triton or Trisis, designed to
disable so-called safety-instrumented systems, which monitor equipment for conditions that might lead to an explosion or chemical leak.

The result could have been a catastrophic lethal accident. Luckily,
the malware simply triggered a shutdown of the plant. Though the

hackers were widely suspected of working for Iran, FireEye in the fall of 2018 linked the malware to a lab at Russia's Central Scientific Research Institute of Chemistry and Mechanics, suggesting Russian developers might have built this cyberweapon, too, though perhaps on behalf of another team of saboteurs. "The threat is becoming bolder," Lee told me. "We're seeing more aggressive, numerous actions than I've seen in ten-plus years of doing this."

A primary reason for that escalation is the one that Lee had been harping on for years, long enough that his outrage had hardened into a kind of static, cynical anger: The U.S. government, and the West as a whole, have failed to set the norms that might keep the march toward cyberwar in check.

The same inaction, negligence, and focus on offense that spurred him to leave the intelligence community, and led him to burn so many of his bridges with government contacts, were now fueling a global digital arms race. In fact, they had become the primary source of growth for his very successful start-up. And he was still unhappy about it. "The government has largely abdicated its responsibility," Lee concluded. The red lines had still not been drawn. "Our adversaries think they can get away with it."

But Lee also viewed the continuing uptick in infrastructure hacking as a kind of self-perpetuating cycle: Every country's intelligence agencies that witness another country's hacking capabilities, he explained, immediately seek to match or overtake their foes. And Russia had demonstrated its blackout malware known as Crash Override or Industroyer more than two years earlier. Since then, it was safe to assume, Sandworm's hackers had developed new ways to wreak havoc in the physical world.

"States like to have parity with each other. If you're any state other than Russia or the U.S. at this point, you're feeling like you're *really* far behind," Lee said. "There will be a rush for everyone to build these capabilities. And the losers will be civilian infrastructure owners."

The powers of disruption Sandworm so recklessly displayed, in other words, weren't an aberration. They're merely the most visible model of a tool kit that every militarized nation and rogue state in the world might soon covet or possess: the new standard arsenal for a global cyberwar standoff.

RESILIENCE

Dan Geer lives in a one-story white house near the border between Tennessee and Alabama, surrounded by his two-hundred-acre farm. Together with his wife, he works that land, growing a strain of heirloom corn, garlic, dahlia blossoms, seeds for field peas, and a particular white bean called *tarbais,* which, he explained to me, any self-respecting chef requires to make a proper cassoulet.

In the other part of his professional life, he works as the chief information security officer for In-Q-Tel, a nonprofit organization that functions as something like a venture capital investor for U.S. spy agencies. "I find it somewhat productive to have one foot in the dirt and one foot in the intelligence community," he tells me.

In-Q-Tel is tasked with investing in companies that both make money and advance the agenda of the CIA, NSA, FBI, and other three-letter agencies. Geer's job, as the overseer of the firm's cyber-security portfolio, is to see the future of security, on behalf of intelligence agencies that pride themselves on seeing everything.

He fits the part of a professional prophet: At sixty-nine, age has bleached his voluminous muttonchop sideburns white, and he pulls his darker hair back into a ponytail. His reputation in the cyber-security community warrants this Jedi master image. The Atlantic Council's Josh Corman described him to me in a reverent tone as "the elder statesman and philosopher" of cybersecurity. Geer emerges semiannually from the hinterlands to give pithy keynotes before hushed audiences at the world's biggest security conferences like

Black Hat and RSA. He's testified five times before Congress on hearings about national security and technological risk.

But for a futurist, Geer acts a lot like a Luddite. When I managed to speak to him after a few weeks of attempts, it was via a copper landline that connects to his house's spiral-cord phone. His only cell phone is turned off and stored in the glove compartment of his rust-covered 2001 Ford F-150. He has no TV, and no radios in his house other than a windup one for emergencies. Even his tractor, an older Korean model, was chosen to minimize automation and software. "If you don't pick up the latest fads, after a while you look like you've discarded modern life, but no, you just haven't adopted it," Geer explained. "I have no exposure."

That last sentence in particular captures why I'd sought Geer out. It hints at a key fact about his digital asceticism: It's not merely the result of a hermit's inflexible habits. It's also his way of living out his security principles. In a short paper published by the Stanford-based think tank the Hoover Institution in early 2018 titled "A Rubicon," Geer made a case for examining an often forgotten variable in the equation of a society's security against cyberattack: resilience.

Long before and after NotPetya, cybersecurity wonks, experts, and salesmen offered strategies to head off catastrophic cyberattacks: Write more secure software and patch it more conscientiously. Monitor networks with machine-learning-honed tools designed to spot intruders or their malicious software. Punish bad actors like Russia and North Korea.

But like the DARPA Plum Island exercise, Geer isn't focused on how to prevent the next massive, cascading security fiasco. Instead, he's determined to figure out how to recover from it quickly and limit its damage. "It may be time to no longer invest further in lengthening time between failures," as he put it to me, "but instead on shortening meantime to repair."

The key to that resilience, Geer had argued in his paper, is a sort of independence. "Because the wellspring of risk is dependence, aggregate risk is a monotonically increasing function of aggregate dependence," Geer had written. Put more simply, a complex system like a digitized civilization is subject to cascading failures, where one thing depends on another, which depends on another thing. If the foundation fails, the whole tower tumbles. If the control systems are hacked, the power turns off, so the gas pumps don't work, so the mail trucks stop, so the bread isn't delivered—or a thousand such unpredictable outcomes flowing from myriad, mind-bending interdependencies too complex to compute.

Geer argued that the problem of potential cascading failures in computer systems might by some measures be more threatening to human life as we know it than even climate change. "Interdependence within society today is centered on the Internet beyond all other dependencies excepting climate, and the Internet has a time constant of change five orders of magnitude smaller than that of climate," he wrote. Or, as he translated to me on the phone, dependence on a stable climate poses at least as much of an existential risk for humanity as dependence on stable computer networks. But a malicious actor doing his or her best to change the climate would need decades of pumping out carbon to do serious damage, while a malicious team of hackers could unleash chaos on the internet in a matter of minutes.

And how to protect society from those dangerous dependencies? "Quenching cascade failure, like quenching a forest fire, requires an otherwise uninvolved area to be cleared of the mechanisms of transit, which is to say it requires the opposite of interdependence," Geer wrote.

Somehow, he argued, societies need to build or maintain backup systems that are disconnected from interdependent, fragile modern networks. Often, that means an analog alternative. Landline phones when cellular networks fail. Paper ballots that can be counted by hand if vote tallies are hacked. Utility operators like those in Ukraine, ready to switch to manual control and turn the power back on by hand, one circuit breaker at a time. The backup domain controller in a blacked-out data center in Ghana, disconnected from your ravaged global shipping network.

∎

Geer's paper reminded me of a conversation I'd had a few months earlier, riding along with the CEO of the Ukrainian postal service as his private driver took him to Kiev's Boryspil airport. That CEO, Igor Smelyansky, had impressed me with the frank way he talked about NotPetya's paralyzing effects on the postal service, which razed thousands of its computers. He had no illusions about whether it could happen again. "I don't think we can really prevent something like this," he'd said calmly. "We can prepare. And we can try to minimize the damage."

As for how to do damage control for the next cyberfiasco, Smelyansky had ideas. For every element of his seventy-four-thousand-person company, Smelyansky said he and his executives were drawing up a plan for how they could fall back to a kind of minimum set of basic services in the event of another tech meltdown. They were weighing the cost of fuel reserves for their trucks and emergency backup systems for key offices. Every mail truck would get a paper packet that explains how to proceed in the event that cell phone networks are taken down. "We'll have sorting centers where we have backup generators, so the system can still work on a smaller scale," Smelyansky said in the Americanized English he'd picked up from years working in New York. "The driver knows he needs to go there. If he can't reach us, that's what he does, one, two, three."

For the post offices' crucial pension disbursements, Smelyansky had proposed a backup system where, in the event of a prolonged mass computer outage, everyone simply gets a monthly pension of 1,000 hryvnias, a rough median allowance of about $36. When the computers come back online, they add to or subtract from the next payment. But in the meantime, no one starves.

In some ways, the Ukrainian postal service had already fared far better in the wake of NotPetya than another, more modernized country's might have. When the database of newspaper subscriptions had been destroyed, local offices had pulled out boxes of paper subscription cards to re-create the distribution lists. Ukraine's pensioners still picked up their pensions in cash, rather than electronic payments. Many offices, particularly in remote regions of Ukraine, still used paper systems to process payments; some employees didn't even touch computers in their daily work.

"We had the biggest issues in the big cities. In the smaller cities, some employees still remember how to work on paper," Smelyansky told me. "In Kiev, we had employees who didn't remember a time before computers. We had to tell them to find someone older to teach them."

Despite the fact that the Ukrainian postal service had one foot safely planted in the analog past, NotPetya had still exacted a huge toll, just as it had for so many organizations in Ukraine and around the world. Preparing for the next one wouldn't be simple, Smelyansky admitted as we arrived at Boryspil airport for his flight. But he was optimistic. "It's a problem of dependencies. You have to work through the dependencies all the way to the end," he said. "We're working through them."

■

When I asked Dan Geer if he expected another NotPetya to hit the internet, he answered before I'd even finished asking the question. "Yes. Yes, yes," he said. "Why would it not? Is there reason to believe North Korea would do something like this? Yes, they have. Would China? Yes. Is the number of countries capable of doing this going up? I would guess so."

But one lesson of the last cybersecurity disaster—that an older generation of Ukrainian postal workers had the analog skills to keep the system running while the younger generation didn't—is the thought that particularly troubles Geer. Those analog fallbacks are slipping away into history, replaced by digitized, automated, and ultimately fragile new systems. Geer sees his own disconnection from modern technology as both a personal preference and a contribution to a "baseload" population that keeps the stable, fallback systems of the past running.

"The societal advantage of having a ready, running, and known-to-work alternative if the current option were to blow up is not easy to measure, but I believe it's important," he said. "But where do you get the baseload to keep the analog thing running? There has to be some body of people that, left to their own devices, would continue to use it. Otherwise we'll have to go back in the future and re-create it, and that's going to be an awful lot harder than keeping it running now."

Without that analog baseload, humanity will have innovated itself onto the precipice of a new, dangerous era, where vast interdependencies decide our fate and the safety nets have been pulled away. Holding back a portion of society's resources from that innovation will have a cost, Geer acknowledged. But the cost of jettisoning the past might be greater. "I don't want to sound like Chicken Little, but I'm trying to thread a needle," Geer insisted. "I want to at least *choose* whether we want to have irretrievable dependence on something."

The time to make that choice is running out. "We will never have a more analog world than we have now," Geer wrote in the concluding paragraphs of his "Rubicon" paper:

> Countries that built complete analog physical plants have a signal advantage over countries that leapfrogged directly to full digitalization. The former countries have preservable and protective firebreaks in place that the latter will never have, but the former countries enjoy their resilience dividend if, and only if, they preserve their physical plant. That such preservation can deliver both resilience for the digitalized and continued freedom for those choosing not to participate in digitalization is unique to this historical moment.
>
> We stand on the bank of our Rubicon.

EPILOGUE

Ukraine remains true to its namesake—"Ukraina," or "borderland." And few places have felt the pressures on Ukraine's borders more acutely than Maryinka. The tiny town, with fewer than ten thousand people, is situated next to a picturesque lake, 350 miles southeast of Kiev in the war-torn region of the country known as Donbas. Maryinka's grid of tree-lined streets and gray buildings, like so many Ukrainian towns, is dotted with ornate cathedrals and Soviet memorials. But toward the south and east edges of the town, the architecture seems to decay, displaying the scars of years of battles that have caught the town in their cross fire—blast marks, burned and abandoned buildings, and spectacularly exploded facades spilling bricks into empty frames.

Then, still within the town limits, a checkpoint appears, manned by soldiers and protected by a maze of concrete blocks. This is what locals call "point zero." On the other side is no-man's-land. The front line between the pro-Ukrainian and the pro-Russian forces cuts through the town itself.

Even so, less than half a mile from that front line, at Maryinka's center, middle-aged ladies are working inside an orange-painted building that once housed a supermarket, baking bread and packing the warm loaves into patriotically colored blue-and-yellow plastic crates. This is the bakery of Oleg Tkachenko, a priest, entrepreneur, and refugee of the Russian invasion.

In Slovyansk, a city farther north in Donbas, Tkachenko had been building an eight-room house for his family in 2014 when soldiers led by a former Russian military official seized the local police station. They shot his neighbor on the balcony of her apartment—the first civilian killed in the city's takeover. "When you live in the twenty-first century and suddenly a war comes to your town and someone is shooting and people are dying, it's hard to believe it's happening," he reminisces. Today he lives with his wife and four of his children just north of Maryinka, squeezed into a two-room apartment covering less than five hundred square feet.

Oleg and his wife, Eugenia, spend much of their time traveling the region along Donbas's front line. Tkachenko acts as a chaplain for Ukrainian soldiers, and the couple often distribute the fresh loaves of wheat and rye bread their bakery produces; the business generates more charity than profit. The local economy has largely collapsed since the war broke out and nearly half of Maryinka's population fled west. "People don't even have enough money to buy bread," Tkachenko laments.

In their travels along Ukraine's war zone, the Tkachenkos have witnessed countless scenes of a broken society. Villages pockmarked with fifteen-foot-deep craters from artillery. Shell-shocked families who have lived in their cellars for weeks or months. Village elders who have taken their own lives rather than face the desolation of war. A widow forced to bury her husband in her own backyard. One family who moved to Donbas from the town of Pripyat after the Chernobyl disaster in 1986, leaving behind all their possessions, only to have their house burned to the ground in the war, thirty years later.

But some of the most appalling conditions, Oleg and Eugenia say, can be found just south of their bakery, in Maryinka itself. In the ghost town on the other side of the army checkpoint, most buildings are deeply damaged, some obliterated to the point that only a chimney remains. Few journalists, aid workers, or even police dare to cross into that wasteland. But twelve families still live there, stubbornly unwilling to leave or simply lacking the means to start a new life elsewhere.

Those families, as the Tkachenkos described it to me, have turned their homes into bunkers, with sandbags piled up outside their windows and religious icons painted inside their walls as a last, desperate form of protection. One man was recently killed by a land mine, and the fighting remained so dangerous he couldn't be buried for two weeks. A twelve-year-old boy living in the neighborhood was hit with shrapnel in the head and, after several surgeries, remains brain damaged.

But like most of the Ukrainians stranded in their country's war zone, the families continue to eke out an existence. "In the first stage, there was fear and panic. Those never go away, but people get used to them. They live in the stress," Tkachenko says, blinking back tears. "People get used to absolutely anything."

■

Low-grade, endless war remains the dystopian reality of a country that straddles the fault line between civilizations. Ukraine has yet to escape the cruelty of its geography.

The story of Sandworm shows how that geography helped make Ukraine a beachhead for cyberwar, too; there's little chance the West would have tolerated the same scale of digital attacks if they had been inflicted beyond Ukraine's embattled borders, against NATO or the EU. But unlike Russia's grinding, centuries-old oppression of its neighbor, there's no reason to believe this new form of conflict will be confined by the contours of geography. Cyberwar, unlike so many other faraway atrocities the West has turned a blind eye to for centuries, takes place not at a comfortable remove but on a global network that reaches into our homes, companies, governments, and infrastructure.

In 2010, Michael Hayden, the former director of the NSA and CIA, made a darkly prescient point in a keynote at the Black Hat security conference in Las Vegas, speaking to a crowd of programmers, security engineers, and hackers. "You guys made the cyber domain look like the north German plain. Then you bitch and moan when you get invaded," he said. "On the Internet, we are all Poland. We all get invaded on the Web. The inherent geography of this domain is that everything plays to the offense."

Nearly a decade later, Hayden's cynical words still ring true—even if he was off by a few hundred miles. On the internet, we are all Ukraine. In a dimension of conflict without borders, we all live on the front line. And if we fail to heed the borderland's warnings, we may all share its fate.

APPENDIX

SANDWORM'S CONNECTION TO FRENCH ELECTION HACKING

The links Michael Matonis made between Olympic Destroyer and the attacks on the U.S. state boards of elections in 2016 represent the most publicly verifiable proof of the GRU's responsibility for that Olympic sabotage. But around the same time, Matonis would find another distinct—if convoluted—link between Sandworm and a different election-focused operation, one that deserves its own explanation.

In May 2018, three months after he'd started looking at Olympic Destroyer, Matonis had begun to dig into another clue in the backdoors Sandworm had used in its run-up to NotPetya. ESET had found that one of those backdoors, the VBS tool that had helped it tie NotPetya back to Sandworm's earlier attacks, had been controlled via a certain server in Bulgaria. And that computer's setup had always struck Matonis as strange. It ran a piece of software called Tor, designed to hide the source of internet traffic by triple-encrypting it and bouncing it through three randomly chosen volunteer servers around the world, known as Tor nodes. The Sandworm command-and-control server was also volunteering as one of those Tor nodes, bouncing strangers' traffic around the internet. Perhaps it was an attempt to create a confusing flood of cover traffic, like a pickpocket trying to get lost in a crowd.

But as Matonis examined the configuration of Sandworm's Tor server, he found that its setup could serve as a kind of fingerprint—not to identify the hackers behind it, but to spot the other, similar servers they had set up for different operations. Instead of allowing the servers to melt away into anonymity, their use of Tor had made them stand out in stark relief.

Matonis refused to reveal to me the details of that fingerprint, just as he'd refused to detail the clues that led him to Olympic Destroyer's connection to the Malicious Macro Generator software. But using that Tor fingerprint as a kind of template, he dug up more than twenty similar servers across the internet that seemed to share its traits, all of which had been brought online in 2017. It seemed to him as if someone within Sandworm or working in its service had been tasked with creating a fresh new collection of back-end servers for the group's attacks.

Once he had identified that collection of Sandworm's back-end machines, Matonis started the same process of scouring the internet's domain name system for domains that had been hosted at those servers' IP addresses. And when he googled one of the first domains that process turned up, the Google-spoofing phishing link drive.googlmail .com.verification.security.login-service.ml, a single, remarkable result appeared. It was a message within the dump of emails hacked from the political party of the French president, Emmanuel Macron.

Just before the 2017 French election, WikiLeaks had published that collection of stolen emails, just as it had with Hillary Clinton's campaign in the U.S. election the year prior. The message that contained the fake "googlmail" domain was a phishing email—likely the same one that the hackers had used to breach the Macron campaign's servers and leak their contents. The hackers appeared to have forgotten to remove that lure email before dumping the whole collection of stolen messages. By leaking the full email trove with the phishing domain included—a domain Matonis had now linked to NotPetya— Sandworm's hackers seemed to have spilled their own secrets along with the now-elected French president's. And they'd definitively revealed they were involved in that 2017 election-hacking incident.

ACKNOWLEDGMENTS

This book would not have been possible without the help of the late Mike Assante, who passed away in July 2019 after battling leukemia. Assante was unparalleled not only in his technical knowledge and analysis, but in the deep generosity with which he shared it. Even in his final months, Assante never hesitated to answer questions about the minutiae of his postmortem of the Ukrainian blackouts or the mechanics of his Aurora research. With both of those contributions and many, many others, Assante made the world a safer place for all of us. I hope that, in sharing those chapters of his life, this book helps honor his memory.

All of *Sandworm*'s central subjects spent countless hours telling me their stories, for which I'll always be grateful. But many other sources spoke to me only to share a single anecdote or experience, often on the condition that their names would never appear in print. In many cases, they were telling me about highly sensitive situations in which they or their employer suffered the consequences of a disastrous cyberattack. I repeatedly heard the refrain that despite the risks to their career or the potential embarrassment of sharing the details of their victimization, they felt that this story "deserved to be told"— that its historical value or lessons for the security of other people and organizations was too great not to share. In an era marked by those in positions of power telling shameless, blatantly self-promotional lies, that sort of selfless truth telling is more admirable and important than ever.

My four translators and fixers from Ukraine to Russia to Korea—Grigory Kuznetsov, Margarita Minasyan, Daria Mykhaylova, and James Yoo—all did crucial work, helping to find many of those sources, allowing me to hear their stories, and shaping the narrative with their own reporting ideas. The amazing Chelsea Leu took on the even more involved and difficult task of retracing that reporting as a fact-checker. Thank you in particular, Chelsea, for the thankless months of work correcting my mistakes and misunderstandings.

My colleagues at *Wired* were all very generous in giving me the time and flexibility to write. They include Jahna Berry, Katie Davies, Erica Jewell, Nick Thompson, and Andrea Valdez. My *Wired* web editor, Brian Barrett, not only signed off on my book leave without hesitation but took on a new workload to help cover for me, writing more stories in my absence than I ever could have. He and Susan Murcko also edited many of the news stories whose events became chunks of the book's narrative. Rob Capps deserves credit for first suggesting that I find *the* big story of cyberwar. John Gravois deftly and thoughtfully edited both the *Wired* piece that inspired this book and the early magazine excerpt adapted from it. Above all, my fellow *Wired* security writer Lily Hay Newman not only took on a huge amount of newswriting to keep *Wired*'s security channel buzzing during my leave but also helped me to think about the book's narrative and ideas, gave the first draft an intensely thorough reading, and most heroically spent a day on Plum Island in the pouring rain to report on a DARPA black start exercise while I comfortably typed at home.

A big thank-you to my agent, Eric Lupfer, who has listened to plenty of half-baked ideas over the years before this one came to fruition and who first suggested the title *Sandworm*. This book's editor at Doubleday, Yaniv Soha, was as patient, critical, and insightful a guide through this process as I could possibly have hoped for. Doubleday's editorial assistant Cara Reilly also gave the book several invaluable rounds of edits. Thanks to both of you—and to Bill Thomas and Edward Kastenmeier—for so quickly seeing the potential of the proposal and choosing to work with me on this. Thanks to Kathy Hourigan for standing outside Yaniv's office door to keep him editing quickly. Extra thanks to Dan Novack for his steel backbone as legal counsel, and others at Doubleday/Penguin Random House, including Sean Yule, Beth Pizio, Kate Hughes, Todd Doughty, Michael Goldsmith, Hannah Engler, and Ingrid Sterner.

Other miscellaneous but heartfelt thanks go out (in no particular order) to Mike Assante, Sam Chambers, James Lewis, Kenneth Geers, Alan Paller, Oleh Derevianko and the staff of ISSP in Kiev, Anne Applebaum, Cliff Stoll, Steven Levy, Alex Gladstein, Maryna Antonova, Khatuna Mshvidobadze, Zurab Akhvlediani, Elena Ostanina, Autumn Maison, Roman Dobrokhotov, Fyodor Mozgovoy, Adrian Chen, Joshua Corman, Trevor Timm, Ben Wizner, Edward Snowden, Patrick Neighorn, Cristiana Brafman Kittner, Marina Krotofil, Ben Miller, Anna Keeve, Ranson Burkette, Ilina Cashiola, Jessica Bettencourt, Sarah Kitsos, Jaime Padilla, Mike Smith, Walter Weiss, Nadya and Stephan Wasylko, Natalie Jaresko, Tom Mayer, Jasmine Lake, Bryan Fogel, Sarahana Shrestha, Sabrina Bezerra, Sam Greenberg, Naima Zouhali, and Steve Worrall, and a very big, special thank-you to Bertha Auquilla.

Thanks to Bilal Greenberg for keeping me entertained and for taking the epic naps that allowed me to write. And the last, immeasurable thank-you goes to my wife, Malika Zouhali-Worrall, my partner in this work and in everything else.

SOURCE NOTES

Many chapters of this book, particularly the historical ones, relied significantly on secondary sources, and I'm especially grateful to the authors of the works I've listed in the bibliography. The central story of *Sandworm,* however, was largely based on hundreds of hours of interviews, whose subjects I've tried to name in the text itself whenever possible. With the exception of stray facts I might have mistakenly failed to cite—my apologies in advance for any omissions—anything not included in the following endnotes should be attributed to my own reporting.

The epigraphs for each part of the book are from Frank Herbert's *Dune,* pages 469, 11, 462, and 451.

CHAPTER 2 BLACKENERGY

10 Around 2007, Oleksiuk had sold: Jose Nazario, "BlackEnergy DDoS Botnet Analysis," Arbor Networks, Oct. 2007, archived: bit.ly/2D0qzQ0.

10 By late 2007, the security firm Arbor Networks: Ibid.

CHAPTER 3 ARRAKIS02

17 Companies from Northrop Grumman to Dow Chemical: Ariana Eujung Cha and Ellen Nakashima, "Google China Cyberattack Part of Vast Espionage Campaign, Experts Say," *Washington Post,* Jan. 14, 2010, www.washingtonpost.com.

CHAPTER 4 FORCE MULTIPLIER

26 Thirteen days after Trend Micro: "Ongoing Sophisticated Malware Campaign Compromising ICS," ICS-CERT website, Dec. 10, 2014, ics-cert.us-cert.gov/.

CHAPTER 6 HOLODOMOR TO CHERNOBYL

35 The nation's name itself: Reid, *Borderland,* 1.

36 By the beginning of the twentieth century: Ibid., 13.

36 Even after Bolshevism swept Russia: Ibid., 97.

37 In total, about 1.5 million Ukrainians: Ibid., 99.

37 The Soviet regime manufactured: Applebaum, *Red Famine,* xxvi.

37 "For God's sake, use all energy": Ibid., 25.

37 The secret police force: Ibid., 31.

37 When American Relief Administration: Ibid., 64.

37 At the same time, the most prosperous peasants: Ibid., 123.

37 They searched systematically: Ibid., 223.

38 The Soviet regime simply starved: Ibid., 236.

38 The Soviet government restricted travel: Ibid., 202.

38 The historian Anne Applebaum's book: Ibid., 257.

38 Raphael Lemkin, the Polish-Jewish lawyer: "Coining a Word and Championing a Cause: The Story of Raphael Lemkin," *Holocaust Encyclopedia,* United States Holocaust Memorial Museum website, www.ushmm.org/.

38 "This is not simply a case": Raphael Lemkin, "Soviet Genocide in the Ukraine," in *Holodomor: Reflections on the Great Famine of 1932–1933 in Soviet Ukraine,* ed. Lubomyr Y. Luciuk (Kingston, Ontario: Kashtan Press, 2008).

39 Stalin and his Ukrainian Communist Party subordinate: Reid, *Borderland,* 150.

39 Between 800,000 and 1.6 million people: Ibid., 151.

39 The Nazis rounded up: Ibid., 162.

39 Even after the Red Army: Ibid., 161.

39 In all, 1 in 6 Ukrainians died: Vadim Erlikhman, *Poteri narodonaseleniia v XX veke: Spravochnik* (Moscow: Russkaia Panorama, 2004), 21–35, via Wikipedia.

39 In the 1950s, through the last years of Stalin's terror: Reid, *Borderland,* 205.

40 On the night of April 25, 1986: Ibid., 194.

40 Exactly what happened next: "New Study Rewrites First Seconds of Chernobyl Accident," *Sci News,* Nov. 21, 2017, www.sci-news.com/.

40 A jet of radioactive material: "Sequence of Events," Chernobyl Accident Appendix 1, World Nuclear Association website, Nov. 2009, www.world-nuclear.org.

40 But no public warning: Reid, *Borderland,* 197.

41 They carried flowers, flags, and portraits: Lev Golinkin, "The Lasting Effects of the Post-Chernobyl Parade," *Time,* April 30, 2016, time.com.

CHAPTER 7 MAIDAN TO DONBAS

43 With the U.S.S.R.'s collapse: Reid, *Borderland,* 216.

43 In the year 2000, a bodyguard released: Ibid., 244.

44 Putin had gone so far: Ibid., 246–47.

44 In 2010, he defeated Tymoshenko: Ibid., 252.

44 As president, Yanukovich proved himself: Ibid., 253–57.

45 On one street near the Maidan: Glib Pakharenko, "Cyber Operations at Maidan: A Firsthand Account," *Cyber War in Perspective: Russian Aggression Against Ukraine,* May 24, 2014, ccdcoe.org/.

45 Many Ukrainians believe the Berkut: Plokhy, *Gates of Europe,* 340.

45 The death toll: Reid, *Borderland,* 268.

46 Before the dust had even settled: Plokhy, *Gates of Europe,* 340.

46 In a blink, thirty-five thousand Russian troops: Reid, *Borderland,* 268.

46 In July 2014, the callousness: Ray Furlong, "Investigators Say Missile from Russian

Unit Downed MH17," Radio Free Europe/Radio Liberty, May 24, 2018, www.rferl .org/.

46 "The anti-people junta is trying": Margaret Coker and Paul Sonne, "Ukraine: Cyberwar's Hottest Front," *Wall Street Journal*, Nov. 9, 2015, www.wsj.com.

47 (The CyberBerkut hackers would be revealed): Andy Greenberg, "Russian Hackers Are Using 'Tainted' Leaks to Sow Disinformation," *Wired*, May 25, 2017, www .wired.com.

CHAPTER 9 THE DELEGATION

59 His unvarnished opinion piece: Robert M. Lee, "The Failing of Air Force Cyber," *Signal*, Nov. 1, 2013, www.afcea.org.

61 "A small number of sources": Michael J. Assante, "Current Reporting on the Cyberattack in Ukraine Resulting in Power Outage," SANS Industrial Control Systems Security Blog, Dec. 30, 2015, ics.sans.org/, archived at bit.ly/2WCU0jt.

61 "The Ukrainian power outage is more likely": Robert M. Lee, "Potential Sample of Malware from the Ukrainian Cyber Attack Uncovered," SANS Industrial Control Systems Security Blog, Jan. 1, 2016, ics.sans.org/, archived at bit.ly/2tll9ib.

64 The fifty-six-second clip: Andy Greenberg, "Watch Hackers Take Over the Mouse of a Power-Grid Computer," *Wired*, June 20, 2017, www.wired.com/.

CHAPTER 10 FLASHBACK: AURORA

70 On the visitor center's screens: "Aurora Test Footage," published by MuckRock, Nov. 9, 2016, www.youtube.com.

CHAPTER 11 FLASHBACK: MOONLIGHT MAZE

72 It began with a seventy-five-cent: Stoll, *Cuckoo's Egg*, 3.

72 He quickly realized the unauthorized user: Ibid., 28.

73 The body of one of those cooperators: Ibid., 370.

73 Though the interlopers routed: Rid, *Rise of the Machines*, 316.

73 By one estimate, the total haul: Ibid., 330.

74 The ministry offered a surprisingly friendly: Ibid.

75 At the end of that second evening: Ibid., 331.

75 "those motherfuckers in intelligence": Kaplan, *Dark Territory*, 87.

76 "The Department of Defense has been at cyberwar": Rid, *Rise of the Machines*, 333.

77 It described flying drones: Ibid., 301.

77 (The exclamation point): "Interview with John Arquilla," *Frontline*, interview conducted on March 4, 2003, www.pbs.org.

77 "It means disrupting if not destroying": John Arquilla and David Ronfeldt, "Cyberwar Is Coming!," in *In Athena's Camp: Preparing for Conflict in the Information Age* (Santa Monica, Calif.: Rand, 1997), www.rand.org/.

77 Hamre had said in a 1997: Pierre Thomas, "Experts Prepare for 'an Electronic Pearl Harbor,' " CNN, Nov. 7, 1997, cnn.com.

78 Rand's analysts imagined catastrophic: Robert H. Anderson and Anthony C. Hearn, "The Day After . . . in Cyberspace II," in *An Exploration of Cyberspace Security R&D Investment Strategies for DARPA* (Santa Monica, Calif.: Rand, 1996), www.rand.org/.

79 "Today, our critical systems": "Transcript: Clinton Remarks on Cyberterrorism on January 7, 2000," *USIS Washington File,* Jan. 7, 2000, fas.org.

CHAPTER 12 FLASHBACK: ESTONIA

84 "You do not agree with the policy": Joshua Davis, "Web War One," *Wired,* Sept. 2007, www.wired.com/.

84 At almost exactly the stroke of midnight: Eneken Tikk, Kadri Kaska, and Liis Vihul, "International Cyber Incidents: Legal Considerations," 2010, 20, ccdcoe.org/.

85 An analysis by the security firm Arbor Networks: Davis, "Web War One."

86 "NATO has put its frontline forces": "Putin's Prepared Remarks at 43rd Munich Conference on Security Policy," *Washington Post,* Feb. 12, 2007, www.washingtonpost .com.

87 "Those who desecrate monuments": Guy Faulconbridge, Reuters, May 9, 2007, uk.reuters.com.

CHAPTER 13 FLASHBACK: GEORGIA

90 Those numbers dwarfed Georgia's army: Ariel Cohen and Robert E. Hamilton, "The Russian Military and the Georgian War: Lessons and Implications," Strategic Studies Institute, June 2011, ssi.armywarcollege.edu.

93 They began within half an hour: Ibid., 45.

93 But the security firm: Jose Nazario and Andre Dimino, "An In-Depth Look at the Russia-Georgia Cyber Conflict of 2008," www.shadowserver.org/.

94 "How did they know that": Joseph Menn, "Expert: Cyber-attacks on Georgia Websites Tied to Mob, Russian Government," *Los Angeles Times,* Aug. 13, 2008, latimesblogs.latimes.com/.

94 It had consolidated pro-Russian: Luke Coffey, "10 Years After Putin's Invasion, Russia Still Occupies Parts of Georgia," *Daily Signal,* March 1, 2018, www.dailysignal.com.

95 Only seven in a hundred: Eneken Tikk, Kadri Kaska, and Liis Vihul, "International Cyber Incidents: Legal Considerations," 2010, 68, ccdcoe.org/.

CHAPTER 14 FLASHBACK: STUXNET

96 On most matters of national security: Sanger, *Confront and Conceal,* 201.

96 But on this, he felt the need: David Sanger, "Obama Order Sped Up Wave of Cyberattacks Against Iran," *New York Times,* June 1, 2012, www.nytimes.com.

96 But international watchdog groups noted: Zetter, *Countdown to Zero Day,* 70.

97 Within two months of Ahmadinejad's election: Ibid., 81.

97 A crisis was looming: Ibid., 83.

97 "I need a third option": Sanger, *Confront and Conceal,* 191.

98 For months, the labs would quietly test: Ibid., 198.

98 Not long after the tests began: Kaplan, *Dark Territory,* 206.

99 A chamber inside the length: Ivan Oelrich and Ivanka Barzashka, "How a Centrifuge Works," Federation of American Scientists, fas.org/.

100 "The intent was that the failures": Sanger, *Confront and Conceal,* 199–200.

100 Out of the 8,700 centrifuges: Zetter, *Countdown to Zero Day,* 3.

101 As soon as an infected USB: Ibid., 6–11.

101 And they'd determined that the malware: Ibid., 28–30.

101 It was only in September 2010: Ibid., 177.

102 (Siemens software engineers might have been): Sanger, *Confront and Conceal,* 196.

102 It would then play that recording: Ibid., 198.

102 But they had blown the ultrasecret: Ibid., 203.

102 (It would be two more years): Sanger, "Obama Order Sped Up Wave of Cyberattacks Against Iran."

103 Instead, the Americans and Israelis behind: Sanger, *Confront and Conceal,* 206.

103 According to some U.S. intelligence analysts: Ibid., 207.

103 Even in spite of its confusion: Zetter, *Countdown to Zero Day,* 361.

104 "Somebody crossed the Rubicon": Sanger, "Obama Order Sped Up Wave of Cyber-attacks Against Iran."

105 "This has a whiff of August 1945": Paul D. Shinkman, "Former CIA Director: Cyber Attack Game-Changers Comparable to Hiroshima," *U.S. News & World Report,* Feb. 20, 2013, www.usnews.com.

CHAPTER 15 WARNINGS

112 The intruders destroyed the contents: Peter Elkind, "Inside the Hack of the Century," *Fortune,* June 25, 2015, fortune.com/.

112 The FBI director, James Comey: Andy Greenberg, "FBI Director: Sony's Sloppy North Korean Hackers Revealed Their IP Addresses," *Wired,* Jan. 7, 2015, www.wired.com.

112 "They caused a lot of damage": "Remarks by the President in Year-End Press Conference," Dec. 19, 2014, www.obamawhitehouse.archives.gov.

113 In 2014, for instance, after Chinese cyberspies: "U.S. Charges Five Chinese Military Hackers for Cyber Espionage Against U.S. Corporations and a Labor Organization for Commercial Advantage," Department of Justice, May 19, 2014, www.justice.gov.

114 Security companies such as CrowdStrike: Andy Greenberg, "Obama Curbed Chinese Hacking, but Russia Won't Be So Easy," *Wired,* Dec. 16, 2016, www.wired.com.

114 (The Bowman Avenue Dam they'd targeted): Joseph Berger, "A Dam, Small and Unsung, Is Caught Up in an Iranian Hacking Case," *New York Times,* March 25, 2016, www.nytimes.com.

CHAPTER 16 FANCY BEAR

116 On June 14, *The Washington Post* revealed: Ellen Nakashima, "Russian Government Hackers Penetrated DNC, Stole Opposition Research on Trump," *Washington Post,* June 14, 2016, www.washingtonpost.com/.

116 Cozy Bear, it would later be revealed: Huib Modderkolk, "Dutch Agencies Provide Crucial Intel About Russia's Interference in US-Elections," *Volksrant,* Jan. 25, 2018, www.volkskrant.nl.

116 "Both adversaries engage in extensive": Dmitri Alperovitch, "Bears in the Midst: Intrusion into the Democratic National Committee, Opposition Research on Trump," *CrowdStrike,* June 15, 2016, www.crowdstrike.com.

117 "Worldwide known cyber security company": Guccifer 2.0, "Guccifer 2.0 DNC'S Servers Hacked by a Lone Hacker," June 15, 2016, guccifer2.wordpress.com, archived at bit.ly/2FOMwEE.

117 The original Guccifer: Matei Rosca, "Exclusive: Jailed Hacker Guccifer Boasts, 'I Used to Read [Clinton's] Memos . . . and Then Do the Gardening,'" *Pando,* March 20, 2015, pando.com.

117 "Personally I think that I'm among": Guccifer 2.0, "FAQ from Guccifer 2.0," June 30, 2016, guccifer2.wordpress.com, archived at bit.ly/2Mwo3V6.

118 The clue was almost comically revealing: Thomas Rid, "How Russia Pulled Off the Biggest Election Hack in U.S. History," *Esquire,* Oct. 20, 2016, www.esquire.com.

118 The Russian hackers seemingly hadn't even bothered: Lorenzo Franceschi-Bicchierai, "Why Does DNC Hacker 'Guccifer 2.0' Talk Like This?," *Motherboard,* June 23, 2016, motherboard.vice.com.

118 The hackers sent the news site *Gawker:* Sam Biddle and Gabrielle Bluestone, "This Looks Like the DNC's Hacked Trump Oppo File," June 15, 2016, gawker.com.

119 DNC officials had furtively discussed: Kristen East, "Top DNC Staffer Apologizes for Email on Sanders' Religion," *Politico,* July 23, 2016, www.politico.com; Mark Paustenbach, "Bernie Narrative," via WikiLeaks, sent May 21, 2016, wikileaks.org, archived at bit.ly/2FoysLh.

119 The stolen emails revealed: Jordain Carney, "Wasserman Schultz Called Top Sanders Aide a 'Damn Liar' in Leaked Email," *Hill,* July 22, 2016, thehill.com; "'This Is a Silly Story. (Sanders) Isn't Going to Be President,'" *Boston Herald,* July 24, 2016, www.bostonherald.com; Dan Roberts, Ben Jacobs, and Alan Yuhas, "Debbie Wasserman Schultz to Resign as DNC Chair as Email Scandal Rocks Democrats," *Guardian,* July 25, 2016, www.theguardian.com.

119 Guccifer 2.0's stolen DNC emails: Lee Fang and Zaid Jilani, "Hacked Emails Reveal NATO General Plotting Against Obama on Russia Policy," *Intercept,* July 1, 2016, theintercept.com/.

119 Despite DCLeaks' attempt to appear: Sean Gallagher, "Candid Camera: Dutch Hacked Russians Hacking DNC, Including Security Cameras," *Ars Technica,* Jan. 26, 2018, arstechnica.com.

119 This time, in a blatant mockery: Andy Greenberg, "Russian Hackers Get Bolder in Anti-Doping Agency Attack," *Wired,* Sept. 14, 2016, www.wired.com.

120 The site, of course: Raphael Satter, "Inside Story: How Russia Hacked the Democrats' Email," Associated Press, Nov. 4, 2017, www.apnews.com.

120 Another seemed to call for "open borders": "HRC Paid Speeches," email via WikiLeaks, sent Jan. 25, 2016, wikileaks.org, archived at bit.ly/2RRtcNA.

121 The security firm Secureworks found the link: "Threat Group 4127 Targets Hillary Clinton Presidential Campaign," June 16, 2016, www.secureworks.com, archived at bit.ly/2RecMtu.

121 "I love WikiLeaks!": Mark Hensch, "Trump: 'I Love WikiLeaks,'" *Hill,* Oct. 10, 2016, thehill.com.

121 But for the most part, Trump: Andy Greenberg, "A Timeline of Trump's Strange, Contradictory Statements on Russian Hacking," *Wired,* Jan. 4, 2017, www.wired.com.

121 Trump's obfuscation served Fancy Bear: Jake Sherman, "POLITICO/Morning Consult Poll: Only One-Third of Americans Say Russia Influenced 2016 Election," *Politico*, Dec. 20, 2016, www.politico.com.

122 "I think they've gotten medals": Andy Greenberg, "Trump's Win Signals Open Season for Russia's Political Hackers," *Wired*, Nov. 9, 2016, www.wired.com.

122 "We know that you are carrying out": Bill Whitaker, "When Russian Hackers Targeted the U.S. Election Infrastructure," CBS News, July 17, 2018, www.cbsnews.com.

122 The same day, the Department of Homeland: "Joint Statement from the Department of Homeland Security and Office of the Director of National Intelligence on Election Security," Oct. 7, 2016, www.dhs.gov.

123 "the biggest retaliatory move": Andy Greenberg, "Obama's Russian Hacking Retaliation Is Biggest 'Since the Cold War,'" *Wired*, Dec. 29, 2016, www.wired.com.

CHAPTER 17 FSOCIETY

127 The picture—first published by researchers: Anton Cherepanov, "The Rise of TeleBots: Analyzing Disruptive KillDisk Attacks," *We Live Security* (ESET blog), Dec. 13, 2016, www.welivesecurity.com, archived at bit.ly/2B6Lgc3.

127 "We are sorry": Chris Bing, "Early Indications Point to Sandworm Hacking Group for Global Ransomware Attack," *Cyberscoop*, June 30, 2017, www.cyberscoop.com.

CHAPTER 18 *POLIGON*

135 "This expensive light flicking": The Grugq, "Cyberwar via Cyberwar During War," *Risky Business*, March 6, 2017, www.risky.biz.

CHAPTER 19 INDUSTROYER/CRASH OVERRIDE

142 ESET named the malware Industroyer: Anton Cherepanov, "Win32/Industroyer: A New Threat for Industrial Control Systems," ESET paper, June 12, 2017, www.welivesecurity.com, archived at bit.ly/2Tan4N2.

143 Dragos had taken the controversial step: "CRASHOVERRIDE: Threat to the Electric Grid Operations," Dragos report, June 12, 2017, dragos.com/, archived at bit.ly/2HyuTuB.

146 "We are deeply concerned": Maria Cantwell, Ron Wyden, Brian Schatz, Sherrod Brown, Tammy Baldwin, Martin Heinrich, Chris Van Hollen, Christopher Coons, Al Franken, Bernard Sanders, Richard Durbin, Jack Reed, Edward Markey, Tammy Duckworth, Mazie K. Hirono, Thomas Carper, Patty Murray, Christopher Murphy, Jeanne Shaheen, Open Letter to President Trump, June 22, 2017, www.energy.senate.gov.

147 Send that one packet of eighteen bytes: "Advisory (ICSA-15-202-01) Siemens SIPROTEC Denial-of-Service Vulnerability," ICS-CERT advisory, July 21, 2015, ics-cert.us-cert.gov.

CHAPTER 21 SHADOW BROKERS

155 "!!! Attention government sponsors of cyber warfare": Shadow Brokers, "Equation Group Cyber Weapons Auction—Invitation," Aug. 13, 2016, originally published on www.pastebin.com, archived at bit.ly/2TfpEBt.

156 And when he opened them on his PC: Andy Greenberg, "The Shadow Brokers Mess Is What Happens When the NSA Hoards Zero Days," *Wired*, Aug. 17, 2016, www .wired.com.

156 Though the files appeared to be dated: David Sanger, "'Shadow Brokers' Leak Raises Alarming Question: Was the N.S.A. Hacked?," *New York Times*, Aug. 16, 2016, www.nytimes.com.

156 Cisco, for instance: "Cisco Adaptive Security Appliance SNMP Remote Code Execution Vulnerability," Cisco Security Advisories and Alerts, Aug. 17, 2018, www.tools .cisco.com, archived at bit.ly/2CnkJAv.

157 Instead, in the first twenty-four hours: Andy Greenberg, "No One Wants to Buy Those Stolen NSA-Linked Cyberweapons," *Wired*, Aug. 16, 2016, www.wired.com.

157 Experts largely agreed the profit motive: Ibid.

158 "Circumstantial evidence and conventional wisdom": Edward Snowden, Twitter post, Aug. 16, 2016, twitter.com, archived at bit.ly/2RdZGwc.

159 This time they offered up: Shadow Brokers, "Message#5—Trick or Treat?" *Medium*, Oct. 30, 2016, Medium.com, archived at bit.ly/2MvthQW.

159 "We're sending a message": William M. Arkin, Ken Dilanian, and Robert Windrem, "CIA Prepping for Possible Cyber Strike Against Russia," NBC News, Oct. 14, 2016, www.nbcnews.com.

159 "TheShadowBrokers is trying": Shadow Brokers, "REPOST: TheShadowBrokers Message#6," Steemit, Dec. 2016, Steemit.com, archived at bit.ly/2FPu4vt.

160 "So long, farewell": Shadow Brokers, "Message Finale," TheShadowBrokers.bit, Jan. 12, 2017, archived at bit.ly/2CJn4wv.

160 Some in the security industry speculated: Kevin Poulsen, "Mystery Hackers Blow Up Secret NSA Hacking Tools in 'Final F——k You,'" *Daily Beast*, Jan. 13, 2017, www.thedailybeast.com/.

160 "The fun is over": Joseph Cox, "NSA Exploit Peddlers the Shadow Brokers Call It Quits," *Motherboard*, Jan. 12, 2017, www.motherboard.vice.com.

160 "We recognize Americans' having more in common": Shadow Brokers, "Don't Forget Your Base," *Medium*, April 8, 2017, medium.com, archived at bit.ly/2CKzBQ5.

161 "Russia is likely using the latest": Jake Williams, "Russia 'Crosses the Rubicon' with Newest Shadow Brokers Dump," *Peerlyst*, April 9, 2017, www.peerlyst.com, archived at bit.ly/2CJTlDG.

161 "@malwarejake You having big mouth": Shadow Brokers, Twitter post, twitter.com, April 9, 2017, archived at bit.ly/2B38u2T.

CHAPTER 22 ETERNALBLUE

163 "Last week theshadowbrokers be trying": Shadow Brokers, "Lost in Translation," Steemit.com, April 14, 2017, www.steemit.com, archived at bit.ly/2FQ7Auy.

164 Or, as my *Wired* colleague Lily Hay Newman: Lily Hay Newman, "The Leaked NSA Spy Tool That Hacked the World," *Wired*, March 7, 2018, www.wired.com.

164 *The Washington Post* would later confirm: Ellen Nakashima and Craig Timberg, "NSA Officials Worried About the Day Its Potent Hacking Tool Would Get Loose. Then It Did," *Washington Post*, May 16, 2016, www.washingtonpost.com.

165 They immediately received tens of thousands: Dan Goodin, ">10,000 Windows Computers May Be Infected by Advanced NSA Backdoor," *Ars Technica*, April 21, 2017, arstechnica.com.

165 Within a week of the Shadow Brokers' release: "DoublePulsar," *Binary Edge* (blog), April 21, 2017, blog.binaryedge.io, archived at bit.ly/2RNPiAq.

166 Researchers were calling the new ransomware WannaCry: Jakub Křoustek, "Wanna-Cry Ransomware That Infected Telefonica and NHS Hospitals Is Spreading Aggressively, with over 50,000 Attacks So Far Today," *Avast* (blog), May 12, 2017, blog.avast.com, archived at bit.ly/2FXxbRz.

166 Thousands of people had their doctors': Amyas Morse, "Investigation: WannaCry Cyber Attack and the NHS," U.K. National Audit Office, Oct. 24, 2017, www.nao.org.uk.

166 The Spanish telecommunications firm: Agamoni Ghosh and India Ashok, "Wanna-Cry: List of Major Companies and Networks Hit by Ransomware Around the Globe," *International Business Times,* May 16, 2017, www.ibtimes.co.uk.

167 "I picked a hell of a fucking week": Marcus Hutchins, Twitter post, May 12, 2017, twitter.com, archived at archive.is/9CkQn.

170 The entire scheme generated: Samuel Gibbs, "WannaCry: Hackers Withdraw £108,000 of Bitcoin Ransom," *Guardian,* Aug. 3, 2017, www.theguardian.com.

170 Perhaps its creators had been testing: Andy Greenberg, "The WannaCry Ransomware Hackers Made Some Real Amateur Mistakes," *Wired,* May 15, 2017, www.wired.com.

170 Within days, security researchers at Google: Andy Greenberg, "The WannaCry Ransomware Has a Link to North Korean Hackers," *Wired,* May 15, 2017, www.wired.com.

170 By December 2017, the Trump White House: "Press Briefing on the Attribution of the WannaCry Malware Attack to North Korea," Whitehouse.gov, Dec. 19, 2017.

171 He'd later tell a Maryland court: Sean Gallagher, "NSA Employee Who Brought Hacking Tools Home Sentenced to 66 Months in Prison," *Ars Technica,* Sept. 25, 2018, arstechnica.com.

171 The contractor, the report stated: Gordon Lubold and Shane Harris, "Russian Hackers Stole NSA Data on U.S. Cyber Defense," *Wall Street Journal,* Oct. 5, 2017, www.wsj.com.

171 It had, the company: "Preliminary Results of the Internal Investigation into Alleged Incidents Reported by US Media (Updated with New Findings)," Kaspersky blog, Oct. 25, 2017, www.kaspersky.com, archived at bit.ly/2B4xnLn.

171 Aside from Nghia Hoang Pho: Josh Gerstein, "Suspect's Twitter Messages Played Role in NSA Hacking-Tools Leak Probe," *Politico,* Dec. 31, 2018, www.politico.com; and Kim Zetter, "Exclusive: How a Russian Firm Helped Catch an Alleged NSA Data Thief," *Politico,* Jan. 9, 2019, www.politico.com.

CHAPTER 23 MIMIKATZ

175 DigiNotar was blacklisted: Kim Zetter, "Diginotar Files for Bankrupty in Wake of Devastating Hack," *Wired,* Sept. 20, 2011, wired.com.

CHAPTER 24 NOTPETYA

179 When he stopped at the intersection: "Car Bomb Kills Senior Intelligence Officer in Central Kyiv," *NTD,* June 27, 2017, mb.ntd.com.

179 He was killed instantly: Christopher Miller, "Colonel in Ukrainian Military Intel-

ligence Killed in Kyiv Car Bombing," Radio Free Europe/Radio Liberty, June 27, 2017, www.rferl.org.

179 Parts of his vehicle flew dozens: Alec Luhn, "Ukrainian Military Intelligence Officer Killed by Car Bomb in Kiev," *Guardian,* June 27, 2017, www.theguardian.com.

182 Instead, its extortion messages seemed: Matt Suiche, "Petya.2017 Is a Wiper Not a Ransomware," Comae blog, June 28, 2017, blog.comae.io/, archived at bit.ly/2UjSdxI.

183 It crippled multinational companies: Eduard Kovacs, "NotPetya Attack Costs Big Companies Millions," *SecurityWeek,* Aug. 17, 2017, wwwsecurityweek.com.

183 It even spread to Russia: "Информационная система Evraz подверглась хакерской атаке," *РИА Новости,* June 27, 2017, www.rbc.ru/; Yuri Zoria, "Ukrainian Banks, Enterprises, Media and Energy Companies Under Powerful Cyber Attack, Including Chornobyl NPP—LiveUpdates," *Euromaidan Press,* June 27, 2017, euromaidanpress.com/; "Malicious Malware: Lessons Learned and What to Expect from Cyber Crime in 2018," *Tass,* Jan. 1, 2018.

CHAPTER 25 NATIONAL DISASTER

184 The monumental mission of the Chernobyl facility's staff: "The New Safe Confinement Made Simple," Chernobyl NPP website, chnpp.gov.ua/.

189 According to ISSP: Raphael Satter, "Ukraine Official: Worm Likely Hit 1 in 10 State, Company PCs," Associated Press, July 6, 2017, dailyherald.com.

CHAPTER 27 THE COST

196 "We overcame the problem": Richard Chirgwin, "IT 'Heroes' Saved Maersk from NotPetya with Ten-Day Reinstallation Bliz," *Register,* Jan. 25, 2018, www.theregister.co.uk.

198 "Without computers these days": Hamza Shaban and Ellen Nakashima, "Pharmaceutical Giant Rocked by Ransomware Attack," *Washington Post,* June 27, 2017, www.washingtonpost.com.

198 In its financial report: "Merck & Co. (MRK) Q3 2017 Results—Earnings Call Transcript," *Seeking Alpha,* Oct. 17, 2017, seekingalpha.com.

198 Two congressmen would write: Alex Keown, "Recent Cyberattack on Merck & Co. Could Lead to Drug Shortage," Biospace.com, Sept. 25, 2017, www.biospace.com.

198 Reckitt Benckiser, the British manufacturer: Chelsea Leu, "The Cost of NotPetya," sidebar to "The Code That Crashed the World," *Wired,* Aug. 2017, www.wired.com.

199 To get a sense of what: Kate Fazzini, "The Landmark Ransomware Campaign That Crippled Atlanta Last March Was Created by Two Iranians, Says DoJ," CNBC, Nov. 28, 2018, www.cnbc.com/.

201 One woman, fifty-six-year-old: "Heritage Valley Health, Drugmaker Merck Hit by Global Ransomware Cyberattack," Associated Press, June 27, 2017, www.post-gazette.com.

203 He points to a *New England Journal of Medicine*: Anupam B. Jena et al., "Delays in Emergency Care and Mortality During Major U.S. Marathons," *New England Journal of Medicine,* April 13, 2017, www.nejm.org.

CHAPTER 29 DISTANCE

213 At the same time, Trump: Philip Bump, "What Trump Was Saying About Russia and Putin—and What the Campaign Was Doing," *Washington Post,* Dec. 14, 2017, www.washingtonpost.com/.

214 "Why should U.S. taxpayers": Nick Wadhams and John Follain, "Tillerson Asks Why U.S. Taxpayers Should Care About Ukraine," *Bloomberg,* April 11, 2017, www.bloomberg.com.

215 Serper, ESET, and Cisco's Talos: David Maynor et al., "The MeDoc Connection," *Talos* (blog), Cisco, July 5, 2017, blog.talosintelligence.com, archived at bit.ly/2S6UpuU.

CHAPTER 30 GRU

222 "NotPetya was probably launched": "NotPetya and WannaCry Call for a Joint Response from International Community," NATO Cooperative Cyber Defence Centre of Excellence, June 30, 2017, ccdcoe.org.

222 In late 2018: Steve Evans, "Mondelez's NotPetya Cyber Attack Claim Disputed by Zurich: Report," *Reinsurance News,* Dec. 17, 2018, www.reinsurancene.ws.

224 "Russian Military Was Behind": Ellen Nakashima, "Russian Military Was Behind 'NotPetya' Cyberattack in Ukraine, CIA Concludes," *Washington Post,* Jan. 12, 2018, www.washingtonpost.com/.

CHAPTER 31 DEFECTORS

227 The military spy agency's mission: Suvorov, *Inside Soviet Military Intelligence,* 8.

227 Nor did it ever take the public blame: Ibid., 39.

228 Vladimir Rezun, a GRU captain: Ibid., 3.

228 On another occasion, he writes: Ibid., 162.

228 The twenty-nine-year-old had grown up: Hart, *CIA's Russians,* 18.

228 Over the next six years: Richard C. S. Trahair and Robert L. Miller, *Encyclopedia of Cold War Espionage, Spies, and Secret Operations* (New York: Enigma Books, 2009), 342.

228 Then, in 1959, after a botched: Hart, *CIA's Russians,* 51.

228 His father had been killed: Schecter and Deriabin, *Spy Who Saved the World,* 59.

229 He also hoped to make enough: Ibid., 87.

229 He'd pass the materials: Ibid., 179.

229 By some accounts, it was that warning: Jerrold Schechter, "A Very Important Spy," *New York Review of Books,* June 24, 1993, www.nybooks.com.

229 Exactly how he was caught: Hart, *CIA's Russians,* 123.

229 At the Brits': Schecter and Deriabin, *Spy Who Saved the World,* 75.

230 As he later described it: Suvorov, *Inside the Aquarium,* 241.

230 In his new life: Dimitri Simes, "A Soviet Defector Cashes In on His Story," *Washington Post,* May 11, 1986, www.washingtonpost.com.

230 His most revelatory books: "*The Aquarium* GRU Headquarters," Federation of American Scientists Intelligence Resource Program, fas.org.

231 He describes a weeklong: Suvorov, *Inside the Aquarium,* 92, 131, 148.

231 Rezun went on to detail: Suvorov, *Inside Soviet Military Intelligence,* 105, 124.

231 According to Rezun: Suvorov, *Inside the Aquarium,* 143.

231 Space, too, was the GRU's: Suvorov, *Inside Soviet Military Intelligence,* 60.

231 Rezun's own innovation: Suvorov, *Inside the Aquarium,* 193.

231 "This company, which numbers 115": Ibid., 33.

231 In some cases, he wrote: Ibid., 38.

232 (While that description): "Torture and Ill-Treatment—Comments on the Second Periodic Report Submitted to the United Nations Committee Against Torture," Amnesty International, Oct. 1, 1996, www.refworld.org.

232 In that volume: Viktor Suvorov, *Spetsnaz: The Inside Story of the Soviet Special Forces* (New York: Norton, 1987), 98.

232 "One likely target would be": Lunev, *Through the Eyes of the Enemy,* 32.

232 After congressional hearings: Nicholas Horrock, "FBI Focusing on Portable Nuke Threat," UPI, Dec. 21, 2001, bit.ly/2TiKvDO.

232 But other Soviet defectors confirmed: Alexander Kouzminov, "False Flags, Ethnic Bombs, and Day X," *California Literary Review,* April 25, 2005, archived at bit.ly/2B7yn1w.

233 "It should not be shocking": Lunev, *Through the Eyes of the Enemy,* 32.

234 By most accounts: Luke Harding, "The Skripal Files by Mark Urban: Review—the Salisbury Spy's Story," *Guardian,* Oct. 17, 2018, www.theguardian.com.

234 Reporting by the BBC: Richard Galpin, "Russian Spy Poisoning: Why Was Sergei Skripal Attacked?," BBC, Oct. 25, 2018, www.bbc.com.

234 The father and daughter: John Lauerman and Caroline Alexander, "Novichok, Russian Nerve Agent Spooking Britain," Bloomberg QuickTake, *Washington Post,* July 5, 2018, www.washingtonpost.com.

234 Tragically, two British: Vikram Dodd and Stephen Morris, "Novichok That Killed Woman Came from Bottle, Police Believe," *The Guardian,* July 13, 2018, theguardian.com.

CHAPTER 32 *INFORMATSIONNOYE PROTIVOBORSTVO*

236 The GRU's spies had missed: S.J., "What Is the GRU?" *Economist,* Sept. 11, 2018, www.economist.com.

236 Attempts to intercept: Mark Galeotti, "Putin's Hydra: Inside Russia's Intelligence Services," European Council on Foreign Relations Policy Brief, May 2016, 6, www.ecfr.eu.

236 Moscow came to see: Mark Galeotti, "Putin's Secret Weapon," July 7, 2014, foreignpolicy.com.

236 (The GRU was even threatened): Mark Galeotti, "We Don't Know What to Call Russian Military Intelligence and That May Be a Problem," *War on the Rocks,* Jan. 19, 2016, warontherocks.com.

236 One clue: "What Is the GRU? Who Gets Recruited to Be a Spy? Why Are They Exposed So Often?" *Meduza,* Nov. 6, 2018, meduza.io/.

237 "seemed more comfortable accompanying": Galeotti, "Putin's Secret Weapon."

237 Korabelnikov was eventually replaced: Galeotti, "Putin's Hydra," 6.

238 It was the GRU that led: Galeotti, "Putin's Secret Weapon."

238 "shown the rest of the world": Ibid.

238 In the spring: "MH17—Russian GRU Commander 'Orion' Identified as Oleg Kannikov," *Bellingcat*, May 25, 2018, www.bellingcat.com; and "Third Suspect in Skripal Poisoning Identified as Denis Sergeev, High Ranking GRU Officer," *Bellingcat*, Feb. 24, 2019, bellingcat.com.

239 It was based on a speech: Valery Gerasimov, "The Value of Science Is in the Foresight: New Challenges Demand Rethinking the Forms and Methods of Carrying Out Combat Operations," *Military-Industrial Courier*, Feb. 27, 2013, translated and reprinted in *Military Review*, Jan./Feb. 2016, usacac.army.mil/.

239 The article was little noticed: Mark Galeotti, "The 'Gerasimov Doctrine' and Russian Non-linear War," *In Moscow's Shadow*, Feb. 27, 2013, inmoscowsshadows .wordpress.com, archived at bit.ly/2G2NsEK.

CHAPTER 33 THE PENALTY

243 "In June 2017, the Russian military": Sarah Huckabee Sanders, "Statement from the Press Secretary," Whitehouse.gov, Feb. 15, 2018, www.whitehouse.gov.

243 By that night: "Russian Military 'Almost Certainly' Responsible for Destructive 2017 Cyber Attack," National Cyber Security Centre website, Feb. 15, 2018, www .ncsc.gov.uk; "CSE Statement on the NotPetya Malware," Communications Security Establishment website, Feb. 15, 2018, www.cse-cst.gc.ca; "New Zealand Joins International Condemnation of NotPetya Cyber-attack," Government Communications Security Bureau, Feb. 16, 2018, www.gcsb.govt.nz; "NotPetya Malware Attributed," CERT Australia website, Feb. 16, 2018, www.cert.gov.au.

244 "We strongly reject such accusations": "Kremlin Slams 'Russophobic' Allegations That Pin NotPetya Cyber Attack on Russia," *TASS*, Feb. 15, 2018, tass.com/.

244 The U.S. Treasury announced: "Treasury Sanctions Russian Cyber Actors for Interference with the 2016 U.S. Elections and Malicious Cyber-attacks," U.S. Department of the Treasury website, March 15, 2018, home.treasury.gov.

245 In an announcement made: "Russian Government Cyber Activity Targeting Energy and Other Critical Infrastructure Sectors," US-CERT website, March 15, 2018, www.us-cert.gov.

246 Kirstjen Nielsen would explain: Blake Sobszak, "DHS on Russian Grid Hackers: 'They Are Doing Research,'" *EnergyWire*, Oct. 3, 2018, www.eenews.net.

246 The security firm Symantec had first detailed: Andy Greenberg, "Hackers Gain Direct Access to U.S. Power Grid Controls," *Wired*, September 6, 2017, wired.com.

CHAPTER 34 BAD RABBIT, OLYMPIC DESTROYER

248 It contained fully 67 percent: Dan Raywood, "The Rabid Ransomware Bunnies Behind #BadRabbit," *Infosecurity*, Oct. 25, 2017, www.infosecurity-magazine.com.

CHAPTER 35 FALSE FLAGS

254 In the run-up to the Olympics: Andy Greenberg, "Hackers Have Already Targeted the Winter Olympics—and May Not Be Done," *Wired*, Feb. 1, 2018, www.wired.com.

254 The North Korean dictator, Kim Jong Un: Joe Sterling, Sheena McKenzie, and Brian Todd, "Kim Jong Un's Sister Is Stealing the Show at the Winter Olympics," CNN, Feb. 10, 2018, www.cnn.com.

255 The two countries had even taken: Ivan Watson, Stella Ko, and Sheena McKenzie, "Joint Korean Ice Hockey Team Plays for First Time Ahead of Olympics," CNN, Feb. 5, 2018, www.cnn.com.

255 Russian athletes could compete: Rebecca R. Ruiz and Tariq Panja, "Russia Banned from Winter Olympics by I.O.C.," *New York Times,* Dec. 5, 2017, www.nytimes.com.

255 "We know that Western media are planning": "Olympics Officials Confirm There Was a Cyber Attack During the Opening Ceremony—and Russia's Already Denying They Did It," Reuters, *Business Insider,* Feb. 11, 2018, www.businessinsider.com.

256 The data-wiping portion of Olympic Destroyer: Juan Andres Guerrero-Saade, Priscilla Moriuchi, and Greg Lesnewich, "Targeting of Olympic Games IT Infrastructure Remains Unattributed," Recorded Future blog, Feb. 14, 2018, www .recordedfuture.com, archived at bit.ly/2CXNGdd.

256 And both destroyed files: Paul Rascagneres and Martin Lee, "Who Wasn't Responsible for Olympic Destroyer?" *Talos* (blog), Feb. 26, 2018, blog.talosintelligence .com, archived at bit.ly/2UuAyDs.

256 The company also traced: Jay Rosenberg, "2018 Winter Cyber Olympics: Code Similarities with Cyber Attacks in Pyeongchang," *Cybersecurity DNA* (blog), Feb. 12, 2018, www.intezer.com, archived at bit.ly/2WvQFCD.

256 Both APT3 and APT10 had been named: "Advanced Persistent Threat Groups: Who's Who of Cyber Threat Actors," FireEye, www.fireeye.com, archived at bit.ly/2MG27qI.

257 "Russian Spies Hacked the Olympics": Ellen Nakashima, "Russian Spies Hacked the Olympics and Tried to Make It Look Like North Korea Did It, U.S. Officials Say," *Washington Post,* Feb. 24, 2018, www.washingtonpost.com/.

258 The metadata: Kaspersky GReAT Team, "OlympicDestroyer Is Here to Trick the Industry," SecureList blog, March 8, 2018, securelist.com, archived at bit.ly/2GcHdhR.

258 "It's a completely verifiable false flag": Kaspersky Lab, "Surprise Keynote," YouTube, April 2, 2018, www.youtube.com.

CHAPTER 37 THE TOWER

267 On July 14: Indictment, Case 1:18-cr-00215-ABJ, U.S. Department of Justice, July 13, 2018, www.justice.gov.

269 In his photograph: "Aleksandr Vladimirovich Osadchuk," Most Wanted, FBI website, www.fbi.gov.

269 On the website of a: "Investigative Report: On the Trail of the 12 Indicted Russian Intelligence Officers," Radio Free Europe/Radio Liberty, July 19, 2018, www.rferl.org.

270 His light blue eyes stared: "Aleksey Aleksandrovich Potemkin," Most Wanted, FBI website, www.fbi.gov.

270 Kovalev, accused of the hands-on: "Anatoliy Sergeyevich Kovalev," Most Wanted, FBI website, www.fbi.gov.

270 He'd noted his affiliation: Kevin Poulsen, "This Hacker Party Is Ground Zero for Russia's Cyberspies," Daily Beast, Aug. 3, 2018. www.dailybeast.com.

CHAPTER 39 THE ELEPHANT AND THE INSURGENT

280 "Our message is clear": "Reckless Campaign of Cyber Attacks by Russian Military Intelligence Service Exposed," National Cyber Security Centre website, Oct. 4, 2018, www.ncsc.gov.uk.

281 Around the same time: Anton Cherepanov and Robert Lipovsky, "GreyEnergy: Updated Arsenal of One of the Most Dangerous Threat Actors," *We Live Security* (ESET blog), Oct. 17, 2018, welivesecurity.com, archived at bit.ly/2D5atDU; and Kaspersky ICS-CERT, "GreyEnergy's Overlap with Zebrocy," *SecureList* (blog), Jan. 24, 2019, securelist.com, archived at bit.ly/2DdFEwK.

283 And even with its outsized spending: Armedforces.eu, "Compare Armed Forces: Military Power of USA and Russia," armedforces.eu/.

CHAPTER 40 GENEVA

292 "It was in Geneva in 1949": "Brad Smith Takes His Call for a Digital Geneva Convention to the United Nations," Official Microsoft Blog, Nov. 9, 2017, blogs .microsoft.com, archived at bit.ly/2t0Ft3c.

293 Clarke's imagined treaty: Clarke and Knake, *Cyber War* (New York: HarperCollins, 2010), 242.

295 In 2017, Trump announced: David Sanger, "Pentagon Puts Cyberwarriors on the Offensive, Increasing the Risk of Conflict," *New York Times,* June 17, 2018, www .nytimes.com.

295 Three months later: Dustin Volz, "Trump, Seeking to Relax Rules on U.S. Cyberattacks, Reverses Obama Directive," *Wall Street Journal,* Aug. 15, 2018, www.wsj.com.

295 "As a deterrent against attacks": Daniel White, "Read Donald Trump's Remarks to a Veterans Group," *Time,* Oct. 3, 2016, time.com.

CHAPTER 41 BLACK START

299 "While we were cleaning things up": Lily Hay Newman, "The Hail Mary Plan to Restart a Hacked US Electric Grid," *Wired,* Nov. 14, 2018, www.wired.com.

302 Hackers of unknown origin: Blake Sobczak, "The Inside Story of the World's Most Dangerous Malware," *E&E News,* March 7, 2019, https://www.eenews.net.

CHAPTER 42 RESILIENCE

305 Geer made a case for examining: Daniel E. Geer Jr., "A Rubicon," National Security, Technology, and Law, Feb. 5, 2018, www.hoover.org.

EPILOGUE

311 Even so, less than half a mile: Lily Hyde, "A Bakery in a War Zone," *Roads and Kingdoms,* Oct. 6, 2017, https://roadsandkingdoms.com.

APPENDIX SANDWORM'S CONNECTION TO FRENCH ELECTION HACKING

315 ESET had found: Anton Cherepanov, "TeleBots Are Back: Supply Chain Attacks Against Ukraine," *We Live Security* (ESET blog), June 30, 2017, www.welivesecurity .com, archived at bit.ly/2UEDQEo.

BIBLIOGRAPHY

Applebaum, Anne. *Red Famine*. New York: Doubleday, 2017.

Clarke, Richard, and Robert Knake. *Cyber War*. New York: HarperCollins, 2010.

Hart, John Limond. *The CIA's Russians*. Annapolis, Md.: Naval Institute Press, 2003.

Herbert, Frank. *Dune*. Annotated reprint, New York: Penguin, 2005. Originally published Philadelphia: Chilton Books, 1965.

Kaplan, Fred. *Dark Territory*. New York: Simon & Schuster, 2016.

Lunev, Stanislav. *Through the Eyes of the Enemy*. With Ira Winkler. Washington, D.C.: Regnery, 1998.

Plokhy, Serhii. *The Gates of Europe*. New York: Basic Books, 2015.

Reid, Anna. *Borderland*. New York: Basic Books, 1997.

Rid, Thomas. *Rise of the Machines*. New York: W. W. Norton, 2016.

Sanger, David. *Confront and Conceal*. New York: Crown, 2012.

Schecter, Jerrold L., and Peter S. Deriabin. *The Spy Who Saved the World*. New York: Macmillan, 1992.

Stoll, Clifford. *The Cuckoo's Egg*. New York: Pocket Books, 1990.

Suvorov, Viktor. *Inside the Aquarium*. New York: Macmillan, 1986.

———. *Inside Soviet Military Intelligence*. New York: Macmillan, 1984.

Zetter, Kim. *Countdown to Zero Day*. New York: Crown, 2014.

INDEX

ABOUT THE AUTHOR

Andy Greenberg is an award-winning senior writer for *Wired* magazine, where he covers security, privacy, information freedom, and hacker culture. He is the author of the 2012 book *This Machine Kills Secrets,* and his stories for *Wired* on Ukraine's cyberwar (including an excerpt from *Sandworm*) have won a Gerald Loeb Award for International Reporting and two Deadline Club Awards from the New York Society of Professional Journalists. He lives in Brooklyn with his wife, documentary filmmaker Malika Zouhali-Worrall.